From Brynamor to ...
Nicko's rugby odyssey

Mike Nicholas

with Gary Slater

London League Publications Ltd

From Swn-y-mor to Seattle
Nicko's rugby odyssey

A CIP catalogue record for this book is available from the British Library.

First published in Great Britain in April 2014 by:
London League Publications Ltd, P.O. Box 65784, London NW2 9NS

ISBN: 978-1909885-04-2

Cover design by: Stephen McCarthy Graphic Design, 46, Clarence Road, London N15 5BB

Layout: Peter Lush

Printed and bound in Great Britain by Charlesworth Press, Wakefield

Foreword

Mike Nicholas, Eddie Cunningham of St Helens and I all went on Wales's World Championship tour of Australia and New Zealand in the summer of 1975. Twenty players made the trip. We had a great time and enjoyed one another's company and you will read about that tour later on. At the airport in Sydney, on the way back, we all took it in turns to say a few words.

I said: "I think we are all blood brothers from now on. When we get back home we are all the best of friends. In games we will never attack one another. We will play fair because we are all the best of mates. As far as I am concerned, we are brothers." Everybody cheered.

A few months later, Widnes played St Helens in the BBC2 Floodlit Trophy at Knowsley Road and Eddie tried to pinch the ball off me and so I gave him a little tap with my head and cut him above an eye. In the bar afterwards, he wasn't speaking to me and I asked: "What's wrong with you Eddie?"

He said: "What about that meeting we had on the way home and you said we were all blood brothers and we don't harm one another? Look at my head." I replied: "Eddie, I didn't include cup ties in that."

Funnily enough, the one time when I really fell out with Mike was in a cup tie too, the final of the John Player Trophy at Knowsley Road in 1979, when I hit him and got sent off. You will read all about that later too. But the Welsh lads were like a bit of a family. Although we got stuck in, we never really had a go at one another.

I didn't know Mike in rugby union. My last game for Cardiff was against Aberavon – Mike's club – in October 1964 when Max Wiltshire and Billy Mainwaring were in the second row and they both went on to play for Wales. Mike didn't play in that game and so I didn't get to know him until he came north in 1972. Then we played against each other and I watched him play as well.

John Warlow of Widnes, Kel Coslett of St Helens, I and a few others went down to Wembley to watch Mike play in the 1974 Challenge Cup Final against Featherstone Rovers. Warrington played really well that day and I remember Nicko scored a try. We had a great time and ran for a taxi afterwards and piled in. The taxi driver turned round and said: "There's only five allowed in this taxi." I said: "Well, you'll have to get out!"

Mike was very unlucky on the international scene because he was picked for the 1974 Great Britain tour of Australia and New Zealand and is on the official tour photograph, but had to withdraw through injury. He was unlucky on the 1975 tour too, because he picked up another injury and didn't play much.

I remember Wales's match against Canterbury at Christchurch which was a very rough and hard game. Mike was carried off injured just after half-time and I had to go on to replace him. I ended up hitting Mark Broadhurst, who went on to play for Hull Kingston Rovers, and put him in hospital for the night. If Mike had just stayed on the field I wouldn't have got into such trouble.

I always enjoyed playing against Mike and we have been mates ever since. He is one of those people who is great at organising things and I have never met anyone who knows as many people as Mike. On one occasion I went down to watch Wales versus Scotland at Bridgend and he introduced me to Rhodri Morgan, the First Minister of Wales, and I thought to myself: "How on earth do you know him?" We got talking and I found out that he lived on the farm where I worked as a boy when I left school. It is a small world.

Mike will do anything for you. My book *Big Jim* came out last year and Mike helped me with that and spoke at the launch at Widnes Rugby League Club. He said it was the first time he had been to Widnes and not been booed. So I am delighted to return the favour and write the foreword for his book. I know you will enjoy it.

Jim Mills

Frodsham, January 2014

(Photo: Jim in action for Wales against Australia in the 1975 World Championship)

Thank You

This book would not have been possible without the help and support of many people and it is only right to thank them all. The sports reporters on the *Port Talbot Guardian*, notably Clive Girton, did an excellent job covering the Aberavon matches featuring Mike Nicholas in the 1960s. Likewise, the *Warrington Guardian* was the best source of information about the Wire in the 1970s and continues to be the place for news about the Wolves. Special thanks to Eddie Fuller, Mike Boden, Mike Parsons and the late John Dickens. Thanks too for allowing the reproduction of some excellent *Warrington Guardian* photographs. Howard Morgan, the Crawshay's archivist, also came up trumps with detailed information about their 1971 tour. Alex Service, Robert Gate and Stephen Wild supplied excellent career statistics for Aberavon players who went North. Eddie Whitham, Mike Peers, George Thornton, Bob Brough, Gordon Myles, Phil Ball, Stan Lewandowski and Neil Dowson also provided invaluable help with photographs.

Thanks also to Steve McCarthy for designing the cover; the staff of Charlesworth for printing the book and Peter Lush and Dave Farrar of London League Publications Ltd for agreeing to publish it.

Take a bow one and all.

Mike Nicholas and Gary Slater

Introduction

My first competitive game of rugby was in about 1958 while I was at Sandfields Comprehensive School in Port Talbot on the Atlantic coast of Wales. Our ground was called Swn-y-Mor, meaning 'sound of the sea'. My final game of rugby was for the London Welsh Veterans side in Seattle on the Pacific coast of the United States in about 1989. I was 43 years old.

It had been quite a journey – from rugby union to rugby league and back; taking in success and failure; good times and bad; tries, goals and injuries; with many friendships made along the way. I hope you will enjoy reading about my rugby odyssey and about my life outside the game.

My co-writer, Gary Slater, and I have been travelling through time and, for me, it has been a cathartic experience. I would like to thank Gary for his efforts and Peter Lush & Dave Farrar, of London League Publications Ltd, for making it all possible.

I would also like to thank all the contributors who have given their time, memories and photographs to build up this picture of my life so far. I hope you enjoy reading it as much as I have working on it.

Mike Nicholas
January 2014

(Photo: Mike in his time at Warrington.)

About Gary Slater

When Gary Slater saw Mike Nicholas make his debut for Warrington in 1972, he could never have imagined that 42 years later he would be collaborating on his autobiography. For a start, until that long gone October afternoon, he had never heard of him. Few Warrington fans had. From that day forward, he followed Mike's career closely and saw him play at Wembley in 1974 and 1975 and witnessed first-hand some of his many sendings-off. In 1998, in a special *Warrington Guardian* publication to mark the centenary of Wilderspool Stadium, he even wrote an article about Mike's "dirty dozen" – his club record number of 'early baths', making him the cleanest player in the club's history.

Mike was furious because he was convinced he had been sent off more times than that – and he was right. At least this book sets the record straight. Gary is a former deputy sports editor of the *Warrington Guardian* and *Birmingham Evening Mail* and is currently employed as a production journalist on the *Daily Telegraph* sports desk in London. He lives in Brixton and must be the only commuter who, on crossing Kellett Road on his way to the tube station, thinks of Cyril Kellett, the goalkicking Featherstone Rovers full-back in the 1973 Challenge Cup Final at Wembley. Gary has written – or co-written – five books about rugby league but regards this as his finest piece of work – so far. He is married to Helen and has four sons – Joe, Tom, Ben and Jack – who are all Warrington Wolves supporters.

Preface

The broadcaster Steve Rider was once described as being "half-man, half-desk" because he spent so long presenting the Saturday afternoon sports programme *Grandstand* on BBC One. In a similar way, Mike Nicholas is "half-man, half-legend" because every rugby fan in Port Talbot or Warrington seems to have a tall tale about his colourful career.

Roy 'Ockher' Aspinall, Warrington's formidable former kit man and groundsman, who died in January 2014, told me about a training match, behind-closed-doors, at Wilderspool soon after Mike had gone North from South Wales.

According to 'Ockher' – and, by the way, 'Ockher' means awkward, Mike was the victim of a high tackle and lost a tooth. Totally incensed, Mike chased the perpetrator – a fellow Warrington player by the name of Dave Cunliffe – up and down the newly-built Wilderspool Leisure Centre in a vain attempt to take his revenge.

It turns out it wasn't Mike at all; it was his team mate Joe Price. But we should have known that for two reasons. First, Mike would have caught him and, secondly, there would be a chapter in the book called: 'The day I murdered a team-mate'!

The book is largely based on 13 two-hour interviews we conducted in the atrium at the Daresbury Park hotel on the outskirts of Warrington over a six-month period. While we talked, Mike would drink cups of cappuccino while I would sink pots of Earl Grey tea.

The young barista became intrigued by our activities, as I tape recorded thousands of words of wisdom, and so she finally asked one day: "Is that man famous?" "Yes he is," I replied. She was thrilled and her little eyes lit up. "Why is he famous?" she continued.

"Well," I confided. "He used to play rugby league for Warrington and rugby union for Aberavon." "Oh," she said, not attempting to hide her disappointment and I felt that we were never served quite as quickly after that.

No matter, in my book, and his book, Mike Nicholas is famous and I feel sure you will enjoy reading about his exploits for Aberavon, Warrington and Wales.

Gary Slater
January 2014

Thank you

London League Publications Ltd would like to thank Steve McCarthy for designing the cover and the staff of Charlesworth Press for printing the book.

Contents

A poetic tribute

'Mike Nic'

Rugby is a game that is mostly all brawn
No brains are required I'm assured,
But one thing for certain if you are to succeed
You need leather balls that's well cured.

I've heard of a player 'Mike Nic' is the name
They call him the 'Wizard from Wales',
The number of times that, that fellow's sent off
No wonder the town's full of tales.

That flat nose of Mike's would make a maid tremble
It's a present from days that are gone,
He'll soon draw a pension, but be kind and don't mention
It'll make him feel old (it's not on).

What does he do when he's not on the field?
And he's not on the field quite a lot,
He works through the night (that could give you a fright)
In a taxi hire firm that he's got.

So, if you have a drink over Xmas
Don't try to get home on a bike,
Give Nicholas a ring for a taxi
You can always rely on 'our Mike'

With thanks to 'Joe Bloke'

1. Wembley joy and pain

Saturday 11 May 1974 was one of the best days of my life – and one of the worst. It was one of the happiest – and one of the saddest – and one of the most significant. It was the date of the Rugby League Challenge Cup final at Wembley between Warrington and Featherstone Rovers. I was 27 years old, in my prime and playing for Warrington.

That week I was inundated with messages of support from staff and former teachers at my old school, Sandfields Comprehensive in Port Talbot, which I found both uplifting and humbling. We left Warrington by coach on the Thursday lunchtime and stayed at the Kensington Palace Hotel. On the Friday morning, we went to Wembley to have a look around and some of the boys practised climbing up the steps leading to the Royal Box and being presented with the cup. That's how confident we were.

On the Friday afternoon, we had a training session at Hyde Park, just a game of tick and pass, and were told to keep off the grass by a park attendant. Roy 'Ockher' Aspinall, our kitman, offered to punch the man's lights out, but thankfully that wasn't necessary. I had had a complete week off alcohol and went to bed early, but I didn't sleep very well. There was a massive buzz around the place.

I remember the team coach driving down Olympic [known as 'Wembley'] Way early on the Saturday afternoon. I looked out of the window and saw Ken Thomas, the former Aberavon winger, in the crowd. Aberavon was my old rugby union club and I knew that Ken was a really cool customer. Ken saw me and broke into a jog. It was the only time I had seen that happen; but then I did have his cup final tickets in my pocket. My mother and father and brothers and mates were all there too.

Kevin Ashcroft, our hooker, had won the Challenge Cup with Leigh in 1971 and I had asked him what Wembley was like. He said that because the dressing rooms were at the back, we wouldn't hear anything until we emerged from the tunnel and then we would be hit by a wall of sound. He was exactly right.

Lining up in the tunnel, I heard Steve Nash, the Featherstone scrum-half, shout "run at the old man" to his forwards. That was a reference to our captain and player-coach Alex Murphy, who was 35 and had battled back from a broken jaw to play in the final. He had already won the Challenge Cup three times – in 1961, 1966 and 1971 – and so a taunt like that wasn't going to upset him; but it set the tone for a bad-tempered match.

Very early on Murph wiped out Dave Hartley, the Featherstone centre, with a high tackle. In a league match Murph might have been sent off, but he had judged the psychology of the situation perfectly. Sam Shepherd, the referee, was a schoolteacher from Oldham. He was taking charge of his first Challenge Cup final and had a crisp white handkerchief in his top pocket. He wasn't going to spoil his big day by sending someone off. He just gave Featherstone a penalty, which Harold Box, their full-back, kicked to put them 2–0 up. Two penalties from our wonderful full-back, Derek Whitehead, made it 4–2 to us before Box struck again for 4–4. It was that sort of game. Two more Whitehead penalties made it 8–4.

Ten minutes before half-time, disaster struck. First, Murph suffered a rib injury and had to go off. Then Steve Nash decided to run a penalty and passed to second-rower Jimmy Thompson who sent his captain John Newlove in for a try by the posts, despite a desperate attempt by me to stop him. Box kicked the goal and they were 9–8 up at the break.

Our scrum-half, Parry Gordon, was carrying a hip injury as well and so Murph, who hated needles, had five pain-killing injections in the dressing room and came out for the second half to finish the job. First, he sent centre Derek Noonan through a gap for Kevin Ashcroft to score our first try. Derek Whitehead added the conversion and kicked two more penalties to put us 17–9 in front. Then Murph kicked two drop-goals to make it 21–9.

I was at my optimum fitness, but copped a high tackle from Billy Harris, their prop forward, which fractured my jaw. It was uncomfortable, but it wasn't displaced and I was so full of adrenalin I didn't really feel it. Things started to turn ugly after that and a brawl erupted. Bobby Wanbon and Barry Philbin traded punches with Les Tonks and Keith Bridges, but no one was sent off. Murph said after the match: "The referee did a great job. He could have sent four men off, but this is Wembley and it's not a girls' game." Derek 'Nobby' Clarke, our assistant coach, added: "We won the match and the brawl."

My big moment came on 75 minutes. I took a pass from Alan Whittle, at speed, 20 yards out, and stepped off my right foot to go inside John Newlove. I then stepped off my right foot again, beat another defender and headed for the line. No one was going to stop me. I touched down and threw my arms up in the air. Dave Chisnall ran in and picked me up. It was a sweet moment; 24–9. Featherstone could not catch us now. We had won the cup.

I was told that I missed out on the Lance Todd Trophy for man-of-the-match by one vote and I scored my try after they picked the winner. It went to Derek Whitehead for his seven goals, which were the difference in a tight match. It was one try apiece before I scored. Jack Bentley, the rugby league writer with the *Daily Express*, didn't go to Wembley. He reported the match from the television coverage, but would have picked me as man-of-the-match. In that case Derek and I could have shared the award. I would have loved that.

If only the full-time hooter had sounded there and then. With just seconds to go, I was running the ball out when my studs caught in the Wembley turf. The pitch was like a fine mesh and a lot of soccer players had had problems with it. There was a Wembley hoodoo. Somebody came in to tackle me and I swivelled to fend them off, but my leg stayed where it was. All of my upper body rotated and my knee just went; my cruciate ligament was ruptured. I was on the deck for about five minutes. The pain was excruciating. At first I didn't realise just how bad it was; I got up, limped around and went up the 39 steps to collect my medal.

There was blood coming out of my mouth from my fractured jaw and my knee was knackered. I was in a bad way and could hardly walk. I even missed the lap of honour. These days it would mean a complete knee reconstruction and being out for a year. Soccer players were finished then if they ruptured a cruciate ligament because they couldn't kick the ball. All I could do was build up my quads, strap the knee and run in straight lines as if I was on a railway track. I played for another seven years like that.

Heading for the line: Slicing through the Featherstone defence at Wembley.
(Courtesy *Warrington Guardian*)

Magic moment: Scoring at Wembley to seal Warrington's Challenge Cup win.
(Photo: courtesy Stan Lewandowski).

Top: Cup kings: In the dressing room after the match and one of the few pictures of Mike with the Challenge Cup. Left to right, back: trainer Derek 'Nobby' Clarke, Kevin Ashcroft, Dave Chisnall, Mike, chief scout Albert White; front: Billy Pickup, Mike Philbin, Brian Brady, Bobby Wanbon, mascot Gary Ashcroft, Barry Philbin.

Below: The menu from the post-match dinner, which was wasted on Mike who had a broken jaw.

Wembley winners: Left to right, back: Derek Noonan, Brian Brady, Derek Whitehead, Billy Pickup; middle: trainer Derek 'Nobby' Clarke, Dave Chisnall, Bobby Wanbon, Dave Wright, Barry Philbin, Mike; front: John Bevan, Mike Philbin, Alex Murphy, Kevin Ashcroft, Parry Gordon & Alan Whittle. (Photo: Eddie Fuller).

Wembley reunion: The team 25 years later in 1999, in exactly the same places, not looking a day older. (Photo: Eddie Whitham).

I remember talking to Parry in the dressing room after the match, discussing backgrounds and where we came from and he asked: "What's it like in Wales, Mike?" I said that rugby in Wales was like a religion. Growing up, I had a ball in my hands all the time and lived and breathed the game. He said: "You're luckier than us in Wigan. I had a bundle of rags in my hands and I used to take it everywhere as well. We couldn't afford a ball."

I went back to the hotel; they had a look at the knee and said they couldn't do anything for me. Arthur Morris, the club's orthopaedic surgeon, said I would just have to wait for it to settle because it was extremely swollen. Even if the ligament had torn they couldn't do anything. I knew I was in serious trouble. Then, stupidly, I went and celebrated with the boys, over-celebrated really. We had a really good night, drinking whisky and brandy and whatever. When I went back to my room I found it had been commandeered by half-a-dozen of my mates from Aberavon and so I went to sleep in Dave Wright's room instead.

I couldn't get out of bed the next morning. Dave said: "Come on, let's go." I said I couldn't get out of bed. He said: "What do you mean?" I said: "I can't move and my knee has gone and my jaw has gone." And all of that was compounded by a huge hangover. I had to be lifted onto a linen trolley and taken downstairs in the lift. Albert White, the Warrington chief scout, produced a walking stick from somewhere. I don't know where he got it from, perhaps he robbed a Chelsea pensioner, but we got on the bus.

I was in a really bad way with fluid coming out of my mouth. We got back to Warrington for the parade around town; 100,000 fans turned out to welcome us, but I didn't want to go anywhere. I just slumped at the back of the bus. I'm not in the celebration photographs.

When we finally arrived at Warrington Town Hall, Parry Gordon fell asleep. We put a curtain over him and left him. I was left behind as well when the bus moved on to Wilderspool. I was out of it, but they sent the mayor's car back to ferry me and Parry to Wilderspool for the celebration banquet. Beautiful pieces of chicken and turkey legs were passed in front of me, but I couldn't eat them because of my fractured jaw. I had some soup. I was laid up for about a month or six weeks after that and on crutches.

Two months before Wembley I had been picked for the Great Britain tour of Australia and New Zealand that summer, which was a dream come true. But I had to pull out of it. Jimmy Thompson was called up as my replacement. My bad luck was his good fortune. I had all the gear for the tour: blazer, jerseys, a map of where I was going, starting off in Darwen, going to Cairns and Rockhampton. I had it all planned out. The worst thing was that the Rugby Football League (RFL) took all the gear back. I thought: "Who is going to fit into my blazer?" They wanted everything, but I said "you're not having the tie" and kept it.

I had also been in touch with Manly, a top Australian club, who were going to offer me a contract. I was to take over from Mal Reilly. They had sent me a dossier, like a draft contract, telling me what I would earn and it worked out at about five times what I was on at Warrington. That didn't happen either. Steve 'Knocker' Norton, the Castleford loose-forward, got that contract instead and went on to win the Australian Grand Final in 1976.

The try at Wembley had been my seventh of the season. Seven tries in seven different matches and we had won them all. But, because of the ruptured knee, my days as a running second-row forward were over. My game had to evolve. I had to become an enforcer, a hit-man, and that would get me into more trouble with the referees.

We were on £350 a man for winning at Wembley and £100 for losing, but we had decided beforehand to share the money between the full first-team squad of 25. So I got a broken jaw and a ruptured cruciate ligament and ended up with £210 – the same money as the 10 squad players who had gone to Wembley for a booze up!

More bad news was waiting for me. A mate of mine, who I was doing some business with, had borrowed my Jaguar XJ6 and blew it up on the motorway on the way down to Wembley. We weren't friends much after that.

I had just started playing golf and some Warrington supporters had a whip round because I had missed the tour and presented me with a set of golf clubs, which was lovely of them. But it wasn't quite the same as three months on tour, £100 a week expenses and a £2,000 share of the profits at the end of it. It was a massive blow and a major crossroads in my life. Things have turned out all right – I have three wonderful kids and a wonderful grandson – but I have often wondered what would have happened if I had signed for Manly. I was single. If I had gone there and liked it, I would probably have stayed.

Dave Wright recalls: "*When I arrived in Warrington, I hadn't even heard of Mike Nicholas; but it only took me one day to find out about him and he and I have been mates ever since. We had a great relationship when I was here both on and off the field, we played in the second row together, and we have kept in touch ever since. Mike was great to play with because he was so tough. I never regarded myself as a really hard player, I could hold my own, but I was never one to look for trouble. Mike was terrific because he protected the rest of the team. He was as tough as they come and talented. We complemented each other.*

When I came to England my reputation in Australia was more as a ball distributor, but when I came into the Warrington set-up we had Chissie who was an excellent ball distributor and Kevin Ashcroft who could offload a ball and so I thought: 'How am I going to balance this side? How am I going to fit in?' So I did a fair bit of tackling. I did Mike's tackling for him. That's why my shoulders are so sore. Interestingly enough, what I was remembered for was my low tackling style. Some of the boys used to go up high in that era. I thought I could tackle and back up a little and follow fellas like Chissie and Mike who could offload the ball. It was a wonderful experience. Wembley was super, super special and it capped off an amazing season. I played 25 games, won 22, only lost three and one of those was against Whitehaven who were bottom of the table and so we weren't focused. We had a super, super season.

Wembley wasn't even on my bucket list because I hadn't thought I could ever get to Wembley, but we did. The final is a blur to a certain extent, but there are some things I remember so vividly. It was terrific. We fell behind and then struck back. Mike had a fantastic game. He was going through gaps. I had a couple of runs. It was just so, so good; but unfortunately Mike got injured late in the game. Injured his knee, injured his jaw, and couldn't walk and couldn't talk after the game. And the not talking bit was difficult for him."

Bennie Crawford, a lifelong friend of Mike Nicholas, remembers: *"I met Alex Murphy in the Kensington Palace Hotel after the final and the first thing he said to me was: 'Have you heard any racing results?' I said I had heard them all. I couldn't live without my racing results. I asked: 'What have you backed?' He showed me his betting slip; he had done a Yankee and all four had won. Murphy was over the moon."*

2. 15 sendings-off

My first sending off was against Leigh at Wilderspool on Boxing Day 1972. I had never experienced a Boxing Day derby before and it was amazing, the speed, the intensity and the crowd were even more volatile than normal. Tony Barrow, the Leigh stand-off, was sent off for flying in on Dave Chisnall for apparently no reason at all and nearly taking his head off. Maybe it was personal from their St Helens days or whatever. I couldn't see any other reason for it, unless it was something that had carried over. In the brawl that followed I ended up getting involved with Tony's brother, Frankie, who I set about and then got sent off by Sam Shepherd. I had picked up an injury shortly before that and if I hadn't been sent off I would have gone off injured. It was very apt that it was Boxing Day. In the tea room after the game I didn't recognise one of their players. I thought: "I don't remember him playing today." But it was Geoff 'Piggy' Fletcher, who was a pig farmer in St Helens. I was new to the game and didn't realise he wore a wig. He looked like two different people on and off the pitch.

I was banned for two matches for that and it set a pattern with holiday fixtures, because I was sent off next at Widnes on Good Friday 1973. I took a short ball off Parry Gordon under the posts and got clattered unceremoniously by two or three Widnes players. Loose-forward Bob Blackwood stood back, on the blindside of the referee, Gerry Kershaw, and let me have it, splattering my face. The ref never saw it. My lip disintegrated in three or four directions and obviously I had to go off for treatment. They did their best to patch it all up, but I couldn't even talk. Alex Murphy sent Gilly Wright on as a substitute and Gilly got injured after about 10 minutes. I remember Murph saying to me: "Get back on." I remember saying to him, in a muffled voice: "Are you sure you want me to go back on?" I went back on, but I had no intention of playing. I only went on for one reason and that was to flatten Bob Blackwood. I never paid any attention to the play. I just followed him; zeroed in and zeroed in and as soon as he got the ball I just piled in and gave him everything. I knew I was going to get sent off and so I jogged off. I broke his nose or whatever. It was a television game and there were pictures of him with blood pouring out of his nose. Murph shouldn't have sent me back on, to be honest. I only had one thing in mind and that was retribution against Mr Blackwood.

We have become very good friends since. He was a hard-as-nails Cumbrian and loved all the hurly-burly. The tougher the game became, the more he revelled in it. He was one tough hombre, a really good competitor.

I got changed, jumped into my MGB and thought: "What the hell have I let myself in for here? What sort of game is rugby league?" I drove straight back to Wales, got to the Grand Hotel in Port Talbot and had a couple of pints. The following day I went to watch Aberavon play London Welsh in the traditional Easter Saturday fixture. I couldn't go in the clubhouse – I was banned because I was a professional – and so I stood with my uncle Grenville in the Shed opposite the main grandstand and watched the match. One wag shouted out: "How's your hand Mike after yesterday? Is it broken?" I really did belt Bob Blackwood and was banned for four matches.

In a funny way, it actually did me a bit of good because other players became wary of me after that. I got a bit of publicity out of it and people started to take notice of me. A few years ago Bob was involved in a car crash and I went to visit him in Whiston Hospital. He must have thought I had come to finish him off.

Bob Blackwood remembers: *"I 'accidentally' made a mess of his mouth; he was escorted off for treatment and a clean-up and to his dismay was ordered back to the field of play by none other than the marvellous Alex Murphy. Mike made a bee line for me and got sent off. That isn't the end of the story and, from what Mike told me years after the event, he drove down to South Wales with the intention of never playing again, but his competitive nature dragged him back. I am pleased he made that decision because we are now firm friends."*

An urban myth has become attached to my third sending off, at Central Park in a Challenge Cup quarter-final in March 1974. There were 21,000 there and it was one of those games you have to win if you are going to get to Wembley. It was a crunch game and it was tense. Colin Clarke, the Wigan captain and hooker, was sent off by Gerry Kershaw 10 minutes into the second half for a high tackle on our centre, Billy Pickup. Ten minutes later Eddie Cunningham, their loose-forward, and I were sent off for fighting, but I felt a bit hard done by because he'd had started it and I was trying to get to him all the way off the pitch. Alan Whittle tried to placate me. I brushed him off and he was in my team. Tempers were really running high and it spilled over into the dressing rooms. There was a bit of toing and froing. At Wigan, the dressing rooms were close together and there was a communal bath, one of the deepest baths I had ever seen in my life. It had a 10 metre board; Tom Daley could have trained in it. Albert White, Warrington's chief scout, perpetuated this myth that I tried to drown Eddie and that Alex Murphy had to jump into the bath, fully clothed, to separate us, but it's not true. We were arguing and stuff and it did carry on into the dressing rooms, but I don't think it ever got to the bath. Well, that's my story anyway.

I shouldn't even have been on the field for my fourth sending off; in a Lancashire Cup tie away to Rochdale Hornets in September 1974. I had ruptured my cruciate ligament at Wembley and pulled out of the Great Britain tour in May, just four months before. I knew I shouldn't have been on the field at Rochdale and was very tentative. The last thing I needed was a local boy from Burtonwood, Tony Cooke, having a go at me. I thought "I don't need this as well as feeling my knee;" butted him and walked off before Fred Lindop could send me off. Tony is a nice guy and we have had a chat about it since. I was banned for four matches for that.

Bob Welding, the Rochdale second row that day, was one of the few opponents I would have a quiet drink with after a game. Jimmy Thompson, of Featherstone Rovers and Bradford Northern, was another. Bob was a warrior, a tough boy, hard as teak and used to wear a head band. On one occasion he was playing for Rochdale against Salford and I went over to watch him to try and pick up a few tips on the game. I got there three minutes after the kick-off and he was leaving the field after being sent off. He was one of the guys I respected and a lovely man too. Years later, I bumped into him a few times, playing golf.

Sending off number five came in a league game against Huddersfield at Wilderspool in November 1975. It was my first game of the season because of injury problems and I wasn't match fit. Things that I would normally have brushed off, I reacted to. I flattened Glenn Knight, their centre, after 28 minutes. Bill Allen sent me off and I was banned for four matches. Two 'A' team games counted towards the ban – even though one of them was actually postponed. Glenn signed for Warrington the following month and when he arrived for training he put his head around the dressing room door and sheepishly asked me: "Am I all right to come in?"

Former team-mate Clive Jones recollects: *"I played against Nicko quite a few times after I signed for Leigh. We beat them a couple of times at Leigh and narrowly missed out at Warrington. Mike and I had a few tussles and I can remember having a bit of a flare-up with Nicko at Leigh. He attacked me and I grabbed him by his shirt collar and held him at bay as he swung three or four punches. Fortunately for me, I have got longer arms than Nicko. Obviously, we had a pie and a pint after the game because when you were at Leigh – or Wigan – you got a pie. He was as hard as nails and wouldn't take a backward step. On numerous occasions he would pile into somebody who was a foot taller and three or four stones heavier. Ask Big Jim Mills about that. Big Jim was sent off 20 times, but he played more games than Nicko. Pro rata, Nicko beat him.*

My sixth sending off came at Featherstone in the first leg of the Premiership semi-final in May 1977 and, again, I felt hard done by. I tackled Peter Smith on the chest and I thought that he did a backward somersault, with two and a half tucks, a tariff three dive. He got me sent off for nothing. It was a harsh decision. It looked far worse than it was. Stan Wall sent me off and I was fined £10, about £100 in today's money. I decided I would give Smith a real stinger the next time we met and let him know what a proper tackle was, but I had to wait until December 1978 and a John Player Trophy game at Featherstone. I made up for lost time though, because I flattened him when we were changing ends before the game started. We won the toss and decided to play up the slope in the first half so that we had the advantage in the second half. We were changing ends and coming through the ranks and Peter Smith walked right across me and I clipped him with my elbow. He went flat out on the floor, prone. I carried on through. The touch judges were combing their hair and the referee, Ronnie Campbell, was stretching his hamstrings. There was a body on the halfway line and they didn't know what to do about it.

When they brought him round, Smith went over to his team-mate Mick Morgan. His nose and his mouth were bust and he said: "Look what this bastard's done to me. What are we going to do about it?" Mick said: "Nothing really, but it looks like we're in for a hard game."

All this delayed the start. I was hiding in the line, keeping out of the way. I should have been sent off before the game started, but the referee had never come across that situation before and didn't know how to apply the laws; so he had to start the game. When the game kicked off the Featherstone players were after me. They knew I had done it and were trying to get me. Keith Bell tried to drop his elbow into my cheekbone; so I reacted to that and was sent off. It was fighting fire with fire. Warrington won 7–0, one of the few times Featherstone have been nilled at home, and I was banned for two matches.

Team-mate Mike Peers remembers: *"On the bus going up to Featherstone, Mike was still bitter about Peter Smith and saying: 'He's going, he's going today'. This was in the days of winning pay and losing pay. If you lost you got £10 and that was taxed. Tommy Martyn and I were saying: "Let's get the game won first and then do what you want." All you could hear in the dressing room was: "He's going today, he's going today." We went out on to the pitch; tossed up and we had to change ends. When we turned around to kick off Peter Smith was flat out on the centre spot and they carried him off on a stretcher. Everybody knew who had done it. We were lining up for the kick-off and Nicko said to me: 'Bloody hell, I didn't think I'd get a chance that early.' He had flattened him before kick-off. The referee Ronnie Campbell knew who had done it, but couldn't send him off because the match hadn't even started."*

In between the two sendings off at Featherstone, I was sent off by John McDonald at York in the first round of the Challenge Cup in February 1978 for leading with an elbow against Terry Ramshaw. But you couldn't miss Ramshaw's jaw; he had a jaw like Desperate Dan. What do you do if you think someone was coming to knock your head off? You protect yourself, don't you?

Sending off number eight came against Widnes at Wilderspool in the quarter-finals of the Challenge Cup in March 1978. My unofficial job was to take the best ball-player out of the game and Doug Laughton was their best ball-player. He was a great player, a fantastic player. If I could nullify him we had a chance. I was having a go at him and, by injury time at the end of the first half, he had had enough. He reacted; we exchanged blows and head butts and Fred Lindop sent us both off. The plan had worked and I had got their most creative player off the field. Big Jim Mills had to separate us, which must be the only time in his career that he acted as the peacemaker. All hell broke loose after that. I gave him another smack on the way off. Alex Murphy had a go at Fred Lindop in the tunnel and had to be restrained by Chief Superintendent Dennis Holland. It looked like they were wrestling each other. Two more Widnes players, Paul Woods and Eric Hughes, were sent off and Warrington won 6–0 with three penalty goals from Steve Hesford. I have still got a copy of Fred Lindop's *Dismissal Report* from that match and it makes fascinating reading. (It is reprinted, in full, in an appendix at the end of the book.)

Shortly afterwards, Doug Laughton rang me up and asked if I wanted to join Widnes. He was looking for an experienced prop. I said I was really honoured and proud to be asked, they were the cup kings, but said I loved Warrington and wanted to stay. I said I had been there six years, was only three or four years off a benefit and so I declined. I think he signed Brian Lockwood instead.

Doug Laughton, the former Widnes captain and coach and 1979 Man of Steel, recalls: *"I was sent off with him at Warrington in a cup match. The swine hit me after I passed the ball and we went at it hammer and tongs. As we were walking off we had another little go. He wasn't a tall man, but he was a wide man. He was like an Oxo cube with legs. He was 5 feet 10 inches in every direction. He was a hard man and a good forward. Murphy must have told him to 'stop that bugger Laughton' and he was a nuisance. Everywhere I went he was after me. In the end I had had enough of it, but he was a good forward as well. I did try to buy him for Widnes, but there was no chance. He was one tough cookie. He had a go at Jim Mills a few times and that takes a brave man. That normally means 'call the ambulance'.*

Later that year Mike had his leg in plaster and was on crutches. I was out with him in Warrington. We went to a nightclub; I knocked on the door and they opened a small window in the door. The nightclub had had some trouble with rugby players a few days before – I don't know if they were professional or amateur – and the man on the door said: 'You are a rugby player aren't you?' I said: 'Yes.' He said I wasn't welcome. Mike was behind me and he said we kept the club going with our custom and told me to knock again. As the man opened the small window Mike launched his crutch straight through and into his face and said 'We're coming in' and in we went."

The RFL's disciplinary committee at Leeds only met once a month in those days and so when I appeared before them on 30 March 1978, I had to answer for two sendings off – the ones against York and Widnes – and two recorded cautions. I almost had a full house. They used to keep me and Big Jim back until last because our files were bigger than the others. They used to bring our files in on a trolley at the end and we used to get booed by the people on the committee. I received a sending off sufficient verdict for the dismissal at York, a two-match ban for the sending off against Widnes and a one-match ban for the two recorded cautions, three matches in all, and that ruled me out of the Challenge Cup semi-final against St Helens.

Grandstand on the BBC used to feature the second half of matches on Saturday afternoons and my mother and father used to switch the television on with some trepidation because they were worried I might have already been sent off. My mam would look at the teams and then say to my dad with a mixture of pride and relief: "He's still on Geoff."

Team-mate Mike Peers recalls: *"I remember Nicko's 10th sending off very well. It was against Barrow at Wilderspool in December 1978. Barrow were top of the league at the time, Ken Gill was playing for them, and they had a very good side. They were top and we were second. In training on the Thursday night Tony Waller pulled his hamstring, so we had no hooker and I got the job. I turned up on the day 45 minutes before kick-off and Nicko was propping. He was going to be number 8. We were getting changed next to each other and he didn't speak to me at all. He just ignored me all the way through the 45 minutes. They had a hooker called Eddie Szymala who was well known as the biggest crackpot in the game. He had such thick arms. I was thinking 'I have got to hook against him and Nicko's not talking to me,' but just as they blew the whistle to go out he grabbed me by the shoulder and said: 'Now look. At the first scrum you nut Szymala and I'll nut Steve Hogan. And if you don't, I'm going to leave you on your own all the game.' Unbelievably there was a knock-on straight from the kick-off and so the first action in the match was a scrum. We were walking to the scrum and Nicko pointed at me and said: 'Right, I've told you.' So we got to the scrum and I looked at Szymala and I looked at Nicko and thought 'I've only got one choice here'. So I put the head on Szymala and Mike put the head on Steve Hogan. A fight broke out, spilled over the wall and in the end the police had to break it up. Ten minutes later, Szymala got sent off which I was very, very pleased about; but 10 minutes after that Mike got sent off as well."*

I remember it a bit differently to Mike. I knew he was going to struggle as a hooker that day and so I took as much pressure off him as I could. I was the one taking Szymala out and Mike was looking after the rest of it. I knew what Szymala was like. We just gave it to him really. I can't even remember the incident John McDonald sent me off for, but there was obviously a build-up with me and Szymala who was, like Mike said, we thought a bit of a crackpot. I was only banned for one match for that.

Anyway, 12 years later, in an interview for the magazine *13*, Szymala included me in his list of 'The 13 meanest men who ever hit me' as follows: "Mike Nicholas: A super-hard, barrel-chested front row for Warrington. His nickname was 'the blond bombshell'. I had watched him play and before I ever played against him I knew we would end up having a do. He was just that sort of player. But, like most, he was very friendly over a pint after the game."

Sending off number 11 came at Leigh during a league match in March 1979 and was a bit of a funny one. They had a ball-playing second row or prop called Mal Yates (now deceased). He was a lovely boy and a very sociable guy, but it was my job to target the ball-player, take him out or disrupt him. He was a very good ball-player, but not very fit. Tommy Grainey, who had been at Warrington, was coaching Leigh then with Colin Clarke as his assistant. Colin Clarke was going mad because I was flying into everybody and banging everybody around, but Tommy was remonstrating with me and saying: "Mike, calm down, calm down." He was the opposition coach, but I had a really good personal relationship with him. One coach was going off his head and wanting to kill me and the other coach was saying: "Take it easy, take it easy." I tackled Mal as much as I could, but I overdid it and eventually Joe Jackson sent me off. That was another one-match ban.

Sending off number 12 came after just three minutes of the Premiership semi-final against Bradford Northern at Wilderspool in May 1979, but all started in the league game at Odsal five weeks before. Some of the Warrington players didn't fancy going to Bradford. It seemed like it was going to be guaranteed losing pay. We took a virtual 'A' team and were so depleted that I had to play at number 8 instead of number 10. They had a juggernaut pack including Keith Bridges, Jeff Grayshon, Len Casey and Jimmy Thompson and I was marking Ian van Bellen. It was a typical Peter Fox-assembled side.

Odsal was a shocking place to play as well. From the dressing rooms and walking down the stand it was like going down into the bowels of the earth. It was almost like going into an amphitheatre. I knew I had to lead from the front and Jimmy Thompson and I had a massive clash early on. It was like a medieval joust and I had my hands full with van Bellen at the scrums, but I never let him get settled. I pulled him all over the shop. Jimmy Thompson came in to do me with his elbow, but I managed to get in ahead of him with my elbow and put him down.

His eyes and his lips popped and he went on the deck. Billy Thompson pointed to the dressing room to send me off, but then he looked around and saw what a young side we had and changed his mind. "Penalty to Bradford," he said, "and look after those kids." I stayed on and we beat them 22–14 with two tries from Ken Kelly and five goals from Steve Hesford. Right on the hooter the Bradford players ganged up on me. I was held up in a tackle; Keith Bridges came from behind and hit me and broke my jaw. A tooth was smashed and the fracture went through my jaw. I had to be helped off the pitch. John Dalgreen, who didn't play that day, and Dougie Hankey, the secretary of the Crosfields club, who was a big Warrington supporter, helped me up through the crowd, one on each shoulder. My jaw had gone and my nose was bust, there was membrane hanging out of my nose, and one of their spectators said: "You dirty Welsh bastard. He should have knocked your head off." I couldn't help it. I pushed Dougie to one side and hit him.

Before the Premiership semi-final our coach, Billy Benyon, said to me "behave yourself today," but I had no intention of listening. I just wanted retribution against Mr Bridges as soon as I could. At the first scrum I thought: "OK, I will give him a smack here and let him know." I missed him and he started laughing to his team-mates. It was the worst thing he could have done. At the next scrum, I managed to control the scrum and collapsed it in a way that I was in a position where I could grab him by the strands of his hair. In no way am I proud of this, but I then booted him straight in the part of the head where he had broken my jaw. Jimmy Thompson saw it and couldn't believe it. He piled into me and I piled into him. Fred Lindop sent us both off and Bridges was carried off. I was fed up with all this gratuitous violence. I went in the dressing room, quickly got changed and walked out down Fletcher Street and passed Jan, Mike Peers' girlfriend. She was late for the game and just arriving. I said "Hi, Jan", went back to my office in my taxi rank and watched the game on television. When Jan got in the stand she turned to Mike and said: "I thought Nicko was playing today." Mike said: "He was, he's just been sent off." She said: "He can't have been. He's just passed me in the street and it's only ten past three."

Parry Gordon said to me later that because Bradford couldn't win any ball without Bridges, who was their hooker, they put him in the shower to bring him around and he came back on to the field for the second half soaking wet. Peter Fox, the Bradford coach, said on television later: "One of my players nearly got decapitated today." He seemed to forget that Len Casey broke Ken Kelly's jaw in the same match and put him out of the Great Britain tour, but never got sent off.

Top: Welcome to rugby league: Three Widnes players tackle Mike at Naughton Park on Good Friday 1973, seconds before Bob Blackwood, number 12, attacked him on the blindside of the referee, but he did take revenge. Ray Dutton is the Widnes full-back and John Warlow is number 8. Barry Briggs is the other Warrington player.
(Photo: Eddie Fuller).

Left: Two of a kind: Mike being tackled by Big Jim Mills of Widnes at Wilderspool in April 1974. Big Jim was sent off 20 times in his career. Mike was sent off 15 times, but only played half as many games.
(Photo: courtesy Stan Lewandowski).

Left: Taking it on the chin: Mike on the receiving end of a high tackle against Workington Town at Wilderspool in October 1978.
(Photo: Eddie Whitham)

Below: Early bath: Mike following Bradford's Jimmy Thompson off the pitch after they were both sent off by referee Fred Lindop for fighting after three minutes of the Premiership Trophy semi-final at Wilderspool in May 1979. Dave Sutton is the Warrington winger with his hands on his hips.
(Photo: Eddie Fuller).

It was all a continuation of the previous game at Odsal; like a blinking saga. That was how it was. It was like a series of events. If you didn't have a go back, it would be a sign of weakness. You had to balance the books. Warrington wrote to the RFL that week, asking that Fred Lindop no longer be allowed to referee Warrington matches. Bradford won 14–11, but lost to Leeds in the final. I was banned for four matches.

Fred Lindop recollects: *"Off the field you couldn't wish to meet a nicer bloke than Mike Nicholas. On the field he was ferocious and played in a very physical Warrington team. He wasn't the tallest of blokes, but he was very broad and never took a backward step, that's for sure. He and Big Jim Mills just didn't like each other. I remember the John Player Trophy final at St Helens in 1979. Big Jim had him down on the floor and was about to punch him, but Mike moved his head at the last minute and Jim missed. I still sent him off and Jim grabbed me after the game and asked: "Why did you send me off?" I said that everybody in the ground had seen it. "Yes," said Jim, "but I missed him. You shouldn't have sent me off for missing him."*

Former referee Billy Thompson recalls: *"I remember one Warrington versus Widnes match at Wilderspool. The two teams were in the tunnel waiting to go onto the pitch. Mike said to Jim: 'How are you doing?' Jim replied: 'How am I doing? I'm going to give you plenty of this (waving his fist) and kick you between the posts.' Mike said to me: 'Billy, are you listening to this?' I replied: 'He's not talking to me...'"*

Sending off number 13 was in my last first team game for Warrington, at Blackpool Borough in April 1980. In the second half, John Corcoran and I were testing each other out and ended up fighting. Harry Hunt sent us both off. There was a dog track at Borough Park and a nightclub called Styx. It was a lovely old ground; I remember walking off and taking tremendous abuse from the crowd. Yet again I had a busted nose and snorted blood over the crowd and sprayed them. I was like a pantomime villain really, taking the crowd on. I was banned for six matches for that.

Sending off number 14 was for the Cardiff City Blue Dragons against Hunslet at Ninian Park in September 1981. Robin Whitfield was the referee and I remembered that he had been sent off in 1974 while playing for Huyton for a high tackle on Derek Noonan. By then I was 35 and was at a time in my career when I didn't care. I was a law unto myself, a coach's nightmare. I did my own thing. I was still professional about training, but it was getting near the time to finish playing. I clipped somebody off the ball, it wasn't that bad actually, but Robin sent me off. I said: "I'm not going Robin." He said: "What do you mean you're not going?" I said: "I'm not going off this field. You put Derek Noonan in Broad Green Hospital for two weeks. You've done 20 times worse than I've just done. I'm staying on." He didn't know what to do. He was beside himself. He stopped the game. In the end he called our captain, George Nicholls, over and said he was going to have to abandon the game because I wouldn't go off. I said: "I've done nothing George." I was playing it right to the hilt, putting him right on the spot. George said: "Mike, you've got to go." I said: "I'm going George, I'm only having a bit of fun with him."

My 15th – and final – sending off came at Tylorstown in the Rhondda Valley in July 1983 in John Bevan's testimonial match. I was still embittered at the way I had left Warrington, but I ended up playing for Warrington against the Cardiff City Blue Dragons. The game was played at Tylorstown Rugby Football Club [John Bevan's old club] whose ground, Penrhys Park, is halfway up "Heart Attack Hill" and was cut into the side of the mountain by unemployed miners at the time of the great depression of the 1930s. From the kick-off, I could see that Chris Seldon was pretty agitated and nervous. They also had a big prop from Merthyr. I didn't hold back, even though it was a friendly and I had played with Cardiff the year before. That's the way I played the game and I clashed with Seldon after a couple of minutes and Frank Tickle sent us both off. We had another go on the way off, which was normal practice for me, and it spilled over into the dressing rooms. They were temporary dressing rooms, Portacabins. I kicked the door down in theirs to get at him and half-a-dozen of his mates jumped on me. I came off second best and the Portacabin nearly turned over. I jumped in my car again, went over the Bwlch and back to Port Talbot. It was two weeks away from my 37th birthday and my rugby league playing days were over.

Ken Kelly, former team-mate and 1981 Man of Steel, writes: *"We went down on a double decker bus to the John Bevan testimonial match on Heart Attack Hill, which put you off straight away. Mike said he wanted to play for the Cardiff team and we said that was fair enough because he was Welsh. When we got there he changed his mind and said he was playing for Warrington. I asked: 'Why? I thought you were playing with your mates.'*

He said: 'Chris Seldon is playing for Cardiff and I owe him something.' It was a testimonial match, but it was one of the hardest games I ever played. It was on Heart Attack Hill, it was a stony hard pitch, like concrete, and Nicko was sent off at the first scrum. Both were sent off. They had to keep them apart in the dressing room and Nicko went home. He got a full Warrington strip out of it. We never saw the strip again.

That's what you got with Nicko. You didn't know what was going through his mind. If he had something on his chest, he would get it off his chest and he would do it with his own team as well. If we were playing tick and pass at Loushers Lane or Wilderspool and somebody didn't stop when they had been ticked, there was trouble. He chased Rick Thackray into the dressing room once because he didn't stop. He had an argument with him; Rick locked himself in the toilet and Nicko was trying to bang the door down to get to him. It was horrendous. He was a colourful character. I like him. We still get on and are good mates, but you would rather have him on your side than against you."

Former team-mate Mike Peers recalls: *"Nicko was a tough guy and a lot of people only remember him for that, but he could play some rugby as well. He had a good pair of hands and was quick. He wasn't Bob Eccles quick, but he was no slouch. People just remember him for his thuggery, but he had a lot more to him than that. I enjoyed playing with him because you could always rely on him."*

Of the 15 matches when I was sent off, my team won 10 and drew one. I wasn't a liability. Still I was sent off 15 times and banned for more than 30 matches. It must have been something in the genes.

Mike leaving the field after another war. In the background, from the left, are Roy Lester, Tommy Martyn, Parry Gordon and John Dalgreen. (Photo: courtesy *Warrington Guardian*).

3. Hannibal Lecter at the door

The Nicholas side of the family originally came from Hereford. They were farming stock, gentlemen, and bred cattle and horses. They had what we would now call a few supermarkets – large grocers – and they sold produce in the South Wales conurbation. I have still got family there and we used to go there as kids for a few weeks in the summer to a village called Welsh Newton, right on the Hereford/Monmouth border. It was like real cowboys and Indians. They had a smallholding on common land; the stock used to roam during the night and so the first job in the morning was to get on a horse and round the cattle up which, for a kid, was marvellous. Then we would go for breakfast in a bunk house, although milking the cows was the priority. Around 1960 I remember going to the Monmouth Show to watch the Welsh show jumper David Broome, after he had won a bronze medal at the Rome Olympics.

Some of the family moved down into Port Talbot and were very affluent. My grandparents had 13 kids, a full rugby league team; my father, Geoffrey, was the youngest. All the other kids went to public school, which must have been a fair old financial outlay. They had the first delivery wagon in the town. They had stables, bred horses and lived in the nicest part of the town, Pentyla. The first house they lived in had five floors and servants and later became the private school, Heathmont, which Sir Anthony Hopkins went to. They downsized later to a house called Mayfield, which was a bit further up the hill. Because of the age gaps my father was only very close to his immediate older brother, Grenville. He was into cricket; he and my father ended up as umpires in the South Wales League, travelling around together for years, umpiring.

Two of my father's older brothers, Fred and Ron, had played rugby for Aberavon. My uncle Fred played on the wing for the combined Aberavon & Neath side who lost 8–3 to South Africa at Neath in November 1931. He also had a Welsh trial. He used to go to matches on his steed. He used to saddle up and go to the ground.

My father served on the Arctic convoys to Russia for about two years during the war. Then he was in the Royal Marines in Germany, house-to-house combat, 'Call of Duty' stuff, but for real. When he died in 2012, there was a full Royal Marine honour guard at his funeral. After the war, it took a while for him to get all this out of his system. My brothers Geoffrey and Clive and I were dragged down to his old haunts for about 10 years: Union Street, Plymouth, the Stonehouse Barracks and Devonport Services. We thought we were in the Marines ourselves. It felt like we had our own green berries by the time we were 10.

Mike's dad on active service in the Royal Marine commandoes during the Second World War.

Above: Happy family – Mum and Dad with Clive (back), Mike and baby Geoff.
Bottom left: Young Mike with a cheeky grin.
Bottom right: Mike making a friend at the Petticoat Lane market in London in the early 1960s.

There was no Severn Bridge in those days and it was a seven-hour journey to Plymouth. He was very proud of being a Marine and all the spit and polish. He used to iron his own clothes and ours too, like we were on parade. He was a disciplinarian, the old-school Victorian type. He didn't show his feelings that much, but then he was from a Victorian family himself. His mother was a schoolteacher and she lived until she was 102, despite having 13 kids.

We identified more with my mother's side of the family, the poor side, and they were great people. My father finished up working in the cold mill at Margam Steelworks. He used to do all the shipment and packing. Before that he had a variety of jobs. He used to be a bus conductor on the ANC express bus from Neath to Cardiff. I used to wait at the bottom of the hill, the bus would pull up and he used to put me on the bus with him. When he drove a lorry for the local sand and gravel company, he used to take me to work with him. You couldn't do that now. My mother's maiden name was Eva Trahar. Her family came from Gwennap and Perranarworthal, near Redruth in Cornwall. They were farmers and tin miners. Trahar is an ancient Cornish name. They came to South Wales to work in the coal mines.

My mother and father met at a dance at St Joseph's Church Hall, when my father was on leave and got married in 1945. He was over in Hong Kong when I was due and they sent him home on compassionate grounds. The war was over and they were all getting demobbed anyway. My parents never swore. We weren't whiter than white, but they were decent people and open-minded. We were allowed to judge everything on its merits and I am eternally grateful for that. They provided me with the values which have stood me in good stead for life in general.

I was born in Margam, a suburb of Port Talbot, on 30 July 1946 and for the first three or four weeks of my life we lived in one of those wartime Nissen huts, made out of corrugated steel, before we moved in with my grandmother at 1 Pellau Road. There were 11 of us in a three-bedroom council house, including my uncle who was an invalid – a cripple – and slept on the landing. I slept with my grandmother and grandfather until I was four and went to school. That's how it was. My grandmother lived next to a massive steelworks, the biggest steelworks in Europe, and I used to think that everyone had a 300ft blast furnace at the bottom of their garden. It was a smoky, smelly town, but it was in the blood and I loved it. Lots of creative people came from there, the actors Richard Burton, Anthony Hopkins, Rob Brydon, Michael Sheen and Ivor Emmanuel, who sang *Men of Harlech* in the film *Zulu*.

On the political side there was the trade union leader Clive Jenkins, the Conservative MP Geoffrey Howe and George Thomas, who was the speaker in the House of Commons; quite an interesting bunch. It was a bit like that film *The Deer Hunter* because of the contrast. There was a massive steelworks and then two miles away the beautiful Margam Estate; with its castle, peacocks and deer. Later on I played cricket there.

I was christened Michael James Nicholas at St Mary's Church, Port Talbot. Dic Penderyn, the Welsh rebel and martyr, who was involved with the Merthyr Rising of 1831, is buried in the churchyard, and I think a bit of his rebellious streak rubbed off on me.

When we lived in Pellau Road, Anthony Hopkins delivered our bread. He had been born and lived in the next street, Wern Road, and his father Dick Hopkins had a bakery in Taibach. My uncle Ron drove the bread van and every morning on the round he used to call in for a cup of tea at our house; but Anthony was always very shy and retiring and hardly came into the house. He would have been 13 or 14 at the time and used to sit in the van. When Anthony had his 70th birthday party in the Orangery at Margam Abbey, he invited my uncle. Once Hannibal Lecter has delivered your bread, it's downhill all the way from there!

Geoff Nicholas, Mike's brother, adds: *"I live across the road from the house where Anthony Hopkins lived as a boy. In 2007 I was outside at the front of the house painting when I saw him and his wife Stella in the road and had a chat with them. I told him my uncle Ron had worked with him in the bakery. 'Ron Trahar', he said straight away and asked for his phone number. Anthony rang him from a film set in Barbados and his wife, Lena, answered. Anthony introduced himself as Tony Hopkins; Lena must have misheard him and said: 'Ron, it's Tony from the club on the phone for you.' Anthony invited him to his 70th birthday party, but Ron was convinced it was all a wind-up until the embossed invitation arrived in the post. They went to the do, but didn't have a chance to speak to Anthony properly and had a long chat with Michael Sheen instead. They had a brilliant night. Ron died nine months later of stomach cancer, but that night was a wonderful memory for him."*

Living in Pellau Road led to my first identity crisis. When I was four or five, I started school at Taibach Infant School, where Richard Burton had gone. We walked to school along the old quarry dram road over the mountain with the other kids. Because I came out of the Trahar house, people assumed I was one of the family and I was referred to as Michael Trahar and so I grew up thinking I was Michael Trahar. When we moved to Sandfields, when my father got a job in the steelworks, I moved to Glan y Mor School. On the first day there the teacher read the register out. She went right through the register, called my name and I never answered it. I didn't know I was Mike Nicholas, I thought I was Michael Trahar. At the end of the register, she said Michael Nicholas again and I still didn't answer. I was still waiting for my name and she said: "I think it's you because everybody else has answered. You are Michael Nicholas." And I said: "Oh, am I?" And that was it; I had my new identity when I was five.

We moved from Margam to 99, Lingfield Avenue, Sandfields. The number 99 turned out to be quite apt, because that was the number the 1974 British Lions shouted out in South Africa to tell them to hit the nearest Springbok. We were close to the beach, where a housing estate was built for the workforce at the steelworks. At one stage, 20,000 to 30,000 people worked there, plus all the ancillary staff. It was a massive complex, but because of the prevailing westerly winds we never got any of the grime. I was always on the beach and it was easy to get a game of cricket or rugby started. The rugby would end up 50-a-side and the tide was the touchline. As the tide came in the pitch got smaller and you needed better skills. We messed about playing rugby in my primary school, but it wasn't that organised. The real structured rugby came after the Eleven Plus exam.

The Sandfields School rugby team with Mike as captain. His mentor Ken Jones is on the right. Mr Williams, the head teacher, is on the left. It was a great school and they were happy days.

In the blood: Mike's uncle Fred Nicholas (seated first left) played for the combined Aberavon & Neath side against South Africa at Neath in 1931. Left to right, back: Mr T.D. Griffiths, G. Prosser, A. Lemon, Supt Rhys Davies; second row: Mr P. Howells, G. Hopkins, M. McGrath, T. Arthur, W. Vicary, E.M. Jenkins, Mr W. Griffiths; seated: Fred Nicholas, G. Moore, Cyril Griffiths (captain), P. Lloyd, G. Daniels, D. Jones; front: Wilf Selby, Tal Harris.

25

My first teacher at junior school, Mr Francis, was excellent. He was mad about the Aberavon rugby team, like me, and so I was a bit of a teachers' pet. The Aberavon constituency was a socialist hot bed, Labour used to get majorities of 30,000, but Mr Francis used to read the *Daily Mail.* I started to read it – not realising it was a Tory rag – and have never stopped;. One day I had been naughty and he was going to give me the cane. I took the cane off him and threw it out of the classroom window. I was seven or eight and that was a sign of things to come. Thankfully, he defused the situation and turned it into a laugh.

We were a sports mad family. My brother Geoff signed as an apprentice with Burnley FC when he was 14, but he only lasted a few weeks. He came home because he was homesick. He signed for them in between Leighton James and Brian Flynn, who both went on to play for Wales. Burnley had a network of scouts in South Wales. Flynn, 'Little Flynny' we called him, was from the next street. His father, Jim, had a lot to do with the FA of Wales. After that Geoff had trials with Charlton and was on Cardiff City's books for a while as an outside-left. He had a great left foot. He was a good soccer player, played rugby and cricket and used to captain the Port Talbot cricket team. My younger brother Clive was a better scrum-half than me. At some stage we have all been single-figure golfers. We were born with a massive hand-eye co-ordination talent. We could swim, run, do anything. We were multi-talented at a high level in all sports, which is something that is difficult now. We were all-rounders and even in cricket we used to bowl and bat.

My father took me to watch Aberavon from when I was six or seven. I knew every player. They played at the Talbot Athletic Ground and I found myself standing on the terraces, next to Richard Burton, watching the match. He was already a Hollywood superstar then. He had made a film called *The Robe* in 1953 which was the first film in CinemaScope. He was becoming a household name. He used to watch the matches and sometimes he'd kick the game off. He was really keen.

He told a couple of good stories about how he'd swap all his worldly goods, his chalet in Gstaad and even Elizabeth Taylor to have played in a Welsh shirt. That was a bit fanciful I think. He wasn't that good a player actually. He played, he was OK, but he also talked about someone I remember very well: Annie Mort. This was before pre-match entertainment.

This woman, in a long dress, came on the pitch and dropped goals with either foot from the halfway line. Unbelievable. She was a show in herself. I remember Cliff Morgan doing a story on her too. What a character. No local cinemas could show *The Robe* because it was in this widescreen CinemaScope and so they had to build a cinema in Swansea. Everybody in Aberavon who wanted to see it would go on a street trip. Richard Burton was the 12th child and sixth son of an alcoholic miner and his father went on one of these street trips to Swansea to watch the film. Amazingly, after 20 minutes he got bored, needed a pint, went out and left the picture house. He got absolutely leathered, then got on the bus and went home. Richard found out about this and wondered what he could do to appease him and so he bought him a television set. He sent it up to Pontrhydyfen, a mining village up the Afan Valley, where he lived.

Aberavon Boys' Club 1963: Left to right, back: Brian Lloyd (assistant coach), Clive Clifford, Gerald Humphries, Norman Thomas, Glyn Owen, Keith Jones, John 'Paco' Rees, Ken Lloyd, Terry Kibble, Aiden Williams (coach); front: Howard Mills, Phil Parry, Dai 'Tonk' Williams, Mike (captain), Pat 'Rudge' Morgan, Lewis Jones, Mike's brother Clive.

The Wales Boys' Clubs side to face England at Bridgewater in Somerset. Mike is on the far right of the front row and played on the wing because he had a sprained ankle. The result was 6–6. Mike Burton, who went on to play for Gloucester, England and the British & Irish Lions, played for England.

Left: Pat 'Rudge' Morgan and Mike in their Wales Boys' Clubs caps. Rudge was Mike's outside-half throughout their schooldays.

His father was very impressed, but he was even more impressed 10 years later when he got electricity put in and could switch it on. A similar thing happened with my father. I got him a CD about the Royal Marine bands, he was into all that, and he put it in the toaster.

I passed the Eleven Plus, but they introduced the comprehensive system for the first time in Wales and I was put in the grammar school stream. We were a new school, Sandfields Comprehensive. It was a really good school and I am very proud of it. It was progressive and the headmaster was Mr Williams. I had a great time there.

I was in Elgar House, named after the composer. The others were Hillary House (after the first man to climb Everest), Stephenson House (after the engineer), Rutherford House (after the explorer), Fleming House (the man who discovered penicillin) and Scott House (the explorer). There were a couple of dodgy teachers though. Mr Jenkins used to clean his shoes in front of you in the geography lessons, polish them while he was watching you. You would be in metalwork, soldering or something, and if the teacher, Mr Morgan, heard you giggling he would hit you on the back of the head. In woodwork, Mr Dai Greenway used to hit you over the head with the job. Someone else used to throw the wooden board duster at you. It was acceptable then. I got caned a few times at Sandfields, but not for anything serious. The deputy head, Mr Arwel Lewis, was pretty sadistic with it and I got caned a few times by him. He had a special rosewood cane which could inflict quite a bit of damage.

For games, we had a great teacher called Ken Jones who had played for Aberavon and Harlequins and went to Loughborough. He was very influential on my career. Being born in late July was a massive drawback in the school system, because you were the youngest and smallest in the year and he put me at scrum-half. I was quite small and broke my collar bone twice before I was 15, once when I was just a kid and once in a Wales secondary schools trial in Bridgend. Even at 15 I was only 5 feet 1 inch and about 10-and-a-half stones. I always felt he should have played me at hooker. I think I would have had a more illustrious career, especially in rugby union, at hooker; but I became captain of the first XV in 1958 and we were unbeaten for three years.

I also had plenty of trials for Wales at junior representative level, but I was always, in effect, a year behind. I even captained the Reds against the Whites in a Welsh youth trial, but I just didn't get into the national team. Stuart Gallacher, who went to Bradford Northern, and Peter Rowe, who went to Wigan, played that day. Roy Mathias (St Helens), Brian Butler (Bradford) and Stuart Ferguson (Leigh) were also around. We were all the same age group. Then, between 15 and 16, I shot up to my present height, 5 feet 9 inches, and put a bit of weight on and things started happening.

The Swansea Bay railway line ran behind our street and it brought the miners down to the beach in the summer on old steam trains. There were only half-a-dozen trains a day. The main line was London to Fishguard; the Swansea Bay branch line emptied the valleys onto the beach and then swung back onto the main line. We used to go over the branch line to play in the fields and did everything: long jump, athletics, golf, five-day test matches. Anything that was on television, we recreated the day after or the week after. We used to call it the 'Street Olympics'. The main opposition was the three Jones brothers – Wes, Byron and Gerald – from number 89.

I knew how late I was for secondary school when the train overtook me. They were always on time. Spot on 8.50am it left Aberavon seaside. If I wasn't at Southdown Road I was going to be late. I still had 600 yards to go. There was an 8.50am train, a 10.30am train, a 12.20pm train and one in the afternoon. They sounded like a boiling coffee pot.

At Sandfields, we didn't have a proper rugby pitch and so we had to play on a gravel pitch. I think I had 14 fillings before I was 15 from playing on that pitch. But once you have played on something like that, the rest is easy.

Soccer was banned at Sandfields. We weren't allowed to play anything but rugby union, cricket in the summer and a bit of athletics. I always felt deep down that that was iniquitous. I was always drawn to rugby league for some reason and I used to watch it on *Grandstand* starring Billy Boston and the boys. My mates and I created our own soccer team and so we had to double up on Saturdays; rugby union in the morning and soccer in the afternoon. I was a midfield chopper. We played for a Salvation Army soccer team called the Yellow Stars. The Salvation Army motto is "blood and fire" and that's the way we played. In the morning we might play rugby for the school and in the afternoon play soccer against someone like Gwynfi, up the Afan Valley; their pitch would be 1,000 feet above sea level. So by the time you had got up there, walked up the mountain to the pitch and played rugby, you could hardly lift your legs. There weren't many soccer skills after that; you hardly had the strength to kick the ball. It's no wonder our soccer suffered.

I got my 'O' levels and did six months in the sixth form, studying geology. My passion was geography and maps. Even now I study and collect maps. I have got a replica of the Mappi Mundi from Hereford, the largest medieval map known to still exist. I even applied for a job as a cartographer with the Ordnance Survey. But there weren't too many jobs as a geographer and so I went into geology instead. After six months, an opportunity came up to be a management trainee at the steelworks at 17 and I took it.

I wish now I had seen it through and gone to university. The trouble was I was totally into sport, every sport you could think of. My first job at the steelworks was in the blast furnaces in administration. I was doing an Ordinary National Certificate in Business Studies on day release, two nights at night school and a day a week at Margam Technical College.

All my mates were playing rugby for Aberavon Boys Club and so I played there, still at scrum-half. The Boys Club produced a lot of good players over the years. We used to train occasionally, but mainly we just played. We were all school friends and knew each other. We were a very good side and could hold our own against anybody. We used to beat Cardiff, Swansea, Newport and teams like that at youth level. One of the coaches, Len Oates, had played rugby league for Hull. Every team I played in was competitive and very tough. Gerard Lewis, the First Division football referee, was one of the people who ran the club.

My boss at the steelworks, AB Matthews, called me into his office one day and said that his son, Phil, was coming home from Marlborough College and was looking for a game of rugby. I said yes, OK, but he had a bit of a rude awakening when he came from public school to play for us. He wasn't a bad player actually and fitted in all right despite his posh accent. Rugby is a great leveller.

I finished playing at youth level at the Boys Club and joined Aberavon Harlequins, with a young centre called Francis Reynolds, Frank Reynolds as he was known later at Warrington. He was quiet, but was a good player and a good bloke. After about half-a-dozen games we both got picked up by Aberavon's first team. Francis made his Aberavon debut against Taibach at the Talbot Athletic Ground in September 1965, and I got selected a month later.

Geoff Nicholas comments: *"Mike always came home from work for dinner, to have a snack and a lie down, and in the last five minutes he would have a rush of blood and have a game of cricket with us in the garden. 'Let me bat,' he'd say. We'd all bowl to him to try to get him out and he would tap it here and tap it there and then, the very last ball before he went back to work, he would smack it down about six gardens and ruin the whole game. We couldn't find the ball and balls were hard to come by in those days."*

When I was a teenager, I spent a lot of time at the Afan Lido on the beach at Port Talbot. The lido was the brainchild of Graham Jenkins, Richard Burton's brother. It had an Olympic-sized swimming pool, sports hall and was way ahead of its time and second only to Crystal Palace in terms of facilities. It was unbelievable. In fact, six years later when I joined Warrington, their facilities were shocking in comparison. They had circus weights at the Parr Hall. All you needed was a silly moustache. It was way behind the times. We were really lucky at the Lido. It staged British boxing title fights, the Welsh Rugby Union had its base there and I played table tennis and badminton with John Simonson. He was my team-mate at Aberavon, a former Welsh table tennis champion and great all-rounder. I even trained with Davis Cup tennis players. One of my mates, Ken Williams, was that good at tennis that he went to train with the great Harry Hopman in Australia. We lived in the same street. I used to be his whipping boy really, but I was that competitive that sometimes I took a few games off him and he reacted badly. Bryn Thomas was the Lido manager; an amazing character and he became another massive influence on my life. Bryn also used to rope me in for stewarding and body guarding at events, so I ended up catching knickers at Tom Jones concerts and keeping women off the stage. It was a pretty good time. The Lido burnt down in December 2009, which was very sad – I'd spent a big part of my life there.

Bryn also had a nightclub in the town, the Carlton Club. There was always something interesting happening and celebrities there. Once, in December 1967, two submarines were on a four-day courtesy visit to Port Talbot docks, the HMS Alaric and the HMS Truncheon, and I got to meet the commander of one of the submarines. Bizarrely, the actress Ann George, who played Amy Turtle on *Crossroads*, was there as well. The commander and I, a couple of girlfriends and Amy Turtle ended up going back to the submarine; got piped on board by the sentry and had a party in his wardroom. It was claustrophobic to say the least. I remember saying to the commander: "Give me a go of your submarine." Imagine that, drunk in charge of a submarine. I drove home after that and shouldn't have. I was all over the shop. I would have done less damage fired from a torpedo tube.

4. B'ravon boy – Aberavon debut

I started watching Aberavon in the 1950s. I remember we played Auvergne, the French province, and it was a bloodbath, the dirtiest game I had seen to that point. They had two particularly tough forwards, Bernard Chevallier and Amedee Domenech, both internationals. It was a brutal game. In 1957 Aberavon & Neath played Australia and lost 5–3 in another stand-out match. A couple of their guys went on to play for the Kangaroos, including Arthur Summons, who featured on the Winfield Cup trophy, which was a bronze statue of a famous photo called *The Gladiators*. We got belted 25–5 by the 1961 South Africans at Neath. The flanker Martin Pelser, who was blind in one eye, played for them.

We were an average team in the 1950s. Then a great team came together; we won the unofficial Welsh Championship in the 1960–61 season and they were all my heroes. I can practically name the team. The great Kel Coslett, who went on to play for St Helens, was the full-back. I'll never forget him putting England flanker Budge Rogers into the Twickenham stands when playing for Wales in 1962. We had a fantastic outside-half called Cliff Ashton; they used to call the team Aber-Ashton because he was so vital to the side. John Collins was on one wing. He played for Wales and was a Royal Marine, like my father. They said he had 11 caps: one for playing rugby and 10 for playing the piano because he was an accomplished pianist.

Ken Thomas scored 26 tries that season. He was a tremendously athletic sprinter and was the strike weapon for that team really, along with John Collins. He knew more about rugby league than anybody else in rugby union. He was so up to date. He was known as Matey and he could sing the South African national anthem in both English and Afrikaans. He organised the trip to my first live game of rugby league, the 1969 Challenge Cup Final between Castleford and Salford at Wembley. We were up in the gods and practically hanging off the girders. It was a full house, over 97,000 there. I was probably in the Castleford end because our tickets came from Pontefract. Some guy who worked with me at the Baglan Bay oil refinery had got them. Three Welshmen – Dai Watkins, Colin Dixon and Ron Hill – played for Salford, but Malcolm Reilly was the man-of-the-match and won the cup for Castleford.

So Kel Coslett, Cliff Ashton, John Collins and Ken Thomas were the stand-out backs, although the others were also good players: Cyril Jones, Brian Jones and Dave Thomas. He got capped against Ireland. They used to call him Dai 'soft centre' Thomas, which I thought wasn't very fair because he was a very talented player. Billy Hullin and Tony O'Connor also played in the backs.

The great Len Cunningham, who won 14 caps for Wales, was the star prop. The other forwards were Phil Morgan, Rhys Loveluck and the Bamsey brothers, John and Alan, who were great characters and the engine room of the team. It was nothing like today, where everything is documented. The league table came out once a month and I couldn't wait for the *Daily Mirror* Monday edition to get it. I listened for the paper to come through the letter box and ran down the stairs to check what position we were. There were 18 first-class clubs and we won. They were a great footballing side. They were a tremendous squad with outstanding players all around the park. Here is the final table:

	Played	Won	Draw	Lost	For	Agst	Ave
Aberavon	**48**	**40**	**4**	**4**	**738**	**191**	**87.5**
Bridgend	45	33	2	10	564	232	75.55
Cardiff	45	31	5	9	518	268	74.44
Ebbw Vale	40	28	1	11	462	189	71.25
Newport	46	30	5	11	520	276	70.65
Pontypool	41	23	8	10	395	262	65.85
Pontypridd	40	23	5	12	328	245	63.75
Cross Keys	45	25	5	15	495	262	61.11
Swansea	45	25	5	15	482	325	61.11
Abertillery	38	20	4	14	289	195	57.89
Neath	36	18	5	13	237	162	56.94
Maesteg	43	22	3	18	420	391	54.65
Llanelli	50	22	6	22	394	285	50
Tredegar	36	16	1	19	256	231	45.83
London Welsh	35	15	2	18	374	346	45.71
Newbridge	44	15	7	22	321	344	42.04
Glamorgan W	32	10	3	19	189	277	35.93
Penarth	40	12	4	23	290	390	35

My cousin, Billy Upton, was a really good centre, but couldn't get into that great Aberavon team. He had a few games, but he wanted regular rugby. He moved on and had a great career at Swansea. He played 129 games for them from 1962 to 1966, scoring 24 tries.

Alan Rees was another excellent player who couldn't get into that great Aberavon team, because he was a fly-half like Cliff Ashton; so he played for Maesteg and then won three caps for Wales in 1962. He was one of the staff at the Afan Lido under Bryn Thomas and was a tremendous all-rounder. He could play any sport you like. He played cricket for Glamorgan and was one of the best cover points in the world, up there with Colin Bland of South Africa. He appeared as a substitute fielder for England against Australia at Headingley in 1964 and took a catch off the bowling of Fred Trueman to dismiss Peter Burge. He also played rugby league for Leeds.

I remember in March 1961, when Aberavon switched on the new floodlights with a match against Cambridge University; a good friend of mine – Dick Greenwood – captained Cambridge that day. We were the first beneficiaries of sponsorship because the new floodlights were paid for by the British Steel Corporation. We were ahead of the game in that period. Aberavon & Neath also played the All Blacks in 1963 and I will never forget it because the game was played in a deluge. They played to the conditions and nicked it 11–6.

We also had two great flankers in Rory O'Connor and Peter Jones. I modelled my game on Rory O'Connor, he was a dirty Welsh blindside. Peter Jones scored three tries in a final Welsh trial and never got capped. His son, Lyn, coached London Welsh in the Aviva Premiership in 2012–13 and is now director of rugby at Newport Gwent Dragons.

The young Bobby Wanbon, Max Wiltshire and the great Billy Mainwaring came along later. Billy played 600 games for Aberavon, but his mother, Mrs Evelyn Mainwaring, was even more famous in Welsh rugby for her inimitable barracking. In one game, the week before an international, Cardiff were playing at Aberavon and Billy picked up Gareth Edwards by his jersey. Mrs Mainwaring shouted out "Put him down Billy, he's playing for Wales on Saturday" and Billy carefully dropped him in the mud.

Aberavon is a great club and I loved it. They play in red and black, but we called it blood and black. I am very proud of it and am very proud of Warrington. They are the only two clubs in my life really. Bobby Wanbon was already at Aberavon when I joined. He was three years older than me and was already established in the team. He had a stunning girlfriend and I remember envying him. He lived in the Railway Tavern in the town and took me under his wing. I used to meet him at the pub and then go up to training.

I played my first game for Aberavon in October 1965, as a scrum-half at Maesteg. I was barely 19. They had tried to get me to play while I was still at school, but I had declined because I didn't think I was experienced enough. I will never forget my debut, because the two hookers – Tony Ware, of Maesteg, and Aberavon's Brian Vincent – were sent off after 25 minutes for persistent scrum offences. It was probably my fault: I couldn't put the ball in the scrum because I was so nervous. Anyway, the match report in the following Friday's *Port Talbot Guardian* said I looked "competent and efficient" and Aberavon won 11–5.

My second game was at home to Cheltenham the following month, but I had gone away with my girlfriend down to Newquay and decided to drive back on the morning of the game. This was in the days before the Severn Bridge and so we left Newquay at three in the morning and got back to Port Talbot at 10. Then I had an hour's kip. I was brilliant, considering the mammoth journey, had a really good game and won the man-of-the-match. Aberavon won 30–3 and our centre Cyril Jones, who was the acting captain, scored two fine tries and kicked three conversions and a penalty goal.

Bryn Thomas even mentioned me in his weekly 'Sporting Chatter' column in the *Port Talbot Guardian* the following week. He said: "Michael Nicholas, the young Aberavon Quins inside-half, again played for Aberavon on Monday evening against Cross Keys and, as on Saturday against Cheltenham, he gave a good account of himself. It now looks as if he will be given an extended trial with the town's premier rugby XV. Michael is a strong boy and has a good rugby background and I have every confidence that he will make the grade in senior rugby and, we hope, maintain the standard set by previous inside-halves such as Tony O'Connor, Billy Darch, Lew Oates, Maxy Williams, Onllwyn Brace and Arthur Evans, but to mention a few who have worn the red and black jersey with great distinction."

In another of my early games, Clive Rowlands, the Wales captain, was playing for Swansea at scrum-half. I was a young pup and him and their Number 8, Clive Dyer, tried to rough me up a bit, but I wasn't having it. I remember giving Rowlands an elbow, despite the fact that he was captain of Wales. Having said that, I was never sent off in rugby union.

That season we reached the final of the Welsh Floodlight Alliance competition against Bridgend. It was a two-legged final with the first leg at the Talbot Athletic Field in front of our biggest crowd of the season. Terry Dunne was the Bridgend scrum-half and was a tough guy who had played for them for years, but was coming to the end of his era. I was up-and-coming. I was all over him, disrupting his game. It was one of my best games at scrum-half and we won 28–8 with two tries from Omri Jones. The return leg was the following Wednesday at Brewery Field and was very different. I was injured, as was our hooker, Morten Howells. We were virtually passengers throughout the game. Bridgend won 9–6, but we had done enough and our captain, Max Wiltshire, received the 'Snelling' Floodlit Alliance Cup after the match. It was my first trophy.

Aberavon's annual dinner dance was held one Friday night in March, but was completely overshadowed by what happened after it: Francis Reynolds crashed his car and it caught fire. As you would expect, the accident was reported in the following Friday's *Port Talbot Guardian*, under the headline "Lucky escape for Aberavon centre": "Aberavon's centre three-quarter, Francis Reynolds, had a lucky escape in the early hours of Saturday morning when a car he was driving overturned and caught fire… He was driving home… [and was] turning into Princess Margaret Way when the vehicle overturned. The only occupant in the car, Francis managed to crawl unaided from the wreckage, although suffering from head and hand injuries. The car caught fire shortly afterwards, but the blaze was not serious and was quickly extinguished. Francis was taken to Neath General Hospital suffering from cuts and abrasions, but was discharged later the same day."

5. The Green Stars

I returned to Aberavon for the 1966–67 season full of enthusiasm. We beat Glamorgan Wanderers, Llanelli and Cross Keys, before we lost narrowly at home to Swansea when Max Wiltshire was sent off. At Pontypool in September, I thought I had scored the winning try when I raced over for a touchdown, but play was recalled when the referee adjudged that the pass I received had been forward. Three days later, Aberavon beat Cardiff 15–12 but I wasn't playing. Aberavon had signed Gareth Thomas from Llanelli and I had lost my place in the team. They just dropped me. Looking back, although I was strong around the scrum, my service was a bit dodgy. All my outside-halves had flat noses from my ballooned passes, as Tony Phillips, my outside half partner, will confirm. Scrum-half was a position for dexterity and smaller guys and I wasn't that agile.

After that I had one game for Bridgend against Neath at scrum-half and it was a nightmare. Francis Reynolds and I had both been dropped by Aberavon. He went to have a game with Neath and I was asked to play with Bridgend. I was reluctant because I only wanted to play for Aberavon, but I had had some good games against Bridgend in the past so I accepted. I was working 12-hour shifts in the dry dock at the time and I mean working, grafting in the belly of the St Gowan lightship which was in for a refit. I went to the Brewery Field for the game and I was shocking. Leighton Davies, their captain/coach, wasn't happy with me and he had good reason. He was on my back throughout the game; I just went from bad to worse and we lost 9–0. Francis played a blinder for Neath.

Years later, I met someone at Old Trafford at a function for Wooden Spoon, the rugby charity I am involved with. He was Scottish and I asked him where he was from and he said: "Near Glasgow." I am into geography and so I asked him where specifically and he said: "Little Cumbrae." I said "There's only a lighthouse on there" and he said yes, his father was the lighthouse keeper in the Firth of Clyde. I told him we had something in common because I had worked on a lightship. He said it was the isolation that was difficult to come to terms with. I said: "It wasn't too bad for me; I used to go home for tea every day because the lightship was in dry dock!" He was a guest of Bob Harris, the Wooden Spoon events chairman, who was instrumental in rugby league players being welcomed by the charity.

The fashion in Welsh rugby in the 1960s was for the scrum-half to dive-pass the ball, which was just little rugby players showing off really. That was all right for Gareth Edwards, he was an outstanding gymnast at school, but I was getting heavier and didn't have the agility. I wasn't going to make it as a scrum-half at Aberavon or Bridgend and I couldn't go back to Aberavon Harlequins because my brother, Clive, had taken over my position. He had played for the Welsh schoolboys and youth team. My friend Tony Phillips, from Cwmavon, had played in the Aberavon schoolboys with me and always said my brother was a better scrum-half than me; and he was.

So I went to play for the Aberavon Green Stars instead. They were a Roman Catholic club and I was one of the first non-Catholics to play for them. Pat O'Brien, a big friend of the family, was the captain/coach and I used to call him 'the pontiff' because he ran everything and kept the club going. I had spent a lot of time with a ball on Vivian Park when I was a kid and the Stars used to train and play there as CYMS (Catholic Yong Men's Society), nicknamed 'The Saints'. They moved to Sitwell Way as Aberavon Green Stars and I went to watch them. I was one of their only supporters so I knew all the boys. They were a really good side, another physical, brutal team. It didn't mean anything to me whether they were Catholic or Protestant. They were just good rugby players. I had supported them; so I went to play for them and had a good couple of years there. Their clubhouse was on the beach at Little Warren and was a good facility. Bobby Wanbon had played for them in the first two of the three seasons when they were invincible between 1962 and 1965 and became the first team to go 100 games without defeat.

If I was feeling a little bit sorry for myself about being dropped by Aberavon, that was all put into perspective by events on 21 October 1966. Just 20 miles away from Port Talbot, 116 children and 28 adults were killed in the Aberfan disaster when a colliery spoil tip collapsed and engulfed a junior school. It was one of those Kennedy assassination moments. Everybody knows where they were when it happened. My friend Clive Jones, who played with me at Aberavon and Warrington, told me later that he was driving lorries in Porthcawl at the time and went up to help in the rescue effort. It was horrific.

I went on a tour with the Green Stars to Munster in 1967. I was struggling to go money-wise and the club sponsored me. We flew from Cardiff to Cork; then got a bus to Limerick in the Golden Vale and stayed in the Cruise's Hotel. It was the first time I had seen beggars in the streets. We played Young Munster at Thomond Park, which was rustic, rural and rundown then, and were well beaten, 14–0. We had been out drinking Porter all the time. It was a good tour, but there was a bit of bother in the hotel when one of the boys, Cyril O'Connor, had his jaw broken by the Garda, the Irish police. We had never seen anything like that before. They didn't mess about; they just hit him with a truncheon. It was gratuitous. There didn't seem to be any reason for it. We flew back home with our tails between our legs. I don't think Cyril played again after that. He was one of my early influences in the physical side of rugby.

The Green Stars played teams such as Tonyrefail, Abercynon, Tredegar Ironsides, RAF St Athan, Haverfordwest, Maesteg Celtic and Llanhilleth. In the 1967–68 season, with John Simonson as captain, the Green Stars hit a purple patch and we won 15 games in a row. It was one of their most successful seasons since their 'Invincible' era.

Chris O'Callaghan, the former Wales RL manager and Aberavon RU coach, says: "It has been my honour and privilege to be a friend, although not a playing contemporary, of Mike Nick. As a young boy, I remember him playing alongside my father for the Aberavon Green Stars, Aberavon and Port Talbot Town Cricket Club where his brothers and father were players and officials. I remember watching him train in the weights room at the Afan Lido Sports Centre – the first rugby player I ever saw shift some weights. That was before he went into the Red Dragon pub and drank a concoction of alcoholic drinks that would stun a *dray horse. He didn't drink much but then again he didn't need to as the stuff he swallowed was Chernobyl strength shandy.*

The Aberavon Green Stars were completely bonkers and it is little wonder that Nicko turned out the way he did. Some of his later antics with Warrington were considered to be acceptable, normal behaviour – if at times a little excessive – by the people he played with at the Stars. It was a team composed entirely of Roman Catholic players, with no Protestants allowed – except Nicko. They were so hard, the SAS used to pay them protection money."

In 1969, when Prince Charles was invested as the Prince of Wales, they decided to have an Aberavon Green Stars swim. Quite a few club members were endurance swimmers. We started off at the clubhouse and ran to the sea; swam out between the piers and back in. It was like 1,000 yards on land and 1,000 yards in the sea. It was like an early triathlon. I was really fit at the time and entered. There were about 40 of us, but they nearly called it off because the sea was too rough. We all ran into the water, but then we couldn't see anybody because the waves were that high. All you could see was a pair of feet in front of you. Only one person failed to finish, a mate of mine named Tony Jones, known as 'The Bush'. He got pulled out of the water and has never been allowed to forget that. It was frightening, like we were swimming for our lives. In the last 200 yards we didn't even swim, we couldn't, because the waves broke along the pier and we just tumbled in, as if we were in a spin drier. When I got back to the beach, there was no one in front of me and I thought: "Bloody hell, I might have won this." The crowd were all shouting and I ran into the clubhouse and there was a bloke in a swimming costume having a pint at the bar. He must have finished five minutes earlier. There were two prizes, one for the serious, endurance swimmers, and one for the 'non-regular swimmers' like me. I was the first 'non-regular swimmer' to finish, about eighth or ninth, but I didn't get the prize because I hadn't paid my subs! They gave it to the next guy, who finished about 11th.

Some of the serious swimmers had done the Mumbles to Aberavon swim, which is about seven miles. I rowed it once as an escort in September 1967. Because the Bristol Channel has the second highest tide in the world, the swimmers had to head out to sea for the tide to bring them back to Port Talbot. So they were going out and out into the Atlantic. One of the swimmers, a man named Ivor Sutton, only had one leg. He had lost the other through a childhood illness. He hopped into the surf and took a while to get going, but he completed it and actually finished second. On the way back I was rowing and really putting it in. I snapped the oar and so I had to use the remnants of it. The swimmer we were escorting wanted to stop, but I was so competitive I said "No. Keep going, keep going" and he finished it too.

Of course, I still followed Aberavon's fortunes and twice during the 1967–68 season they had four players in the Wales team. Full-back Paul Wheeler, centre Ian Hall and the second-row pair of Billy Mainwaring and Max Wiltshire lined up against the All Blacks at the National Stadium in November. We lost 13–6.

Then, on Saturday, 20 January 1968, Paul Wheeler, Billy Mainwaring, Max Wiltshire and Bobby Wanbon were in the Wales team at Twickenham. I went to watch and it finished as an 11–11 draw, with Bobby scoring a try on his debut. After the match we all went to the Berners Hotel, where the Welsh team were staying, to celebrate. Bobby brought Nigel Horton back with him, who was a substitute for England that day. He went on to play for England many times as a lock forward and later opened a bar in Toulouse, but that night he was absolutely paralytic. Bobby had done a job on him; Bobby was one of those guys who could eat and drink for Wales as well as playing for them.

A few days later Wales named their team to play Scotland and, bizarrely, Bobby was dropped because he wasn't supposed to have scored. It was a planned move that should have ended up with Gareth Edwards scoring; but the move broke down. Bobby picked up the scraps, scored and he wasn't picked for the next game. He had already been approached by St Helens and signed for them for £4,500 – about £100,000 in today's money. I was going out with Bobby's cousin, Rosemary Jones, and we went to visit him in St Helens a couple of times. She was at college in Wrexham.

The England match was one of the first games Wales played under a coach, the former Ebbw Vale Number 8, David Nash. It was the early days of coaching, but Wales were ahead of England and Ireland and everybody else, getting together before internationals at the Afan Lido and training together. This was revolutionary at the time, instead of just warming up by putting a car heater on. Wales stole a march on the rest with their professional attitude. It really showed in the 1970s.

Twenty-eight years later, Bobby and I got tickets to watch England versus Wales at Twickenham. When we arrived in the West car park Bobby said it was the first time he had been back since he played and scored. With that, the legendary former Welsh centre Ray Gravell approached us. He was doing some media work and was very passionate. He stopped us and said to his mate: "Bobby Wanbon and Mike Nicholas. Don't mess with them. They've got tough toe nails."

Events moved quickly for me in August 1968. Aberavon scrum-half Gareth Thomas returned to Llanelli and so I returned to Aberavon. I had just turned 22. I even scored a try on the opening day of the season as we thrashed Glamorgan Wanderers 41–3. We then lost 9–6 at Llanelli, but the match report said: "The man the Scarlets could not contain was scrum-half Mike Nicholas." The next week we thrashed Cheltenham 32–17, scored eight tries, and the headline in the *Port Talbot Guardian* said "Nicholas and Locke build the foundation for great Aberavon try-scoring blitz". The Locke was Bernard Locke, my outside-half and a friend of the family. His father, Morgan, was a member of Port Talbot Cricket Club. I always liked the Welsh word Morgannwg, meaning Glamorgan, and I eventually named my youngest son Morgan.

By now I was super fit; it was decided to maximise this and play me where I had a free role, instead of being a specialist. I ended up fitting in the back row, at Number 6, blindside wing forward. Omri Jones was Aberavon's star player at the time, even though he never got capped. He was known as 'Om the Bomb' and was a top openside wing forward, rumbustious and aggressive. He came from the same village as Richard Burton up the valley. He had a lot going for him and I enjoyed playing with him. We did a job on Phil Bennett in a Floodlit Alliance game at Stradey Park that November. We didn't touch him. We did a pincer movement on him and he just backtracked until he was right up against the fence behind the goal and trying to jump into the crowd. Only tries counted in the competition and we beat them by three tries to nil, 9–0. It was one of my best ever victories. Omri always flew out of the back of the line-out and terrorised outside-halves. He was good at that. He had close-cropped hair and they were frightened of him. But his bark was worse than his bite; he was a very religious boy. Certainly, when it came to tackling, he thought it was better to give than to receive.

Another impressive Aberavon forward at the time was John Luff, who was an archetypal public schoolboy. He had been there since he was eight and not experienced much family life. He was from Stroud in the Cotswolds, was shy and retiring and a real gentleman. His family had a quarry business and they put him out to run one of their quarries in South Wales. He joined Aberavon; I used to take him home for tea and he loved it. My mother was delighted to look after him and took him under her wing.

We played a lot of games, especially over Easter. On Good Friday 1969 we faced a good Northampton side in a night match and beat them 19–6. Less than 18 hours later we took to the field again with already-injured players against a superb London Welsh side, which was packed with internationals and half-a-dozen British Lions. Then, after only three minutes, our centre Stuart Forrester suffered a shoulder injury and had to be taken to hospital by ambulance. There were no subs in those days; so we had to reshuffle the side and I was put out on the wing to mark the great Gerald Davies. We were thrashed 52–8. It was the first time Aberavon had conceded 50 points. It was embarrassing, even though there were mitigating circumstances. I remember hurting so bad that I disappeared out of town after the match. I took my girlfriend down to the Gower Peninsula for a quiet meal, hiding out of sight. That's how seriously I took it. We played again on the Monday, two days later, and drew 9–9 with Neath. We had to be fit to do that.

Prop Phil Morgan, one of my heroes from the great Aberavon team of 1960–61, retired at the end of that season. He was one of the few players from the championship-winning side that I played with. He was a lovely man and ended up coaching us. He died too young.

Before the start of the 1969–70 season, Francis Reynolds rejoined Aberavon from Aberavon Quins and Ken Whelan rejoined from Maesteg, but all eyes were on Glamorgan and their pursuit of the cricket County Championship under Tony Lewis. They clinched the title against Worcestershire at Sofia Gardens on Friday 5 September amid scenes of jubilation by thousands of supporters.

Sadly, I was on holiday in Spain with my girlfriend at the time and was upset about missing it, but kept in touch with events through the English papers. It was a memorable summer because I was a massive Glamorgan fan. The off-spinner, Don Shepherd, took his 2,000th first-class wicket that year. All-rounder Peter Walker was a brilliant fielder, taking 73 close catches to go with his 101 wickets and more than 1,000 runs.

Wednesday 1 October was another significant date for me. Aberavon played Cross Keys in the Floodlight Alliance. I scored a try as we won 21–3, but when I went down on the ball I was kicked in the back and suffered fractured ribs – but I didn't know they were fractured at the time. A week later we played Bristol and I made a big effort to play; I knew the Welsh selectors would be there and wanted to impress them. But because of the rib injury I did myself a disservice and had to go off midway through the second half. I slipped down the pecking order with the selectors. Weeks later I went to the doctor's because my ribs weren't getting any better. I had an X-ray that revealed I had fractured ribs, but I kept on playing.

Ken Whelan was another amazing character in the Aberavon back row. He was very proud of never being injured and carried off, but in one game at Neath was really struggling with concussion. Not to be outdone, he went to sit with the spectators for the last 20 minutes and then walked off with the team at the final whistle in a totally deranged state.

I went to pick him up once to play for an invitation XV against Belmont Abbey public school in Hereford. Ken had a young family, but just did his own thing. His wife and kids weren't too happy that he was going away to play again. He said: "I won't bother today love. I'll just see Mike off and bring the coal in for the fire." I said "We are going to be one player short" but he whispered "Don't worry". He went into the coal house and his boots were buried under the coal. He picked them up, sneaked out and got in the car with me. We shot up to Hereford, got to the abbey and had to find out where the game was being played. We were shown to the abbot's study where he was sat behind his desk in his monastic robes, and looked like Friar Tuck. He welcomed us and asked: "Would you like a drink boys?" We said 'yes', thinking he meant soft drinks, but he had a barrel of beer under his desk and started pulling pints for us. We had three or four pints with him before the game. I think he did it for us to be a bit drunk and not play as well against his first XV.

Ken's brothers, Jimmy and Justin, played for the Aberavon Green Stars and gave Barry John a hard time when he was at Trinity College, Carmarthen, and playing for them.

Clive Jones made his Aberavon debut at Pontypool that season and we formed a really good wing-forward partnership straight away. He would fly out from the scrum and the line-out while I roamed the blindside, picking up the scraps and getting the dirty work done. One match report called us the "tearaway twins".

Clive Jones recalls: *"I played against Nicko for Bridgend against Aberavon around 1968. We had an injury and I ended up on the wing. I can remember Mike bombing up and down the pitch. He didn't have blond hair then, he had his natural brown hair, but disappeared for a spell in the summer, spent some time in Spain and came back with flowing golden locks which we all teased him about as being peroxide. He said 'no', his hair had been bleached by the sun. We were both wing forwards, I was openside and Mike was blindside. We hit it off and ended up as a good partnership at Aberavon. There weren't many half-backs, scrum-halves, stand-offs or outside-halves that could get past us. Internationals like Barry John, Gareth Edwards (Cardiff), Chico Hopkins (Maesteg) and Phil Bennett didn't like playing against Aberavon because we did a good job on them. We had a bit of a reputation; we trained hard and played hard."*

Hard men: Aberavon Green Stars following the 1967-68 season. Back: Peter Smith, Justin Whelan, Philip Davies, David Winters, Franco Ruggierio; second row: Brian Donovan, Haydn Bennett, Colin Walters, David Condon, John Arnold, David Paskin; seated: Mike, Vivian Jenkins, Patrick O'Brian, John Simonson (captain), Bryn Thomas, Denis Richards, Colin Potts, Anthony Lewis; front: Granville Pugh, Ian Purchase.

Combined Aberavon & Neath team to play South Africa in December 1969: Left to right, back: Glynn Overton (Aberavon secretary), Mike, Alan Davies, John Luff, Dai Whitlock, Brian Thomas, Alan Mages, Wilson Lauder, Dai 'Pigs' Thomas, Morton Howells, Lord Heycock; middle: Denzil Lloyd (touch judge), Bob Fleay, Francis Reynolds, Omri Jones, Billy Mainwaring (captain), John Simonson, Ian Hall, John Poole, touch judge; front: Dai Parker, Martyn Davies, Graham Hodgson.

Blood and black: Aberavon training was more serious than it looked. (Picture restored by Bob Brough).

Fans' favourite: Mike was Aberavon's player-of-the-year for the 1969–70 season and is standing on the left. He received the award from the famous rugby writer Clem Thomas (centre). Also pictured are team-mates Clive Jones (far right) and Alan Martin (second left) and coach Phil Morgan (second right). At the front are Mrs Martin, Mrs Morgan and Clive's partner Judith Clarke. When Paul Cullen first saw this photograph he thought Mike was a member of the New Seekers!
(Picture restored by Bob Brough).

In action for Aberavon.

Below: Aberavon 1965-66: Left to right, back: Bobby Wanbon, Omri Jones, Ron Staddon; second row: Gwyn Price (trainer), Arthur Roberts (treasurer), Morton Howells, Alan Hughes, Phil Morgan, Billy Mainwaring, Eric Jones, Meirion Prosser, Brian Gittins, Graham Hughes, Miah McGrath; seated: Gareth Mainwaring, Alan John, Cyril Jones, Llewellyn Heycock (chairman), Max Wiltshire (captain), Glynn Overton (secretary), David Thomas, Bryan Jones, John Davies; front: Huw Harries, Mike Nicholas.

43

I looked like Adrian Street, the Welsh professional wrestler, who dyed his hair and was famous for his flamboyant persona; it helped me to stand out in games. I remember John Taylor, the London Welsh flanker, wearing a skullcap once in a Welsh trial two years earlier. It made him stand out and helped his cause no end. He was selected ahead of Omri Jones.

I started in the centres against Pontypridd because of an injury crisis and then moved to full-back when Stuart Forrester suffered a broken leg. Whenever we were short I used to fill in. I played full-back, centre, wing, Number 8, hooker and prop. The only position I didn't play was second row, obviously, because I wasn't tall enough; but even then I used to dominate the back of the line-outs because I jumped on a player's shoulders to win the ball.

During a night match at Ebbw Vale, I suffered a cut above my eye and a piece of turf must have been left in when the doctor, who we thought liked a drink, sewed me up. Next morning my head had swollen to the size of a football and I didn't even realise. When my mother came in to get me up for work all she could see was my head, like something out of *The Elephant Man*, and she screamed. My head was swollen for about a month after that.

In December a combined Aberavon and Neath XV played the touring South Africans and I was on the bench. I think it was the first time we had substitutes, but I never got on. Francis Reynolds played and it was 0–0 at half-time before the Springboks pulled away in the second half to win 27–0 in front of a big crowd. There was a small anti-Apartheid demonstration beforehand and there were dozens of police on duty. Earlier on in the tour, at Swansea, there had been a pitch invasion and my Aberavon team-mate Omri Jones, who was a police constable, was on duty. He couldn't resist the opportunity, knocked his helmet off and tore into the fray, taking out half-a-dozen protesters. Later on in the tour, at Bristol, the demonstrators put tacks and drawing pins on the pitch to try to stop the game.

After the South Africa game I had my first experience of a free bar, courtesy of the Welsh Rugby Union. Anyway, human nature took over and we ended up drinking pints of brandy. You can imagine what we were like for the next few days. The reception was at the Afan Lido and the Springboks were wearing their old-fashioned university-style blazers with beading on the edges. They were under siege really and there was almost a laager mentality. They crowded together, stuck to themselves and didn't engage in conversation. It was obviously a very controversial tour and they didn't feel welcome. One or two guys did communicate and I had a chat with a wing forward called Piet van Deventer. He asked what I did and I told him that I was employed in the steelworks. He said he was from Kimberley, the diamond mining region, and added in his strong Afrikaans accent: "I look after 6,000 blacks (he pronounced it 'blicks') in a compound." He was quite a nice guy and more sociable than the rest. He said they sometimes had visits from the rugby union hierarchy and their partners, and they used to spoil them with gifts of diamonds. No wonder the hierarchy wanted the tours and junkets to South Africa to continue. Talk about blood diamonds. A lot of the amateur game was like that at the time: a charade.

Just before Christmas, the reporter Clive Girton gave me another good write-up in the *Port Talbot Guardian* after we had beaten Maesteg 18–9. He said: "Mike Nicholas is fast making a name for himself as one of the finest utility players Aberavon has ever had. He started off his playing career as a scrum-half, switched to the wing-forward berth, and in a number of matches this season has found himself playing at full-back. His courage and skill is unquestionable, and Aberavon are extremely fortunate to have a player of his quality. On Monday of last week it was thanks to some desperate and resolute covering from him that the Wizards line was only crossed once, and he contributed in no small way to the evening's success." I couldn't have said it better myself.

My good form continued until the end of the season and in April I was named Player-of-the-Year. I was still only 23. My mentor Bryn Thomas recorded the fact in his 'Sporting Chatter' column in the *Port Talbot Guardian*. "Aberavon Rugby Football Supporters' Club made their Player-of-the-Year award this week, and the player selected was Mike Nicholas, who this season has established himself as one of the most powerful and determined back row forwards playing in senior Welsh Rugby. I have watched Mike this season set about his task of establishing himself as a first-choice player in any Aberavon line-up, and he has no one to thank, no one but himself for his single-mindedness of purpose to be 100 per cent fit to carry out his intentions. He has spent hours and hours in training at the Lido and this well-deserved award is a fitting tribute to a sportsman who has refused to be side-tracked in the course he has set for himself."

My niece Emma's husband, the fly-half Jamie Davies, was Aberavon's Player-of-the-Year in 2005–06. He has scored more than 4,000 points for Aberavon now and there are interesting parallels between our careers because, like me, he was rejected as a young player and then came back and won the Player-of-the-Year award.

I was pretty introverted at the time, like Shaun Edwards was in his youth, with tunnel vision and in my own bubble, my own zone, for years. I gave up my job in administration at the steelworks to go out onto the plant so that I could do more physical labour to augment my training. My mother used to say I was like a number six blast furnace. (The steelworks had five.) I used to eat unbelievable amounts because I was training, training, training. One summer I took a job building a basic oxygen plant which was 250 to 300 feet high. Instead of using the lifts I used to run up the steelworks and work out with metal bars. We were putting sheeting and cladding and steel up. I was on nearly £100 a week in the 1960s. It was more like danger money. If my mother had known what I was doing she would have gone mad. I rewarded myself with a blue MGB sports car, my favourite car.

A normal day then would have been to get up at about five. My mother would have filled a huge Tupperware box with half-a-pound of bacon, 10 sausages, 10 boiled eggs and six yoghurts and that was my breakfast. Then we'd all cram into my brother's Ford Popular to get to work for six. At lunchtime I'd do a short work-out, have a full dinner and a pound of apples. After work I'd go home for my tea and then go training with Aberavon. After that we would go out and have about five or six pints of Strongbow cider, which was the natural drink of rugby players, to quench the thirst. Then I'd have a whole chicken and chips on the way home, go to bed about 12 and then get up at five again.

I used to take on menial jobs because it was physical work. I dug trenches for £2 a day, 10 hours a day. It was all about preparation and conditioning for rugby. Even when I was working I would take a break and do a work-out: sit-ups and press-ups and all that stuff. You could stand on a traffic island, Briton Ferry island, if you wanted a day's work and the contractors going west would pick you up.

The first day I went there we went to Morriston, outside Swansea, to build the Morganite factory. When we arrived on the site at about 6.30am there was an old wooden canteen wagon that a steam roller used to pull behind it. I went in and they said: "What do you want to eat then?" There was a man with a shovel on a stove, frying eggs and bacon on the back of the shovel. I said: "Whatever you've got." I was in my element. One of the lads with me, Michael, had been in and out of jail. He was gritty. He was chuffed when I played at Wembley, he told all his mates in prison that he had worked with me.

Finally, I made a big decision to pack in the steelworks altogether and was on the dole for about nine months, but didn't waste that time. I hammered the training. I really became like a full-time professional and my game improved even more. After nine months I got a job as chief safety officer at the BP refinery at Baglan Bay. It was the early days of safety officers, but it was becoming mandatory for companies to have them. Six thousand men worked there, including Lennie 'The Lion' Williams, the boxer from Maesteg, who used the phone in my office. He fought twice against Frankie 'The Tiger' Taylor for the British title. Derek Quinnell, who went on three British Lions tours, and Roy Mathias, who joined St Helens, worked there as electricians.

I used to run the safety meetings. All the companies had to have a safety officer because there were different units within the refinery. John Charles, 'Il Gigante Buono', 'the Gentle Giant', the former Wales, Leeds United and Juventus centre forward or centre half, was one of the safety officers with Wimpey Construction and used to turn up for meetings on his bicycle. His helmet looked like a peanut on his head. It was a token job, but he was a lovely man, really down to earth and humble. He used to regale us with stories: in one game someone tried to clear the ball, he was 40 yards out, it hit him on the head and he scored.

I met him at various events after that, anything with a Welsh connection, and once at the Welsh FA Golf Day at Conwy. I went to his funeral and memorial service at Elland Road on St David's Day, 2004, with my good friend Ken Jones, the sports feature writer with *The Independent*. It was amazing; there must have been 10,000 people there. Eddie Gray was the Leeds caretaker-manager at the time and gave an emotional tribute.

At Baglan Bay I got good local press, became quite well known and people on the site became aware I was playing. There was a site newspaper and I was in that. This guy came to me and said: "I am connected with Featherstone Rovers. Come to my digs tonight and I will make a phone call for you." I went along and he made the call. He said: "I have got this young lad here. He is getting rave reviews and is interested in rugby league." I went on the phone and the man at the other end asked "How old are you?" I said "24." Then he asked "How tall are you?" and I said "About 5 feet 9 inches." Then he asked "How heavy are you?" I said "About 13-and-a-half stones" and he put the phone down. In other words, he did not think I was big enough – or perhaps he was just the social club secretary. Three years later I played against Featherstone at Wembley and scored one of the tries that beat them.

6. Crawshay's and Wolfhounds

We made an embarrassing start to the 1970–71 season, when we were beaten 12–6 at home by the junior club Taibach in September. It was the first time in Aberavon's history we had been beaten by our little neighbours and they deserved it, even though we fielded an experimental side.

All that was forgotten the following month when we achieved a famous victory of our own over Llanelli, the so-called 'West Wales wonder team', at the Athletic Ground. Ray Gravell, who went on to be a Welsh great, made his debut for them in the centres and we were so short of players that Clive Jones stepped in to play at prop. Clive had a blinder against Barry Llewellyn, who was one of the Welsh props at the time. There must have been more than 6,000 there, and we beat them 9–6 despite a late try from Phil Bennett. It was a great win and a real shot in the arm for the club. Everybody was happy. Cliff David, the Aberavon treasurer, was delighted with the large crowd that had poured through the turnstiles and Lord Heycock, the Aberavon chairman, was overjoyed with the victory. Outside-half Jeff Jones and centre Robert Stevens scored our tries and centre John Simonson, who was with me at the Green Stars, kicked a drop-goal. It was Llanelli's first defeat of the season.

Shortly after that, we lost another player to rugby league when our winger Bob Fleay, a former youth international, signed for Swinton. He was only 21 and had been a regular member of the side since he joined us from youth rugby in 1968. He was a swimming instructor at the Afan Lido. He scored two tries for Swinton in a trial match and signed straight after the game. He received £2,000 with another £1,000 to follow if he made the grade – which he most certainly did. Bob was replaced by a young winger from Pyle, near Bridgend. His name was Dennis Curling. He was lightning fast, quick off the mark and with a deceptive body swerve. More of him later.

Stephen Wild, the Swinton Lions historian, commented: *"Bob Fleay holds the distinction of making 150 consecutive club appearances between 19 March 1972 and 22 August 1976 (his last game for Swinton). It is an all-time club record for an unbroken sequence in the first team. He'll be remembered as a decent winger in a difficult period for the club. He still comes to the odd game and is a real gent."*

When Aberavon went to London, say to play against Wasps, Rosslyn Park or London Welsh, we would book one room at the Regents Palace Hotel, near Piccadilly Circus, which was the room of shame. If you had to go back to that you obviously hadn't managed to get fixed up with a girl or get to a party somewhere. Invariably, the team would end up in all parts of London and it was a tradition that we all met in a pub in Petticoat Lane on the Sunday morning to compare notes. Then we'd all get back on the train and go home singing on the Underground, like miners in the pits, which was unusual for people on a Sunday morning to be greeted with. Very occasionally, we would catch the 1.01, the last train out of Paddington on a Saturday night, at one minute past one, which got into Swansea at about seven in the morning. We would sleep in the luggage racks.

I remember going to play London Irish when the actors Richard Harris and Oliver Reed and comedian Dave Allen were having a drink in the bar. That November, London Irish had eight doctors playing for them. Our outside-half Jeff Jones was a former Welsh youth international and a good player. He got flattened and suffered a bad cut. After the game, the London Irish prop called Moloney, who had flattened him, came into the dressing room and said: "Where's the outside-half I injured? Come here, I'll stitch you up." And he stitched him up there and then. I had never seen that before or since. You could say that Jeff was literally stitched up.

Monday 15 February 1971 was Decimal Day, when the United Kingdom decimalised the pound. Port Talbot did its bit too. The Olympic pool at the Afan Lido was shortened by 11 inches – from 55 yards to 50 metres – to make it conform to international standards. The cost of shortening the 165ft-long pool was about £2,000 – about £40,000 in today's money – and took four weeks. I bet they wished they had made it 50 metres long in the first place.

As usual, there was a hectic finish to the season with the Snelling Sevens at Cardiff Arms Park on Saturday 24 April, followed by our traditional tour of Devon on the Monday and Tuesday. We didn't do too badly. We reached the semi-finals of the Sevens before losing to Llanelli and then beat Torquay and Paignton on successive days.

Team-mate Clive Jones recalls: *"On one tour we were down in Devon or Cornwall and, as you do, we were fraternising with the local females and were lucky enough to take some very lovely ladies back to our hotel for 'tea and cake'. Mike was in the adjoining room to me. Another of our friends, a centre called John Simonson, said 'Let's see how Mike is getting on with his female friend' and so we sneaked into his bedroom. She was sitting on the bed fully clothed and Mike was doing press-ups. He never lived that down. He couldn't deny it because there were two witnesses to that very strange act. She was fully clothed sat on the bed and Mike was going for gold with his press-ups. She was obviously testing his stamina and strength, but it was hilarious because this was one o'clock in the morning. We expected him to be carousing or having some social interaction with this beautiful Cornish woman but, no, he was concentrating on his fitness and his chest and forearms."*

It was a great tour every year: soft opposition (we could play with hangovers) on the English Riviera with palm trees all around. Even the dustmen wore bowler hats. We stayed in the Palm Court Hotel, Torquay and at four o'clock one morning, after a night out, we decided to have a drinking contest. Now four o'clock in the morning is not a good time to have a drinking contest, but Clive Jones set the tone and drank four pints of lager straight down. Our big mate, John Richardson, decided that the only way to top that was to fill a bucket up with lager and drink that. After a while, John was struggling, but he was really stubborn. In the end he regurgitated the lot, but still continued to finish the bucket off. That's the depths we had sunk to!

I got in trouble one year by 'borrowing' a turkey from the kitchen and putting it in the bed of our captain, Billy Mainwaring. So Billy got into bed next to a turkey and wasn't too pleased. Cold turkey, not recommended.

On one tour we all had to wear bowler hats. I was working in the cold mill at the steelworks at the time, in the safety department, and I didn't have a bowler hat. One of the guys felt sorry for me and lent me his grandfather's funeral bowler hat which was a big mistake. Off I went on tour with it and, unfortunately, I swapped it for a favour off a young lady. He never saw the bowler again and never spoke to me again.

For the 1971–72 season, we had a new coach in Max Wiltshire, a new captain in Ian Hall and I was honoured to be named vice-captain. We started the season in style too by reaching the final of the Welsh Rugby Sevens at Cardiff Arms Park on Saturday 28 August.

I enjoyed playing sevens because I had a good engine and my whole game was based on my stamina and energy. I used to over-train. Instead of training for 80 minutes, I would train for another 10 minutes on each half. I would come into my own in the last 20 minutes of games. One of my big heroes at sevens was the scrum-half Bernard 'Slogger' Templeman, from Penarth. Penarth were the whipping boys really in the 15-a-side game but came into their own at sevens.

We beat University College Swansea 10–5 in the first round, Cardiff 13–10 in the second round and Swansea 20–9 in the semi-finals. I scored a try and kicked eight conversions along the way.

We lost 23–8 to Phil Bennett's Llanelli in the final, but made a little bit of history at the same time. Dai Condon scored both of our tries – I kicked the conversion after the first – and his second try was the last one of the game. The value of a try was raised from three points to four at the start of the 1971–72 season, but the Welsh Sevens were being played under the 1970–71 Laws and so Dai scored the last three-point try in the world. To my horror, I missed the kick, even though it was under the posts, because I was so exhausted. It was the only kick I missed all day. *The Port Talbot Guardian* described me as "easily the best forward on view all afternoon".

The teams and scoring details from the final were as follows:
Aberavon: Dennis Curling, Danny Sheehy, Ian Hall (captain), Clive Shell; Dai Condon, Mike Nicholas, Clive Jones.
Llanelli: Andy Hill, Roy Bergiers, Phil Bennett (captain), John Thomas; Hefin Jenkins, A. Reynolds, Roy Mathias.
Andy Hill (2), Hefin Jenkins, John Thomas and Roy Mathias scored the Llanelli tries, with Phil Bennett converting four of them.

The Condon family were the Port Talbot undertakers and massive Aberavon fans. Dai, who later became the Aberavon chairman, had a wicked sense of humour and he would often be seen on all fours in the cinema, crawling in and out of the aisles, up to some mischief or, like me, up in the balcony, throwing rotten apples from the fruit shop next door during the Saturday morning matinee. They used to explode on people's heads, but do no lasting damage because they were so rotten. Dai wasn't renowned for his bravery, but he could run and was a great sevens player. He used to sit next to you on the way to night matches and regale you with stories about working for the family firm, how he had just embalmed somebody, how he had laid somebody out, and took great delight in all the gory details. One day I stopped him and said: "I don't want to hear any more of your stories. All I want to know is the best coffin to have when you die." Dai said that was easy to answer because there were only two types: solid oak with brass handles, the full Monty, the real McCoy, with all the lining, or the orange box type, the cheapest ones. "Which one do you recommend?" I asked him. "Definitely go for the more expensive one," he said, "your arse will be out of the bottom of the other one in six months."

Dai Condon recalls: *"I scored the last three-point try. Dennis Curling ran 20 yards and was tackled on the line. I just picked up the ball, put it down and the whistle went. I get reminded about that a lot. I was lucky enough to play with Mike at Aberavon Green Stars, when he was a scrum-half, and at Aberavon, when we were both in the back row. I had the legs and lived off the scraps that people like Mike and Clive Jones gave me. I got a few tries off that. Mike and Clive were both mean players. They didn't give an inch. They were similar in lots of ways and had a similar attitude. They took training seriously, which people didn't do in those days, and would want to beat each other. Mike's philosophy was that he didn't like any other side – 'Let's go out and beat them' – he always personalised it and went out there to nail certain players, not in an underhand way, but sometime during the game there would be a bit of a flare-up and you had a rough idea from who was sitting on the floor what had happened. Mike just couldn't help himself. In the old days, wing forwards used to go for the outside-half, but Mike would select other forwards to give a good lumping to. I learned a lot from watching him do that.*

Warrington took a clutch of players from us and it meant I could stay at Aberavon a couple of years longer in my position, because Clive and Mike were better players than me in the back row. The cupboard was bare when they both went. Bobby Wanbon had gone earlier and Dennis Curling followed. Dennis was fast; he could shift. One Sunday, Dennis and I went down to Morfa Beach to shoot rabbits, but we forgot the guns. We still caught two because that's how fast Dennis was. He was great on the wing.

The money they received was a lot then and – apart from Dennis Curling, who lives in London now – they have all stayed up there and made their family lives up there. They haven't come skulking back. The steelworks was going strong then and I suppose they could have stayed down and had positions in the works, but they wanted to pursue their rugby and up they went. It took a long time to replace them at Aberavon. They were that good as a pair.

I remember we played at Cardiff one Wednesday night and Clive was asked to go from back row to prop because we were short. Come half-time we were having a team talk; one of Clive's eyes was swollen and shutting and he said: 'Help me out boys.' At the start of the second half we went down for a scrum and Mike said to Alan Martin, who was in the second row: 'Let's swap for a minute.' I knew why, but Alan said: 'Is there a move on? No one has told me.' It was the early days of moves. The scrum was set and the next thing 'boom' and the Cardiff hooker had to be carried from the field. I knew it was Mike.

50

Aberavon 1970–71: Left to right, back: Mike, Ray Wilkins, Colin Stevens, Jeff Jones; middle: David Condon, Phil Bell, Terry Diaper, Len Ford, John Richardson, Allan Fall, Ken Jones (treasurer), T.O. James; front: John Griffiths (trainer), Dennis Curling, John Simonson, Ian Hall, Lord Heycock (chairman), Billy Mainwaring (captain), Morton Howells, Robert Stevens.

To be Frank: Francis Reynolds of Aberavon became Frank Reynolds of Warrington
(Photo: Eddie Fuller).

Whenever we were on tour in Torquay and places like that, there were drinking games or races on the prom and he would still want to win. He was very competitive and was a handful. You wanted to be on the same side as him.

Len Ford was a big lump from the Aberavon Quins. He played for Aberavon for a while and was very strong. Me and Mike were the wing forwards and Len was the Number 8. I had a patch when I scored quite a few tries and before one match Len said to me: 'Dai, why don't you push in the scrums?' I said: 'Len, where does it say in the Sunday papers who pushes in the scrums? It just says who scores the tries.' Len wanted to give me a clip round the ear after that, but Mike intervened.

Aberavon reached the Welsh Rugby Union Challenge Cup final in 1974 and lost 12–10 to Llanelli. Billy Mainwaring and I are convinced that if we had not lost three such experienced and streetwise forwards as Clive, Mike and Bobby we would have won.

Clive Jones and I were then invited to join Captain Geoffrey Crawshay's Welsh XV 40th annual tour to Devon and Cornwall. It was a big honour for us and for Aberavon because selection for the tour was seen as a stepping stone to the national side.

The tour captain was another Aberavon player; centre Ian Hall, who had already won the first of his eight caps. The stand-off was Phil Bennett, the man with the famous sidestep, who had made history two years earlier when he won his first cap against France in Paris. He had replaced Gerald Davies on the wing, becoming Wales' first substitute. He sat next to me for the team photograph. The scrum-half was Billy Hullin, a former Aberavon player, who was playing for London Welsh at the time and had been capped in 1967. Pontypool's Tommy David, a future dual code international, was in the back row.

Swansea prop Mel James, who later joined St Helens, was in the front row. He worked for the National Coal Board and was famous for his chat-up line. The lucky ladies would be entitled to three loads of coal a year, courtesy of the NCB. The honorary secretary was Doug Ackerman, whose son Rob would go on to become a dual code international and play rugby league for Whitehaven, Leeds, Carlisle and Salford. The chairman was Arthur Rees, who had won 13 caps for Wales and was the Chief Constable of Staffordshire. In 1975, he led the hunt to find the Black Panther, Donald Neilson, who had kidnapped and murdered Lesley Whittle, whose body was found hanging in a drainage shaft at Bathpool Park in Kidsgrove. The High Court Judge Rowe Harding, who had played for Swansea, Wales and the British Lions, was one of the life vice presidents.

We boarded a train at Port Talbot at 9.44am on Monday, 6 September and headed to Newport where a coach left at 10.50am to take us to the County Hotel, Taunton for lunch. I have still got a copy of the itinerary. After lunch, we headed to Plymouth for a match against Plymouth Albion which kicked off at 6.15pm. After the match we headed to the Regent Hotel in Penzance.

The next day we visited the Prince of Wales oyster beds on the Helford River and I won an oyster eating contest. There were crates of Guinness, brown bread and as many fresh oysters as you could eat. I had about six dozen and was ill for months afterwards. That night we had dinner at the Regent Hotel and that was followed by an initiation ceremony which has remained secret – until now. I was stripped down to my jock strap, blind-folded and led to believe that I would be circumcised. Some players returned home rather than go through with the ceremony. I was disorientated and touched with blocks of ice that felt like sharp knives. Somehow I ended up on Penzance High Street, blindfolded in a jock strap. The following day we played Cornwall at Redruth before returning by train to Port Talbot on the Thursday. What an experience!

There was a fantastic camaraderie involved with the Crawshay's. The Crawshays, the Guests and the Keanes had been the powerful families who controlled the industrial revolution in South Wales. The Crawshay family had a place called Llanvair Grange, not far from Blainavon, and Clive Jones and I were invited to a garden party there. We thought we would be a bit unconventional and turned up in my MGB in string vests and miner's helmets. That caused a bit of a stir and we had a bit of fun – as usual.

I was in demand now and was next asked to play for the Irish Wolfhounds invitation side in the Neath Centenary Sevens. There were four Irish backs and three Welsh forwards. There was an out-and-out sprinter on the wing called Vincent Becker, Tom Grace, who became a British Lion in 1974, John Moloney and Dick Milliken. I was picked with Peter Williams and Gareth Thomas. Peter was J.J. Williams' brother and played for Bridgend. He was a very good sevens player. Gareth's father was J.B.G. Thomas, the doyen of rugby union writers in Wales. Gareth's brother, Craig, wrote the international best-seller *Firefox*, which Clint Eastwood made into a film. Ireland supplied the backs, Wales supplied the forwards. It was a very good tournament. We beat Gala and Public School Wanderers in the early rounds and met Neath in the final. We went 8–0 up after putting Becker away twice. He was a flier, but as I recall had no stamina and went off at half-time, leaving us with six players. We lost 10–8.

I had another good day for Aberavon on Saturday, 25 September, despite us losing 22–16 at Cardiff. I scored two tries, set up another for Dennis Curling and generally impressed John Billot, the reporter from the *Western Mail* – 'The National Newspaper of Wales'.

Writing in Monday's paper, he said: "Aberavon had Cardiff worried as the Wizards hit back from 12–0 down to 12–10 in the second half, with acting skipper Mike Nicholas in tremendous form again. His value could not be overestimated as he scored two tries and made the other. He also found time for a wrestling match with Cardiff prop Gerry Wallace and for a series of cover tackles that referee Jeff Kelleher found more acceptable than the two-man tangle."

John Billot was also impressed with the Cardiff Number 8 Roger Lane and concluded his article as follows: "Note for the WRU. If there are better players about for the Wales 'B' team to play France 'B' next month than Mike Nicholas and Roger Lane, snap them up. They must be supermen."

But I hardly had time to catch my breath because I had been picked for the Wolfhounds for the Ulster 1971 celebrations, which was another real honour. The team was packed with

British Lions. We had All Black half-backs in Chris Laidlaw and Earle Kirton, who went on to play for Harlequins. We had an international second rower in Max Wiltshire. The plane tickets arrived and we flew to Dublin. Karl Mullen, who had captained the 1950 British Lions and was a consultant gynaecologist, met us at the airport. We had lunch and were chauffeur driven in Mercedes up to the Mountains of Mourne and met up with Fergus Slattery, Billy Steele and a few others. The man in charge, Des Scaife, ran Butlin's Mosney in County Meath and we had to stop there to pick up the kit before we drove up to the beautiful Slieve Donard Hotel. I remember the Irish players were apprehensive about going up to the North because of the Troubles.

It was in 1971, at the height of the Troubles. We went to Ballymena, which was a Protestant enclave, where Willie John McBride, who was fresh off the Lions tour of New Zealand, had arranged a game for us. Only he could have put this game on. Instead of going through Belfast, we skirted around Aldergrove, which is now Belfast International Airport, and then went up to Ballymena.

We had a fantastic side. Tom Kiernan was at full-back, Ken Kennedy played, Mike Gibson, Bill Mulcahy, Dick Milliken and I were in the back row and we won 66–0. The celebrations afterwards were fantastic and McBride got us all drunk and directed the chauffeur to take us back through Belfast, instead of taking us round. "Give them a real tour of the city," he said. It was a nightmare. There were road blocks and armed squaddies every couple of hundred yards, stopping us and getting us out. It took us hours and hours to get through the road blocks of Belfast. It was a real insight into what was going on.

I think it's fantastic that Ireland play rugby as a united team. The Irish Rugby Football Union has to be applauded for sticking to that.

Dennis Curling was having a fine season as well and wrote his name into the Aberavon record books against Nantymoel in the first round of the Welsh Challenge Cup on Wednesday, 17 November. He scored seven tries to equal Johnny Ring's club record which had stood alone for 50 years, since 1921, before he joined Wigan. He also set one up for Number 8 Dai Condon.

Nantymoel stopped us from scoring for 26 minutes and then Dennis scored four tries in nine minutes. Once we realised he needed only one try to break the record we spent most of the last 20 minutes trying to give him his eighth try. Right at the end Dai Condon was over the Nantymoel line and aimed a pass towards Curling only to see it go astray. The final score was 44–0. We had scored 10 tries and kicked just two conversions.

Another rugby player who worked with me at Baglan Bay, a back-row forward called Jimmy Owen, was not enjoying himself quite as much. He clocked on one Monday morning with his mouth full of stitches. He had had a trial for Warrington at Hull the day before. Keith Boxall had given him an elbow and his teeth had come up through his mouth. He had gone up there badly prepared, slept in his car overnight and played. He had gone on the bench and been dropped in the complete deep end. Perhaps rugby league was best avoided.

Not many people know this, but they built Offa's Dyke between Wales and England to keep the rugby league scouts out. But it did not stop Dennis Maddock, who was

Warrington's Welsh scout and a long-distance lorry driver. He would park his lorry in club car parks and you could see a Warrington sticker in the window. He was outrageous and would try to sit next to you in the dug-outs. He gave me Alex Murphy's number and I remember speaking to him from a red telephone box on the edge of town. Contact with rugby league people had to be clandestine. It was like a spy film: press button A for rugby league. Murph told me about his plans for the club and he must have sewn a seed of interest.

Francis Reynolds played for Aberavon Harlequins in the 1970–71 season and scored 27 tries – which is still a club record for one season – and signed for Warrington soon afterwards, with Dennis no doubt getting his fee.

Officially, anybody who went north was supposed to be taboo and persona non grata. You had crossed the great divide and become tainted and all that rubbish. Rugby league had become the forbidden fruit. In truth, with anybody who went north, the Welsh public kept an eye on them and their progress. We were willing them to do well. We didn't want them to fail and if they did fail and came home they had let us down. A good friend of mine, Peter Davies, who was known as the Ironman, and sadly passed away in 2012, went to Wigan from Neath in 1964. He was a second row but he wasn't cut out for rugby league. He accepted their offer and unfortunately came with this tag that he was the Ironman and only played once for them. He came back quickly and wasn't allowed to play rugby union again, which was iniquitous. He was a victim of the system.

Another guy who played for Neath and Wales, Don Devereux, signed for Huddersfield in 1958 and when he finished playing for them and went back to Wales he wasn't allowed to teach rugby union. Nobody should have the right to ruin someone's career like that and I always felt deep down that it was wrong.

Lots of players went up north and didn't quite make it. One was Danny Harris, a Welsh international who played at Leigh from 1961 to 1967 and taught at Lymm Grammar School. He was a second row and wasn't cut out for rugby league at the top level. They weren't running forwards, back rowers had a better chance, but weren't guaranteed to make it, such as Colin Standing who was a Number 8 and went from Bridgend to Wigan in 1967 and was on Warrington's books until just before I signed. He only made 18 appearances for Wigan (and half of those were as a substitute) and one appearance for Warrington. I was very surprised he didn't make a bigger impact because he was very mobile.

Other unheralded players went up north and had great careers, like Charlie Winslade with Oldham and Warrington and Don Vines who played for that fabulous Wakefield team in the 1960s and ended up as a professional wrestler on the BBC. Berwyn Jones was another example. He only played second-class rugby in Wales with Rhymney, but ended up getting picked for the Great Britain tour of Australia in 1966 after signing for Wakefield. Some great Welsh players confirmed to me that they relished the challenge, while others felt incomplete because they hadn't played rugby league. J.P.R. Williams nearly signed for Hull and Cliff Morgan was offered £5,000 to sign for St Helens. What great signings they would have been. From the birth of rugby league in 1895, Welshmen have made a massive contribution to the Great Britain team and every club.

John Simonson, the former Swansea, Aberavon and London Welsh centre, remembers: "I was captain of the Aberavon Green Stars for two seasons [1966–67 and 1967–68] and Mike played for two seasons with me there. We always trained together and went on holidays together. Mike was a very shy and retiring boy, lacked confidence and started off playing at scrum-half. He suddenly decided he wasn't going to make it as a scrum-half and decided to try the back row instead. He wasn't physically big enough to play in the back row and so started weight training. It paid off and he became more confident. He knew then he could handle anything and anybody that came along. He was always the first name on the team sheet at Aberavon. He cut bread out of his diet and after the games you had to get to the refreshments before Mike did because he would nick the meat out of the sandwiches because he was on a protein diet.

One time Bristol were playing at Aberavon in midweek; it was pouring down and we beat them comfortably. Mike showered quickly, got into the canteen and got all the meat out of the sandwiches. The Bristol boys were a bit posh, university boys; I was standing next to one guy, he opened his sandwich and said: 'This is a bit of a bad show: bread and butter sandwiches.'

One summer Mike and I went to Ibiza together on holiday. It was the first time I had gone on a package holiday. It was a package deal with Clarkson's and we flew out from Cardiff. We landed in Ibiza, got in the hotel and Mike came up with this cock-and-bull story that we were island hoppers, we weren't on a package tour, that was too low for us, and I was an antiques collector with an antiques shop. Come the last day when the package tour bus was leaving for the airport we had to leave earlier on the Number 9 public transport bus to get to the airport before them and keep the story alive.

Mike and I were called into the Welsh training sessions at the Afan Lido every Sunday. We were super fit and Bryn Thomas had to tell us to calm down because we were too fit for them. Mike should have got a Welsh cap. In rugby union he got himself so fit that when the game broke down he would be the first there, picking the ball up, and that was absolutely invaluable. He was a brilliant guy to have on your team, especially in inhospitable places like Ebbw Vale in midweek when it was peeing down with rain. He didn't care if it was home or away, he just wanted to stamp his authority on the game. We were born too soon really because the money that is in the game now is just incredible. We played for the pride and because you wanted to strut your stuff up and down the main street after a good win on a Saturday. You had fame in the town.

I wasn't surprised when he went to rugby league because a couple of guys had already gone. He was ideally suited for rugby league, because he was a dynamo and never stopped running. Mike invited me to the 1974 Challenge Cup Final. I was living in London then, playing for London Welsh and working as a cab driver. At the after-match dinner I was on the same table as Alex Murphy and I remember him pointing to Mike and saying: 'That's the man who should have won the Lance Todd Trophy.'"

7. Not guilty and going north

By 1972, I was used to appearing on the back page of the *Port Talbot Guardian* but on Friday 28 January I appeared on the front page as well. The headline was: 'RUGBY STAR IS CLEARED OF ASSAULT CHARGE'. The *Port Talbot Guardian* cost 4p back then and I have still got a copy of the report: "Aberavon's star wing forward and vice-captain, Mike Nicholas, was cleared of an assault charge at Swansea Crown Court on Monday – without the jury having to retire to deliberate on the issue. The judge, Mr Justice Talbot … told the jury it would be unsafe to convict on the evidence.

Nicholas … had denied assaulting off-duty police officer Keith Morgan on June 26 occasioning actual bodily harm. Mr Roger Garfield, prosecuting, said the case involved the events of Saturday, June 26. On Friday, June 25 and into the early hours of Saturday morning, a barn dance was being held at Gelli Deg farm, Tonna, Neath, organised by Neath Round Table. These young men were seen to leave the dance … holding a box and it was thought they were making off with the raffle money. They went out into the dark. A committee man, Mr Hale, followed them and called on the help of other committee members and an off-duty police officer.

Mr Hale came upon a group of persons and spoke to one of them. Hale was assaulted and the off-duty PC Keith Morgan and others saw him in trouble and closed on the group when Morgan was struck. He grappled with the person who delivered the blow and it is alleged that person was Nicholas.

Mr Anthony Evans, defending, said the defence admitted the officer had been assaulted and sustained an eye injury as a result. The issue, he added, would be one of identity.

Detective Sergeant Norman Hopkins said when Nicholas was interviewed at Neath Police Station on July 20 he denied all knowledge of the attack and said: 'I don't know what you are talking about, I have never been there, I was in Port Talbot all night in the Sportsman and Casino.'

The officer told Nicholas that he had been identified by two people who had seen him at the dance and Nicholas replied: 'I can't understand that, because I have not been to Neath for ages.'

Less than an hour after the interview, Nicholas returned to Neath Police Station, said Sgt Hopkins, with a man who said he … had been at the barn dance, but Nicholas had not. … the officer said statements had also been taken from four other people who had attended the dance, but none of them had been in a position to identify anyone.

Nicholas told the jury he had spent the evening of June 25 at Port Talbot, firstly in a training session at the Afan Lido. He then went to the Sportsman's Bar and later to the Casino Club. In the early hours … he went to his mother's home to listen to the live broadcast of the first British Lions test in New Zealand and went to sleep on the sofa. He did not attend the barn dance and recalled that the test match he heard resulted in a win for the Lions... Mr Justice Talbot told the jury he considered it unsafe to convict and directed that they return a verdict of not guilty. Nicholas was acquitted."

It was a horrible experience and the court report only tells half of the story. It all started when some of my former team-mates, who were police constables, told me that I needed to go to Neath Police Station to answer some questions and clear something up. I had no idea what I was walking into. I will never forget the interview. I went over to Neath and introduced myself to the desk sergeant. This bloke came from behind the desk and said to me: "You don't know me, do you?"

"No I don't," I replied. "Well I know you," he added. "You are a dirty bastard." I was shocked and said: "Excuse me." He continued: "I know you, the way you play on the field, you are a dirty bastard. If they can't do you on the field, I will do you off the field."

That was my introduction to John Williams of South Wales CID, who later became chairman of Neath RFC and a Detective Chief Superintendent and who died, aged 73, in 2012. After the interview I made my own inquiries into what had happened at the barn dance, because I knew they were trying to set me up for something I hadn't done. A few names came into the frame and I went to the police with the information, but they never took any notice and the case went to court.

I had to go down to the cells to answer bail and was put in a holding cell. The man in the next cell was visibly upset and I asked what was wrong with him. He said: "I've just got two years for grievous bodily harm." I told him that I was charged with something similar, but that I didn't do it. "No," he said. "Neither did I." That got me really worried because I thought I was facing a two-year sentence for something I didn't do.

After the judge heard the prosecution case, he suggested that they needed to rethink it and go back to someone higher up the force to see if it was worth pursuing. In other words, the judge was saying they needed to drop the case because they had no evidence. The police came back and said no, they were carrying on. Whoever was guiding them – and I suspect it was this John Williams – made them continue with the case.

After the judge heard the defence, he turned straight to the jury and directed them. He said the case was unsafe and he would not even let them consider it. I was acquitted there and then. But it still left a very bitter taste in my mouth and was one of the reasons why I got out of Welsh rugby altogether and signed for Warrington.

There was a lot of this stuff going on in South Wales at the time. Peter Hain, the anti-apartheid campaigner, was wrongly arrested and the police tried to fabricate evidence against him. He set up a group called JAIL – Justice Against Identification Laws – to fight back. I wrote to him to lend my support and tell him what had happened to me. The police were getting away with everything.

The Darvell brothers, Wayne and Paul, spent seven years in prison for murder. They were freed by the Court of Appeal in 1992, after it heard claims that South Wales detectives had doctored confession statements and notes, and suppressed scientific evidence.

A prostitute called Lynette White was stabbed to death in Cardiff in 1988 and three men, who became known as the Cardiff Three, were jailed for her murder in 1990. They were later cleared on appeal and the real murderer was eventually jailed in 2003. John Williams himself was later investigated for his part in the botched inquiry and it looked at one stage that he was going to get done for it, but he got off with it in the end.

Max Wiltshire, the Aberavon captain, thought I had done it. He lived in Skewen, a village near Swansea, and later found out through the grapevine who had assaulted the police constable at the barn dance, the crime I was accused of committing. It was a rugby player from Swansea – who I am not allowed to name for legal reasons – and who had immediately emigrated to Australia to get out of the way.

After following the Great Britain tour of Australia in 1988 in a Winnebago campervan, I spent a couple of weeks parked up on Manly beach. Every morning I went to a cafe bar for breakfast which was run by a guy connected with Manly rugby union club. We were outside one morning and a man came past in his car, beeping his horn. He was about to stop and come in when he saw me and shot off. I realised it was the rugby player from Swansea who had committed the assault. I didn't let on and the cafe bar owner said: "That's strange. He normally comes in here and I was going to introduce you to him because he's Welsh." I went there for breakfast every day after that, but the man from Swansea never came back.

We drew 3–3 at Neath in February 1972 and the match report in the *Port Talbot Guardian* quoted one angry Neath fan who thought that referee Ernie Lewis had awarded us too many penalties. "He was like a canary," said the irate supporter. "He wore a yellow jersey and kept whistling all the time." We also drew 7–7 with South Wales Police in April in a match that I remember well because I suffered a broken nose in the first half, but carried on playing until the final whistle.

At least we were still going strong in the Welsh Cup. After beating Nantymoel in the first round, we defeated Penclawdd 16–6 in the second round, Bridgend 15–3 in the third and Newport 28–6 in the quarter-finals. Our reward was a semi-final against Llanelli in front of a big crowd at the St Helen's ground in Swansea. Clive Jones scored a try in the corner after five minutes and we were still leading 7–3 approaching half-time when we lost our hooker Morton Howells with a dislocated elbow. Not only were we down to 14 men, but we couldn't get any ball out of the scrum. I tried hooking and so did Clive, but it was no use. We were starved of possession and forced to tackle like demons. In the second half, wing Roy Mathias scored a try for Llanelli, which Phil Bennett converted to make the score 9–7 to them before their Number 8 Hefin Jenkins scored a try to put the result beyond doubt. But we were given a great reception by the Aberavon fans at the end, because they thought we did not deserve to lose.

Our end-of-season tour to Devon took us to Torquay and Newton Abbott. We won both games and staged a pitch-and-putt competition at Torquay which was won by scrum-half Clive Shell, our player-of-the-year.

Up north, former Aberavon full-back Kel Coslett made headlines by winning the Lance Todd Trophy as man-of-the-match in the Challenge Cup Final. Coslett, the St Helens loose-forward and captain, kicked five great goals as the Saints beat Leeds 16–13 in May.

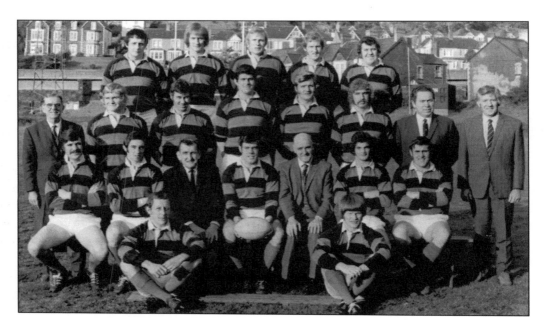

Top: Aberavon 1971-72. Left to right, back: John Richardson, Dai Condon, Max Wiltshire, Huw Jenkins, John Mahoney; second row: T.O. James, Mike Nicholas, Peter Hunt, Alan Martin, Phil Bell, Ken Lloyd, Cliff David (treasurer), Len Cunningham; seated: Phil Bessant, Jeff Thomas, Glynn Overton (sec), Ian Hall (capt), Lord Heycock (chairman), Dennis Curling, Morton Howells; front: Clive Shell, John Bevan.

Left: Kel Coslett (Photo: courtesy Robert Gate).

Below: Captain Geoffrey Crawshay's Welsh XV 1972, 41st tour. Back: left to right: Bobby Windsor, Ken Jones, Phil Bennett, Vivian Jenkins, Mike, Stuart Lane, Alan Martin, Lyn Jones, Tom David, Graham Price, Phillip Chater, Geoff Evans, Del Haines; seated: Wilf Jones, John Williams, Bill Hullin, Colonel Sir William Crawshay, John Dawes, A.M. Rees, Denzil Williams, Ian Hall, Bryan Wilkins, Gwyn Bayliss, Doug Ackerman.

Little did I know at the time, but four months later I would be joining him in rugby league. Dennis Curling beat me to it. He had scored 28 tries for Aberavon that season – a post-war record – and signed for Warrington in August for £5,000. Clive Jones gave him a lift up to Wilderspool, but met Alex Murphy and ended up signing for Warrington as well.

The Crawshay's invited me back to tour with them again in September. It was their 50th anniversary tour, a special occasion, and Colonel Sir William Crawshay, the president, joined us. This really was a 'galacticos' tour and the peerless J.P.R. Williams, of London Welsh, the Barbarians, Wales and the British Lions, was the full-back. Phil Bennett was back again. It was also the start of the famous Pontypool front row of Charlie Faulkner, Graham Price and Bobby Windsor that Max Boyce sang about. Graham and Bobby were both on the tour, although Bobby was still at Cross Keys then. The other prop was Denzil Williams, from Ebbw Vale, who was coming to the end of his career. He had won 36 Wales caps between 1963 and 1971 and played five times for the British Lions. In many ways it was the lead up to the halcyon days of Welsh rugby, another golden era. It was a privilege to play with them.

Clive Jones had been invited, but couldn't tour this time because he had signed for Warrington and it wasn't quite as interesting without my top tourist Clive. Thankfully, this time I did not have to go through the initiation ceremony. We became the perpetrators, building up the suspense – not the victims. Another Aberavon player and schoolboy friend, Alan Martin, came instead. He had gone to Sandfields Comprehensive as well and was a great athlete. He was six feet five inches tall and weighed 17 stone 10 pounds; was a tremendous shot putter and a prolific goalkicker. His nickname was 'Panther' because that was the way he moved around. We beat Plymouth 45–3 and a Cornwall County XV 40–3.

Two days after the tour finished I was off to Scotland to play for the Public School Wanderers in the Selkirk Sevens. Brigadier Rolf James picked me, even though I hadn't been to public school. I have been breaking barriers down all my life and we won the tournament. It was the first time the Wanderers had won the Selkirk Sevens. John Thomas, from Amman United, travelled with me in my MGB. He was only 5 feet 4 inches tall and was said to be too small for the 15-a-side game, but was a great sevens player. Captain Phil Davies, of Richmond and the Army, played for us along with a powerful winger from Morley, Dave Hoyland, who Leeds were interested in. He would have made a great rugby league player.

We had a really good team and we beat Hawick and Gala. A young George Fairbairn played for Kelso. The Brown brothers, Peter and Gordon, both Scotland internationals, also played. It was a prestigious tournament to win and it was the first time the trophy had been taken out of Scotland since before the war. We were staying in the Buccleuch Arms Hotel at St Boswells, near Melrose, and we had a good night. We always celebrated hard after matches when we were on the sevens tour. Next morning I was a bit hung-over and saw in the paper that Warrington were playing Wigan. I spoke to John and we decided to head back down to England and break the journey up by watching the match, have a bit of a rest and then continue home. We got to Wilderspool just before kick-off and managed to blag our way in on the sports centre side by saying we had come to watch some of the Welsh boys playing.

I watched the game peeping through my fingers and thinking: "How tough is this?" Wigan forward Bill Ashurst went off injured and Warrington stand-off Wilf Briggs had a blinder, scoring two tremendous tries. I fell in love with the set-up straight away. It was way ahead of its time with the sports centre on one side of the ground. The atmosphere was brilliant too. It was more like a football crowd than a rugby union crowd, who were more silent and analytical. I thought I was missing out on something. After the match, I dropped in at the dressing rooms to say hello to the boys and so long and then go home.

I went in and said "See you boys" and was walking out with John when I bumped into Dennis Maddock, who was Warrington's Welsh scout. "What are you doing here?" he asked. I explained and he said "Wait a minute" and went into the dressing room. I was stood there like a lemon and next thing he emerged with Alex Murphy. "Alex," he said: "This is the lad we have been talking about. This is the lad you have spoken to on the phone." Murphy looked me up and down. It was like being assessed by Vincent O'Brien, the famous racehorse trainer, and having my fetlocks checked.

Murphy asked me if I would stay in Warrington for the week, train with them and play for the 'A' team on the Saturday. I was flexible, single and didn't take much convincing actually. I thought "The boys are doing all right up here and I like the set-up". John had to open the saw mills in the morning, but he said: "It's OK Mike, I'll get the train." I trained with Warrington all week and stayed in digs in Bewsey with Dennis Curling and Clive Jones.

My first game of rugby league was as a trialist for Warrington 'A' against Barrow 'A' at Wilderspool on the Saturday afternoon. Before the match a photographer took a team picture and so I stood at the back, with my head bowed, trying not to be recognised. I must have ruined the picture, but if the rugby union authorities had seen me I would have been classed as a professional and banned for life. We beat them 46–2 and fans were shouting from the terraces "Get him signed, get him signed".

I signed on the Sunday, but didn't have a clue about negotiating and haggling for money. Murph tells a story that he asked me: "What do you think you are worth?" I am supposed to have replied: "Whatever Clive Jones got, I am worth more because I am a better player than him." Murph never forgot that and kept bringing it up. It came across as arrogant and I didn't want it to come out like that, but I got £4,000 with another £1,000 to come later. I was happy with that. You could buy a house for £5,000 or £6,000. We were also on £30 a match for a win and £10 a match for losing and we would almost kill for winning pay. In the 'A' team it was £10 for winning and £5 for losing. Murph said later it was one of the best signings he ever made and that's good enough for me.

I rang home and spoke to my mum and she said: "Where've you been?" I hadn't been home for a week and explained about the sevens and staying with Dennis and Clive. "When are you coming home then?" she asked. "It will be lovely to see you." I said I would be back the following day to hand my notice in at the oil refinery and collect my things because I was now a professional rugby player. There was a long pause on the other end of the line and then she said: "OK then, see you tomorrow." It was a massive shock for the family to come to terms with, but they never showed it really.

I went home on the Monday and by then the news of my signing had broken. Aberavon were playing Pontypridd and I popped my head around the dressing room door and said "See you boys, thanks for everything" and went in the clubhouse with my girlfriend. I had a cheque for £2,000 in my pocket. The rest was to come later. I was stood there for a while in the lounge and my former woodwork teacher Brian Tashara, who was the club secretary, came over and gave me a brown envelope. It was a note from one of the Aberavon fans wishing me good luck in rugby league.

I said: "For a minute I thought you were going to ask me to leave." He said: "As a matter of fact, I am asking you to leave. You are a professional now and you can't stay here." He said that Jack Young, one of the 'big five' Wales selectors, was in the club and had told him to "Get him out". I left. I didn't want to cause any problems. I was friendly with Brian's daughter and she told me years later that it was one of his biggest regrets that he had to do that. I just shrugged my shoulders and got on with it. I headed back up to Warrington in my MGB to the great adventure.

The *Port Talbot Guardian* covered the news of my signing under the headline: "Aberavon's star player goes north". There was another article for my scrapbook the following week when Clive Girton carried out a "compelling investigation" with the headline: "Just what is it that Warrington RL has to offer?" Part of the article said: "What exactly is the attraction which makes the Warrington Rugby League club so irresistible to Aberavon players? ... Mike Nicholas has become the fifth Wizard to join the northern club. The five wizards on the Warrington books are: Bobby Wanbon, Francis Reynolds, Dennis Curling, Clive Jones and now Mike Nicholas... has joined his former team-mates who could form an Aberavon Exiles club.

In an interview last week before leaving for Warrington for a reported fee in excess of £4,000, Mike told me of his impression of what he called 'the tremendous set-up at Warrington.' The club is owned by a millionaire who has adopted the 'expense no object' policy in getting Warrington among the top trio of league clubs in this country. This millionaire has begun with a team building programme on similar lines to those adopted by first division soccer clubs. He has bought several key players for sums in excess of £6,000 and given the whole side many glorious incentives.

'For instance, the club is involved in about half-a-dozen cup competitions including the ... Challenge Cup and if we can win any of these competitions we stand to gain holidays in Cyprus in addition to our match bonuses,' said Mike... [He] explained that although a couple of other clubs were adopting a similar policy the Warrington plan was in fact the prototype which the others have followed. Turning to the physical set-up, Mike said there sauna baths, masseur and two doctors provided by the club. A sports centre, dance hall, directors' lounge and several other facilities are all in the massive complex.

Club trainer Alex Murphy decided to bring together a pool of top flight players... 'He believes in strength in depth to carry Warrington through their rigorous fixture list,' added Mike... "It's a really fantastic club and the Aberavon boys are very highly thought of by the club and officials alike. Bobby Wanbon is regarded as the king and Curling has really captured the imagination of the supporters and is already one of their firm favourites. Reynolds is playing exceptionally well as is Jones and I am sure I will be very happy up there. 'They are going to find me the same type of job as I have at the moment,' said Mike, who is a safety officer, 'and I felt I couldn't turn down this golden opportunity.'"

We won the Challenge Cup in May 1974 but, sadly, we never got to go to Cyprus as promised. Ossie Davies was the Warrington chairman and one of his companies was building hotels on the Turkish side of the island – but lost them after the Turkish invasion that July.

Three months after I signed for Warrington, Brigadier Rolph James rang again and asked me to play for the Public School Wanderers in a sevens tournament in – guess where – Cyprus. I said: "I can't play, I'm playing against Oldham on New Year's Eve; I'm a rugby league player now." He couldn't believe it. Years after I was at Twickenham for an England Wales game. I was in a hospitality function at Kneller Hall, home of the Royal Military School of Music, and this voice boomed out: "Mike Nicholas, what are you doing here?" It was Rolf and he said "Good grief man. Come and have a drink in the officers' mess with me." I said I wasn't dressed properly, but he got me a jacket and a tie.

When I signed for Warrington one of the conditions was that they found me an equivalent job to the one I had, site safety officer at Baglan Bay. Brian Pitchford, the Warrington vice-chairman, said I could be a trainee manager at Locker Industries wire weaving, but I would have to learn the business first. I asked: "What does that mean?" He replied: "You will have to go in the factory." So they put me in the factory and moved me around the various departments. It was so noisy that I learned how to lip read. It was 18 months of hell and, in the end, I hated going in. I couldn't wait to get out. It was like being in a penitentiary, but I was so impressed with the work ethic of the staff, especially the women, and their humility. I learned a lot about the wire weaving business and loved the connection with the club's nickname – the Wire. Warrington will always be the Wire to me. I understand the marketing of the Warrington Wolves, but they will always be the Wire to me.

I guess I was lucky really. When the 18 stone Cardiff forward Frank Whitcombe joined Broughton Rangers in 1935, the club found him a job as a zoo keeper at Belle Vue Zoological Gardens. Frank joined Bradford Northern in 1938 and started working as a coach driver, which came in handy when Bradford reached the Challenge Cup final against Wigan in 1948. The coach driver taking Bradford to Wembley from their hotel got lost and Frank said: "Out of the way, I'll take over." He jumped into the driver's seat, took the team to Wembley and became the first player to win the Lance Todd Trophy despite being on the losing side. Belle Vue was a leisure complex with speedway and rugby as well as the zoo. Broughton Rangers became Belle Vue Rangers after the war and Stan McCormick, the former St Helens and Warrington winger, started his career with them. Stan told me once that Belle Vue put him on the transfer list in 1948 for £4,000 – which was then the world record transfer fee. He asked: "Why have you put me on the transfer list?" The club secretary replied: "We need to buy another lion and you are our most valuable player."

8. Top of the league

My first game as a fully-fledged professional was for Warrington's 'A' team at Leigh on Saturday 30 September. I got on the bus, a small bus, not a mini-bus, and I thought half the team was missing. Then I realised it was only 13-a-side and then a half-back called Jimmy Green got on. He was a trialist and looked like he weighed about five stones. I thought: "What kind of side have we got here?" Leigh had a couple of Aussies playing for them, who were dishing it out, and I gave it to them. Start as you mean to go on. Tommy Grainey was the Leigh 'A' team coach at the time and he reminded of it years later. I scored a try, my first in rugby league; we beat them 19–13 and I made my first-team debut against Barrow the week after. So I was thrown in at the deep end really. Frankie Jones was the Barrow scrum-half and he did a Cumberland throw on me. I resisted, twisted ligaments in my knee and had to go off injured after half an hour. Warrington still won comfortably, 55–17, and our reserve full-back Ken Hindley, who was only aged 18, kicked 11 goals.

An Irish mate of ours from Aberavon, Bennie Crawford, was working in Connah's Quay at the time. He picked the paper up that morning and saw I was making my debut for Warrington that afternoon and turned up to watch the game. He met us after the match, we all went out for the night and we took him back to our digs in Folly Lane. The landlady, Mrs Daniels, was already on my case because I used to nick the cream off the top of the milk. Clive Jones was always her favourite. We put Bennie on the settee for the night. When Mrs Daniels came down in the morning she put her foot on the settee to open the curtains and woke him up. He said "Top of the morning to you" and she screamed for her husband "Jim, Jim, there's an Irishman on the settee" and all hell broke loose. The IRA was in the news every day at the time. I had to leave Folly Lane after that. The club then put me on to a Mrs McIntyre, who had a flat to rent in Whitefield Road, Stockton Heath, and was a great lady. Her son, Alan, played for Warrington Rugby Union Club and was connected with the Greenall Whitley brewery. I spent the next 30 years there and ended up buying the place when she died. I renamed the house 'Margam', where I was born, and had an engraved window with the Welsh three feathers put in.

Team-mate Bobby Wanbon recalls: *"I joined Warrington from St Helens in 1971 and told Mike 'it's great up here' and he signed in 1972. When I joined Warrington they had already signed Frankie Reynolds from Aberavon. Then Clive Jones and Dennis Curling signed from Aberavon, and then Mike signed from Aberavon. That was five of us from Aberavon. They must have been cursing Warrington. Mike adapted to rugby league straight away and started playing some of his best rugby. He had aggression – obviously – speed around the park and a good pass because he had been a scrum-half. He had everything. Everybody looked up to him. I am glad to say I never played against him. The Wilderspool crowd took to him – and all the Welsh lads – straight away. If you gave 100 per cent, like Mike did, you were always going to get the respect of the crowd. He was brilliant to play with as well as being a good friend."*

The class of 1972: the Warrington team Mike joined. Left to right, back: Kevin Ashcroft, Geoff Clarkson, Derek Whitehead, Alex Murphy, Brian Gregory, Bobby Wanbon, Brian Brady, George Herd, Brian Larkin, Dave Chisnall; seated: Frank Gregory, Parry Gordon, Conrad Barton, Wilf Briggs, Tommy Conroy, Dave Cunliffe, Derek Noonan, Toby Du Toit.
Mike took over from Geoff Clarkson and Brian Gregory. (Photo: Eddie Fuller).

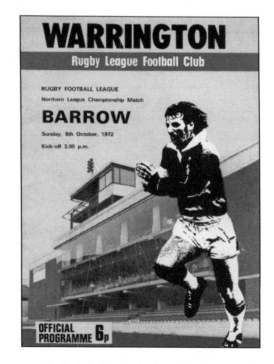

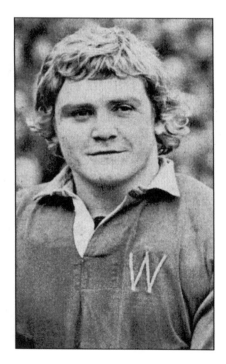

Left: Mike's Warrington debut was against Barrow at Wilderspool on Sunday 8 October 1972. (Courtesy Warrington Wolves RLFC). Right: Baby face: How Mike looked when he first signed for Warrington. Now he says he looks like Mrs Brown. (Photo: Eddie Fuller).

Warrington legends from when Mike joined the club: Clockwise from top left: Parry Gordon; Kevin Ashcroft; Dave Chisnall and Derek Noonan. (Photos: Eddie Fuller)

My second game for Warrington was as a substitute against York at Wilderspool. I came on at half-time for scrum-half John Lowe who had suffered a broken arm and had actually played with it broken for 20 minutes. York had a prop playing for them, big Malcolm Dixon. I was new to the game and he knew I was new to the game. He said: "I am going to pick you up and throw you down to the ground and listen to the crowd react." And he did and the crowd went mad. We still won 34–16. It was the team's 10th successive victory.

My first try for the first team came against Huddersfield at Wilderspool. An Australian centre called John Grant was making his debut as a guest player. I sent him away for a try before scoring myself, a swift handling cross-field move left me with a gap and I powered in from 15 yards. Almost 40 years later, in 2011, John became the inaugural chairman of the Australian Rugby League Commission. Also playing that day, on the wing for Huddersfield, was Wayne Bennett, who has become one of Australia's greatest ever coaches.

Sadly, my new injury jinx was about to strike again – and it was my team-mate Bobby Wanbon who was responsible. Bobby had a really distinctive style of tackling where the top half of his body, his head and his shoulders used to drop across the player he was tackling. Against Whitehaven, he came across the player, landed awkwardly, fell on my leg and I had to be stretchered off. Over the years, Bobby did more damage to me than any of the opposition. Thankfully, in this case, the injury was not as serious as first thought. I was back in training the next week, ready for the match which became known as the Boxing Day brawl against Leigh. I have described it elsewhere because I ended up getting sent off.

One of my first away games was against Hull at the Boulevard and there was a really poor crowd there, about 1,500. We beat them comfortably 36–8 with two tries for Bobby Wanbon and two for Frank Reynolds. I could hear some people shouting: "Nicholas, you traitor. You left us." After the match I went into the clubhouse and there they were, Les Savini and some of his mates from Port Talbot, who had come up to see me play and wind me up. Les was a very popular guy in Port Talbot. He weighed about 27 stones and you couldn't miss him. He was into horse racing and ran a book in the Royal Exchange pub in the days before betting shops were legalised. He was also the projectionist in the Grand cinema. His routine was to put the film on, then go over to the pub, collect all his bets and have a few pints. Usually he had an hour and a half to do all this in.

The early projectors used to get very hot and the film would start to move around and expand. Invariably, one of the cinema goers would have to get him out of the pub because the film had slipped and everybody was watching the film on the wall instead of the screen. He would then have to go over and correct it. One time he was arrested for his bookmaking activities and taken to the police station at the other end of the town, but he was too big to get into a Black Maria. So he had to be escorted down the main street and was such a popular guy people booed, hissed and called the police, saying: "Leave him alone. He's our hero." Les loved it and lapped it all up. He was a great character. He moved on to the Plaza cinema at the other end of town after that and invited me up to the projectionist booth. I had always been interested to see how it was done. He got me to look at the film he was showing and I said: "Bloody hell Les, the film is upside down." He said: "Don't be stupid, it's

The Poseidon Adventure." And for anyone who doesn't know about *The Poseidon Adventure* it is the story of a ship that turns upside down.

Team-mate Clive Jones recollects: "*Our first winter in Warrington, 1972, was freezing. It was the fashion at the time to have bri-nylon sheets and quilts – duvets hadn't been invented – and there was a load of static in the morning. I can remember Mike sliding out of the bed because of the bri-nylon. It was freezing and, on numerous occasions, Nicko went to bed wearing his pumps, his trousers and his donkey jacket because the nylon sheets weren't warm enough. They said the north of England was an overcoat colder than South Wales but, in Nicko's case, it was a donkey jacket colder. Nicko was with me when I met my first wife, Joy, the mother of my children, in a night club in Warrington. Nicko and I had been drinking some concoction of barley wine and Strongbow and were inebriated. She told her mother she had met two nice Welshmen, but she thought they must be a bit retarded because they couldn't speak. Mike must have been drunk that night because he gave me the keys to his MGB to take this young lady home, but I survived to tell the tale.*"

Ossie Davies, the Warrington chairman, was made a CBE in the New Year honours for services to industry. He was the chairman and managing director of Leonard Fairclough Ltd, the builders and civil engineers. He was a magistrate, a former councillor and served with the Royal Engineers in the Second World War, first on bomb disposal and later as a deep-sea diver. He won the Distinguished Conduct Medal in the Anzio beachhead landing in 1944.

He was very relaxed, just let Murph get on with the job and never interfered. He was a nice man and the club's saviour. He rescued it and took it into a new era, which was very exciting and I was proud to be part of that. He was as good as his word, came in, brought Murph in and shook everything up. Murph went on record to say he was going to deliver success – and he did. He created a tremendous side in a short time; with unprecedented success after the club had been in the doldrums for years. I believe the nadir was a 50–0 defeat at home to Salford in November 1970. The club had less than 2,000 watching them.

I didn't know at the time but, as the New Year dawned, I was about to have my first big bust-up with Murph. In the Boxing Day brawl, I had picked up an injury and I knew there was no way I could play against Oldham on New Year's Eve, but I didn't let Murph know that I was injured. I went home to Aberavon and went out with my mates on the Saturday night and then rang Warrington with a weak excuse for not playing, which wasn't like me really. I didn't want to declare the injury because I had already suffered a few knocks and didn't want to get a reputation for being injury-prone. I hid the injury. When I got back to Warrington, Murph pulled me in and carpeted me. My feet never touched the ground. It had the desired effect. I thought I was professional; I had a professional outlook when I was an amateur, but this was new. That's when I realised I couldn't get away with things anymore, not that I tried to. I should have been more forthcoming. He told me in no uncertain terms what he thought. Murph wanted you to play all the time and if you played carrying an injury he never made any allowances. You learned how to play injured. He was the ultimate professional coach – demanding and ruthless.

Left: Dennis Curling goes in for another try.

Below left: Alex Murphy makes a break against St Helens, with Mike, Dave Cunliffe and Bobby Wanbon in support. Referee Fred Lindop is keeping an eye on things.

Below right: Clive Jones runs out at Wilderspool.
(Photos: Eddie Fuller)

First try: Mike heading for the line against Huddersfield at Wilderspool in December 1972. Greg Veivers is the Huddersfield player who cannot stop him. (Photo: Eddie Fuller).

Touching down: Mike scoring that all-important first try with Frank Reynolds looking on. (Photo: courtesy Stuart Ritchie).

In another incident against Leigh I was dropped on my head, my square head, and something sprang, the sternoclavicular joint. The doctor fitted me with a dog collar and when Murph saw it, he ripped it off, saying: "There's no need for that. You are not delivering a sermon." That was how tough he was.

Clive Jones recalls: *"I remember one match at Warrington we were in the dressing room getting changed and Mike looked like the mummy. He had bandaged his knees, his shoulders were bandaged and his elbows were bandaged and Mike said to Alex Murphy: 'I don't really feel like playing today.' Murph thought he was a bit of a hypochondriac and said: 'Nicko, you take a bloody aspirin when your shoes laces are undone, you're bloody playing.'"*

Former groundsman Roy 'Ockher' Aspinall remembers: *"Me and Alex grew up together in Thatto Heath in the 1950s. He went to the Catholic school and I went to the C of E school. We used to wait for them and knock the stuffing out of them when they were coming home from school. Alex came to see me about it and we have been friends ever since. Mike and Alex are similar personalities. It was Murph's way or no way and it was Nicko's way or no way."*

By the start of February we were unbeaten for 19 games in the league – 18 wins and a draw – and about to play second-placed St Helens in a match that would go a long way to deciding who won the League Leaders' trophy. I had been banned for two matches for the sending-off against Leigh and was put in the 'A' team at St Helens on the Friday night to prove my fitness. I scored a try and we won 10–5, but I was concussed. In fact, I played against St Helens on the Sunday with concussion. It was like being in a telephone box with everyone else outside, but I had my best game for the club so far. It was a big part of my development as a player. It was a great game with a brilliant crescendo involving three former Aberavon players. Kel Coslett put St Helens 11–10 ahead with a drop-goal two minutes from time before Dennis Curling scored in the corner after Frank Reynolds drew two men to create space and then delivered a perfectly-timed pass. We won 13–11. The Welsh boys who played for St Helens, Kel Coslett and John Mantle, came to me afterwards and said 'well done'. It felt like I had broken into the scene.

One week later we beat Widnes 20–8 at Wilderspool in the second round of the Challenge Cup in front of another huge crowd – 16,000 – but I suffered torn shoulder muscles. The following week I came on at half-time against Rochdale Hornets in the league and got through the game, but I wasn't right. I also came on too late to change the game. We were already behind and lost 17–5. That was the end of our 20-match unbeaten run, which is still a record for one season.

The next game was against Featherstone Rovers at Wilderspool in the quarter-finals of the Challenge Cup. I started when I shouldn't even have played. I remember going on the field, stretching my arms and feeling pain in my shoulder. I think I cost Warrington the game. Steve Nash, the Featherstone scrum-half, put his stand-off Mel Mason into a gap at the Scoreboard End. Frank Reynolds and I collided, knocked each other over and Mason scored. It was either great rugby league by those two, or inexperienced rugby union type positioning by Frank and me. Featherstone won 18–14 and went on to win the cup.

John Grant recalls: *"I came over off the back of the World Cup tour in France in 1972. I had won a Queensland player-of-the-year scholarship and had a year with Warrington. The first thing that happened was the Welsh guys turned up: Dennis Curling, Clive Jones and Mike Nicholas, who was the leader of the gang. We became best mates because we were all single guys. We had a fabulous time. Mike may have given me the ball for my first try for Warrington, I can't remember, but let's stick with that story. It sounds like a good story. It was 10 minutes into the game, we were playing Huddersfield, a gap opened up and I scored a try. I turned around and the crowd starting singing* Waltzing Matilda. *It was wonderful. It made the hairs on the back of my neck stand up.*

A lot of Australians came over, young blokes, not necessarily making any money out of it but playing good footy, with good clubs, with great guys. I loved playing in England. I loved the cold and I loved the softer grounds. I loved the defence. I was a strong defensive player. I loved the physicality of it. We unfortunately lost our Challenge Cup quarter-final to Featherstone Rovers. We should never, ever have lost that match. That was my one disappointment. I had a fantastic year and enjoyed every moment of it. Luckily I wasn't working and so we had a lifestyle that started at 11 o'clock in the middle of the day and finished at two o'clock in the morning. We worked hard, trained hard and played hard."

We bounced back from that Challenge Cup defeat with a comfortable 44–5 win over Huyton and a victory that really was made in Aberavon: Frank Reynolds scored two tries, Dennis Curling scored two tries, Bobby Wanbon scored one and I scored one. It was a pity that Clive Jones wasn't playing and that no one took a photograph of the four of us together.

We were still top of the league, but had to visit Salford one Friday night. They had a fabulous side, a team of 'galacticos,' and we always had brilliant games at the Willows. George Best used to watch them. I slipped going in for a tackle and the great Colin Dixon ran 60 yards up the field. Luckily he didn't score and we won 10–7. Colin played more than 700 games for Halifax, Salford and Hull Kingston Rovers between 1961 and 1981 and was another one who died too young, aged just 49, in 1993.

We also had to play Wigan at Central Park. As I got off the coach this quite distinguished elderly gentleman approached me and asked: "Who are the boys from Aberavon?" I said I was one and then he asked: "Which one is Curling?" Dennis was still on the bus, but as he came off I told him that someone wanted to meet him. "Hi Dennis," said the man, "I want to congratulate you on equalling my record, seven tries in a game for Aberavon." It was Johnny Ring himself and he made the point that he had also scored seven tries in a match three times for Wigan: twice in 1925 and once in 1927! Dennis must have been inspired, because he scored a try that afternoon and we won 18–8. Aberavon fans used to sing a ditty in praise of Johnny Ring. It started off "Aberavon! Aberavon! You've got to beat Neath on Saturday. Aberavon! Aberavon!" and then had a line about "Johnny Ring was on the wing and Dai Hunt Davies in the centre".

Official photograph: Warrington's squad from the 1972–73 season with the League Leaders' trophy. Mike is sitting on the right of the front row. (Photo: Eddie Fuller).

Lap of honour: Alex Murphy parades around Wilderspool with the League Leaders' trophy. From the right: Frank Reynolds, Kevin Ashcroft, Mike Philbin, Wilf Briggs, Brian Brady, mascot Steve Walsh, Dennis Curling, Murph, Dave Chisnall, Tommy Conroy and Derek Noonan. (Phone: Eddie Fuller).

We went 50 points up against Blackpool Borough at Wilderspool and then let them score three tries near the end. The crowd went mad, stamping their feet in the wooden main stand. They wanted more blood, they weren't happy because we only won 51–20. Two days later we clinched the League Leaders' trophy without even playing. Featherstone thrashed Leeds 30–17 in a night match at Post Office Road and, just seven months after signing, I had my first trophy as a rugby league player. Here is the top 10 from the final league table:

	Pl	Won	Drew	Lost	For	Agst	Pts
Warrington	34	27	2	5	816	400	56
Featherstone Rovers	34	27	0	7	768	436	54
Leeds	34	26	1	7	810	324	53
St Helens	34	24	2	8	623	298	50
Wakefield Trinity	34	25	0	9	814	398	50
Salford	34	25	0	9	723	383	50
Castleford	34	25	0	9	704	404	50
Dewsbury	34	23	0	11	534	354	46
Oldham	34	20	2	12	604	349	42
Hull Kingston Rovers	34	20	1	13	731	522	41

In August 1973, at the start of my first full season with Warrington, a player turned up for the pre-season team photograph and I thought "I haven't seen him before" and so I said to him: "Are you a new signing then?" "No," he said: "I have been suspended for 18 months." I thought: "That's interesting, to be suspended for that long." His name was Joe Price and he said: "I've been watching thee while I've been away. You are doing all right." It was like getting the seal of approval from Albert Pierrepoint, the hangman.

You couldn't believe that Joe was such an executioner because off the pitch he was an affable, rotund and funny guy, a really nice guy, and I got on great with him. I remember him telling Bobby Wanbon: "It's all about winning pay and losing pay, Bobby, and if I can get winning pay by hook or by crook, then I'll get it." That was his philosophy. He wasn't an outstanding player, he was a squad player. He would fill in and never let you down. He was very workmanlike and then all of a sudden the monster would appear. He made one of the worst high tackles I ever saw on the St Helens forward Graham Liptrot at Wilderspool in January 1974. Liptrot had to be carried off and the story goes that he went into the bath and nearly drowned because he was slipping in-and-out of consciousness. Joe was banned until the end of December for that and although the ban was reduced on appeal until the end of May it still cost him a chance of playing at Wembley.

Aberavon handful: This is the Warrington team who played St Helens at Wilderspool on 11 February 1973. It is the only time all five of the Aberavon boys – Frank Reynolds, Bobby Wanbon, Dennis Curling, Clive Jones and Mike – played together. The Wire won a thrilling game 13–11. Left to right, back: Derek Whitehead, Parry Gordon, John Hart, Dave Chisnall, Barry Briggs, Bobby Wanbon, Brian Gregory, Mike, Clive Jones; front: Wilf Briggs, Frank Reynolds, Derek Noonan, Alex Murphy, mascot Gary Ashcroft, Kevin Ashcroft, Dennis Curling.

Past Welsh rugby league legends: Jim Sullivan, Jerry Shea and Aberavon's Johnny Ring.
(Photo: courtesy Robert Gate)

9. Wembley at the double

The 1972–73 season had been a great success. We had won the League Leaders' trophy. Our stand-off Wilf Briggs had scored 23 tries in 25 matches and our full-back Derek Whitehead had kicked 136 goals. But we had missed out on the two main trophies, the Challenge Cup which went to Featherstone and the Championship which went to Dewsbury, and so Murph wanted to strengthen the squad still further.

We had a powerful winger called Toby Du Toit, the only South African ever to play for Warrington. He was a former Springbok under–23 international and had played for Transvaal when they won the Currie Cup. He scored a wonderful try for Warrington in the 1972 Challenge Cup semi-final against St Helens, but Murph didn't rate him and he was out of favour when I signed. He had the South African mentality. He was very much a loner and had his own lifestyle. He didn't mix with the other players. He lived in Lymm and played golf when a lot of the other guys didn't. I got quite friendly with him and liked him. I identified more with him than some of the others because he was an all-round sportsman. He was obviously talented, but Murph didn't rate him. But it is like with the present Warrington coach, Tony Smith, now. With his record, how can you question his judgment?

That was certainly true when I found out who Warrington were going to sign next: John Bevan. I knew John had played for Cardiff, Wales, the Barbarians and the British Lions. I admired him and had played against him for Aberavon, but I didn't know him. I didn't even realise that Warrington were in for him, although there were rumours the previous year that Wigan had tried to sign him, but he had returned their cheque for £12,000. Next thing, Murph said: "We are going to sign John Bevan."

He was in the main stand to watch us play Oldham in the first round of the Player's No. 6 Trophy and must have noticed me because I scored a try as we won 31–14. John had come up on the Friday to discuss terms and Ossie Davies made a loudspeaker announcement that he was likely to sign the following week. He did sign, for £12,000, and then went back home for a few days to sort things out.

Warrington needed somebody to go down to South Wales to collect him. So I went down with Murph and Roy Aspinall to pick him up. Obviously, they didn't know their way around South Wales. The date was set and off we went. John was from Tylorstown, a mining village in the little Rhondda that had also produced a famous flyweight boxer, Jimmy Wilde, the 'Ghost with the Hammer in his Hand', and 'The Tylorstown Terror'.

We went to John's house and his mother came to the door. She wasn't too happy about him going to rugby league – you could sense it. We said "Where's John? We've come to collect him." She said "He's up there" and pointed to a huge coal tip. John was training, running up and down the coal tip, and so we waited for him to come back down and change. Then we took him back to Warrington. He was a great signing. He scored on his debut against Castleford, but then only scored one try in his next eight matches. He was playing well, but it was a big fee and he was under pressure.

Somebody was going to suffer and it turned out to be Leigh at Hilton Park on Boxing Day when he scored four tries. It was a massive breakthrough game for him. Scrum-half Parry Gordon scored two tries that afternoon, made one for John and was presented with a bottle of champagne as our man-of-the-match, but he immediately gave it to John and we drank it in the dressing room. It was the first match in which John gave his famous clenched-fist salute as he scored a try.

Another unusual incident in that match involved me and the Leigh forward Denis Boyd. He had a big reputation and was a fantastic tackler, but somehow I dislocated his shoulder. When he came in to hit me with his shoulder, I picked up speed and ran through him. But as his shoulder came in, I countered it and it popped out of its socket. In the wooden hut tea room after the match, his wife wasn't too happy and had a go at me while he was standing pretty sheepishly behind her.

It was around this time that Murph gave me the nickname 'Clunk'. There was an advert on television which encouraged people to use seat belts. It had the slogan "Clunk, Click, Every Trip" and the nickname was Murph's way of saying that if you were playing against me, you needed to be strapped in for a bumpy ride. "Clunk, click, Mike Nic."

We were already through to the final of the Captain Morgan Trophy against Featherstone Rovers at the Willows in January, but I had to miss the match with an ankle ligament injury I had suffered at Whitehaven. Warrington won 4–0 thanks to two Derek Whitehead penalties. Two weeks later, it was the Player's No. 6 Trophy Final against Rochdale Hornets at Central Park. I started off on the bench, but went on when Dave Chisnall had to go off with a badly cut ear. Minutes later, I scored the opening try. Bobby Wanbon and Brian Brady were tackled near the posts before I crashed over.

We won 27–16 and were starting to feel invincible. We were also starting to wonder about the Great Britain tour to Australia and New Zealand that summer. The last chance to impress the selectors was Sunday 3 March, when Warrington were at home to Dewsbury, the champions. Alan Bates, the Dewsbury scrum-half who went on tour, did not play. Parry Gordon was outstanding and scored five tries as we won 26–10, but was not in the Great Britain squad that was announced the next day. Kevin Ashcroft, John Bevan and I were named, but we were all desperately disappointed for Parry. What more could he have done?

"I still cannot believe it," I said in an interview at the time. "I had been hoping to go, but thought I had missed the chance when I was not included in either of the teams against France." I told the reporter about the excitement in Port Talbot when I phoned them with the news. "My father was at work, but they will let him know and my mother is completely overwhelmed. My two brothers, Geoff and Clive, have gone out for a few drinks to celebrate."

Murph was delighted that three of us had been chosen, but added: "I am very disappointed that Derek Whitehead, Parry Gordon, Derek Noonan and Bobby Wanbon are not going. Parry Gordon is playing better now than at any time in his fine career. There are not many good scrum-halves around, so I just cannot understand why he is not included. He must have killed a black cat at some time.

Kevin Ashcroft (left), John Bevan (centre) and Mike were picked for the 1974 Great Britain tour of Australia and New Zealand. It was a wonderful moment. It vindicated Mike's decision to switch codes. (Photo: *Warrington Guardian*)

Derek Whitehead is in brilliant form and Derek Noonan and Bobby Wanbon would have been an asset to any touring side. They are very unlucky not to be going."

Two days later I received a telegram from the Aberavon Harlequins congratulating me on my selection. I was chuffed to bits. After missing out on a Welsh cap, being selected for the tour vindicated my move to rugby league.

We were still going strong in the Challenge Cup after wins over Huddersfield and Huyton and had to travel to Wigan in the quarter-finals for a match I have covered earlier because I was sent off. We still won 10–6 and were drawn against Dewsbury in the semi-final at Central Park. Before the semi, John Bevan, Kevin Ashcroft and I had all the injections ready for the tour of Australia and so were probably not at our best. I went off at half-time, but came back on for the last few minutes. We won 17–7, were going to Wembley and were going to win the cup.

A lot of football teams were making records and one record producer, who was a big Warrington fan, came up with this song, *Primrose and Blue,* for us. We recorded it in the banqueting suite at the Wilderspool Leisure Centre. We all got together. I have no singing voice whatsoever and so I mimed, but Clive Jones is quite a good singer and figured prominently in it. It was a bit of fun, a chance to get away from the routine of training and playing and made us feel more important.

Two league games in the run-up to Wembley are worth mentioning. Against Featherstone, Dave Chisnall had the end of his nose bitten in a tackle and complained bitterly to referee Billy Thompson about it – and don't forget we were playing Featherstone in the final. I spoke to the Featherstone forward responsible later and he said that Chissie had him completely pinned down. He could not move his arms or his legs, the only thing he could do to get free was to bite him – and the nearest thing was his nose. Then, at home to Widnes on Good Friday, one of their players, Brian Hogan, had a real go at me. Normally I would have done something about it there and then. But I just whispered to him: "I'm going to the Twin Towers boyo, I'll catch up with you later."

Looking back, the 1974 Wembley team was the best side I ever played in. It was really well-balanced, everybody worked for each other and because we shared the workload nobody got stretched or out of their comfort zone and, as a result, we did not pick up that many injuries. We were very competitive and very honest.

Derek Whitehead was terrific at full-back. He had everything, including a great sidestep, and he was a good goalkicker. Mike Philbin was only a makeshift right winger, but he was a massive talent. He could play anywhere in the backs and did a cracking job. Derek Noonan was excellent at right centre. He was so dependable. Defensively, he was tremendous, never let us down and was a good support player.

I was disappointed that Frank Reynolds didn't play at left centre at Wembley. He played in all four rounds leading up to the final and scored our first try in the semi-final against Dewsbury, but then got injured. Murph then put him on the transfer list for £6,000 because he was unhappy that he kept getting injured. Frank was not too particular about designer labels. He just got on with the job. His kit bags were carrier bags from different shops.

Alan Whittle played at left centre at Wembley, even though he was a stand-off really. He was a St Helens lad, like Murph, and a very good player in his own right. Murph had taken him on trial from Barrow in December. He deserved to be in the line-up.

John Bevan was on the left wing. He was a huge addition to our team, a great player and an out-and-out powerhouse. He was unstoppable at times. Keith Fielding of Salford, Stuart Wright of Widnes and John had a race at Wilderspool. Keith was the fastest player I ever played against and he won it, finishing about two yards ahead of Stuart Wright, and he finished about two yards ahead of John. But John had other stuff in his armoury: raw power. Murph missed the four rounds leading up to Wembley, but played at stand-off in the final and brought so much to the side in terms of leadership. Scrum-half Parry Gordon was my hero. He had such talent and such humility. I had so much respect for him. He was a great guy and sadly passed away too young. When I first signed for Warrington, Parry was on the transfer list and in dispute with the club. Johnny Lowe was playing at scrum-half and I thought he was a decent player. He never let us down.

Start of something big: The Warrington team for the Locker Cup match at Wigan in August 1973.
Left to right, back: Brian Brady, Clive Jones, Barry Briggs, Brian Gregory, Billy Pickup, Derek Noonan,
Dave Chisnall, Mike; front: Parry Gordon, Derek Finnigan, Kevin Ashcroft, Frank Reynolds,
Dennis Curling, Wilf Briggs, Derek Whitehead.

Left: Mike on the front foot against Wigan at Central Park
in the 1973 Locker Cup match. Wigan prop Alan Bence is tackling him.
Right: On the charge against Dewsbury at Wilderspool in the all-conquering 1973–74 season.
(All photos: Eddie Fuller).

Left: Dave Wright was Queensland's player of the year (Photo: Eddie Fuller).
Right: Strong as a bull: Brian Brady pictured in 1973. (Photo: Eddie Fuller).
Below: Warrington RLFC 1973-74 signed by the team, but without player-coach and captain Alex Murphy. (Photo: Eddie Whitham).

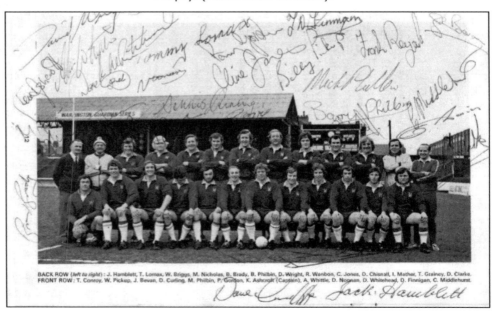

BACK ROW (*left to right*): J. Hamblett, T. Lomax, W. Briggs, M. Nicholas, B. Brady, B. Philbin, D. Wright, R. Wanbon, C. Jones, D. Chisnall, I. Mather, T. Grainey, D. Clarke.
FRONT ROW: T. Conroy, W. Pickup, J. Bevan, D. Curling, M. Philbin, P. Gordon, K. Ashcroft (Captain), A. Whittle, D. Noonan, D. Whitehead, D. Finnigan, C. Middlehurst.

Then when I first saw Parry he looked so pale and fragile and I thought to myself: "What's all the fuss about? Why are they raving about him?" It didn't take me long to find out why. As far as I am concerned he was up there with all the great half-backs: Gareth Edwards, Andy Gregory and Murph. He used to knock big guys down and clamp them. He scampered through gaps, he was like lightning.

People used to call our forwards the 'Panzer Pack'. Murph would use us like Panzer Tanks and the backs stormed through after the blitzkrieg. The front row of Dave Chisnall, Kevin Ashcroft and Brian Brady was brilliant. Chissie was a great competitor, Brady was as strong as a bull, the cornerstone of the pack, and nobody could subdue Kevin Ashcroft. Dave Wright and I played in the second row. Dave was a guest player from the Brisbane Brothers and Queensland's player-of-the-year. He gave us a master-class in tackling that season and he backed up and supported play. He was terrific. Murph said we were one of the best second-row partnerships ever to play at Wembley. We are still friends to this day and it was a privilege to play with him that season. Murph had a simple game plan: don't drop the ball. If anybody did drop the ball – even in training – there was an inquest and that used to intimidate some players.

Loose-forward Barry Philbin was Mike's brother and was one of the best pound-for-pound players I have ever known. He was only 13-and-a-half stones, but he was unbelievable. Murphy signed him from Swinton in January and he was unheralded really, but fitted in fantastically. He was the final piece in the jigsaw. One week after Wembley, Barry won the Harry Sunderland Trophy as man-of-the-match in the Championship Final at Central Park as Warrington beat St Helens 13–12 to win cup number four and crown an amazing year. Ian Mather took my place because I was on crutches. Legend has it that somebody asked Barry Philbin at the end of the season how much winning pay was and he told them. The man then asked: "How much is losing pay?" Barry replied: "I don't know. I haven't lost yet." Played 16, won 16, not a bad record.

Billy Pickup and Bobby Wanbon were the Wembley substitutes and both played important parts. Billy was a typical Murph-type player: six feet two inches, 14 stones, solid and totally reliable. Billy punched Keith Bridges with a cracking straight left during the final and there is an excellent photograph of the punch in the following year's *John Player Rugby League Yearbook*. Then Bobby flattened him and Barry Philbin took care of Les Tonks who was reluctant to return to the action after being substituted. I have already said how much I looked up to Bobby – and how he injured me more than any other individual on a rugby pitch despite the fact that we were playing on the same side. Another example came in a match against Salford at Wilderspool in January 1976. We both went in hard to tackle Colin Dixon, a Wales team-mate of ours, and we clashed heads and fell to the floor. Colin was left holding the ball and we were both flat out under the fish tank window of the Wilderspool centre. Poor Colin didn't know what to do. We both went off injured and Bobby had a nasty gash on the top of his head. I bet he has still got the scar. I returned to the field later. I must have a thicker skull.

I arranged for the Challenge Cup winning team to all get together again at Wilderspool 25 years later, in May 1999, to celebrate the silver anniversary of our success, before Warrington played Sheffield Eagles in a Super League game. We had our photograph taken, standing and sitting in exactly the same places as in May 1974 and both pictures are in this book. When it got to 1.30pm everybody was present, except Brian Brady who was having a new kitchen fitted and didn't know if he could make it. Murph got him on the phone and said: "Dave Wright has come 10,000 miles from Australia and you're saying you can't make it from Wigan. Get over here right away." Brian did as he was told. Murph made a fine speech afterwards. He said we may not have been the best players in the world, but we would die for each other out on the pitch. That was why we had won the cup and that was why we were all there at the reunion.

While I was still on the road to recovery after injuring my knee at Wembley, another Warrington sportsman was starting to make headlines. Mike Slater, the professional at Walton Hall Golf Club, played in all four rounds of the Open at Royal Lytham in July, the only club pro to do so. He shot rounds of 77, 74, 80 and 77 for a total of 308, which earned him a prize of £125 – about £2,000 in today's money. He finished his second round with a birdie 3 in front of the packed stands.

Mike needed that because he was in the dog house with his wife Sue. Mike was a huge Warrington fan and went to Wembley to see us win the Challenge Cup. Warrington had not been to Wembley for 20 years and Mike loved the big occasion. While he was at the match Sue gave birth to their daughter Sally and Mike, obviously, missed it. She was born about kick-off time and Sue was not too happy. Every time I see Sally now we laugh about it, because we are still friends. She says: "How's your knee?" And I say: "Shame your father didn't turn up for your birth."

I started back in light training in July. In August I played cricket for a Warrington RL XI against Greenall Whitley at Walton to raise funds for former Wire players Peter Cannon and Conrad Barton, whose careers had been cut short by injury. I top scored with a breezy 33. We won by one wicket and my picture was in the Warrington programme to prove it.

My comeback game was away to Rochdale Hornets in the Lancashire Cup and ended with me being sent off, as described earlier. But as I continued my recovery from injury – and suspension – I was replaced on the injury list by Derek Noonan who was the victim of a vicious high tackle against Huyton in the second round of the Player's No. 6 Trophy at Wilderspool. Derek was injured early in the match and carried off on a stretcher with a badly broken jaw and taken to hospital. He was out of the team for 10 weeks after that. Huyton full-back Robin Whitfield was sent off for the challenge and later became a referee.

We weren't playing as well as the previous season. Murph wasn't happy and matters came to a head on the way back from Whitehaven after the Player's No. 6 Trophy quarter-final. The game shouldn't have been played – the pitch was a morass, like a paddy field. We got changed in the cricket pavilion as usual, entered the ground at the corner and then the teams went two ways – one behind the posts and one round the 25-yard line – because there was a lake in between. The water was three inches deep.

Derek Whitehead follows up his own kick to score a try against Rochdale Hornets in the 1974 Player's No.6 Trophy Final at Central Park, outpacing Billy Sheffield. (Photo: Eddie Fuller).

Ossie Davies, the Warrington chairman, with a silver tray from the Holly Confectionery Company Limited – the prize for winning at Leigh on Boxing Day 1973. Standing at the back: Derek Whitehead and Ian Mather. Also pictured from left: Tommy Lomax (physio), Derek Noonan, John Bevan, who scored four tries that afternoon, Parry Gordon, Brian Pitchford (vice-chairman), Dave Cunliffe, Derek 'Nobby' Clarke (trainer), Joe Price, Mike, Tommy Grainey, groundsman Jack Hamblett and Dave Wright. Front: mascot Gary Ashcroft, Brian Brady. (Photo: courtesy Stan Lewandowski).

Mike with the Mayor and Mayoress of Warrington, Councillor and Mrs Gordon Myles, at Warrington Town Hall in March 1974.

A civic reception at Warrington Town Hall in March 1974 to mark winning the Captain Morgan and Player's No. 6 Trophies. Left to right, back: Charlie Middlehurst, Dave Sutton, Bobby Wanbon, John Lowe, Dave Wright, Frank Reynolds, Mike Philbin, Tommy Grainey, Dave Cunliffe; second row: Derek Whitehead, Billy Pickup, Dennis Curling, the Mayor & Mayoress of Warrington, Councillor & Mrs Gordon Myles, Barry Philbin, Ronnie Clark, Derek Finnigan; third row: Brian Brady, Dave Chisnall, Kevin Ashcroft, Mike, John Bevan; front: Parry Gordon, Derek 'Nobby' Clarke, Alex Murphy, Alan Whittle, Derek Noonan (Both photos: courtesy Gordon Myles).

Opening a sports shop on Bridge Street, Warrington in 1975 with Alex Murphy (second right) and the Manchester City strikers Joe Royle (first left) and Rodney Marsh (centre). Also pictured are friends Geoff Myatt and Mal Thorniley. The shop owner is giving Murph a playful punch. The shop was called Warrington Sports Centre and was at 113 Bridge Street. (Photo: Eddie Fuller).

Bobby Wanbon scores against York at Wilderspool in 1975 with Tommy Martyn in support. Derek Noonan and Mike Philbin applaud. (Photo: Eddie Fuller).

The pitch quickly became like a World War One battlefield and even John Bevan, with all his power, couldn't get going. We lost 5–0 and went out for a few drinks after the game. Murph took us back to John Tembey's pub – he had played with him at St Helens – but Chissie and I didn't fancy that because Murph was in a mood. We went somewhere else close by and that put him in a worse mood. We all got back on the bus and Murph was still really upset about us losing. There was no toilet on the bus and inevitably, after a while, we had to stop for people to have a pee. We all got off and Murph was ranting and raving and, after only a few minutes, the bus started pulling away. I ran and just about managed to get back on, but half-a-dozen players were left behind in the middle of nowhere on the side of a dual carriageway at Keswick and it was absolutely pouring down.

I said to Murph: "What's all this about?" I was nose-to-nose and eyeball-to-eyeball with him. We came close to fighting. I said: "You can't leave players behind." "Can't I?" he asked and told the driver to carry on. "Let them find their own way home. That'll teach them." Ossie Davies, the chairman, was asleep, and Brian Pitchford, the vice-chairman, didn't want to know; nor did Phil Worthington, the secretary. "Carry on driver," shouted Murphy. I said: "This is ridiculous." We carried on for what felt like 20 minutes before a police car pulled the bus over. Ossie, who was a magistrate and chairman of the bench, woke up to find players missing and police on the bus. The police kept the bus where it was and ferried the missing players to us. They had to do a couple of shuttle runs with the police car.

Murph got away with things you couldn't get away with now. I thought that he used to bully people. There was a fear element. He was like Sir Alex Ferguson with the hairdryer treatment, except with Murphy it was the pointed finger. Bob Eccles tells a story about Murph and Roy Lester in the changing room at half-time when Warrington were losing. Murph launched into his half-time team talk and pointed to Roy and said: "You Roy, you haven't put a tackle in all day and if you don't buck your ideas up you won't be playing next week." Roy said: "Sorry Murph, I'm not playing this week." He was just sat there in his overcoat. Whoever came into the dressing room first got it in the neck from Murph, literally so in Dennis Curling's case, but more of that later.

Despite everything we reached the final of the BBC2 Floodlit Trophy against Salford at the Willows. I was injured and so were a few others, but squad players such as Dave Sutton, Dave Cunliffe, Gilly Wright and Peter Jewitt came in and we got a 0–0 draw, the last goalless draw in Warrington's history. The replay was at Wilderspool in January when Keith Fielding scored for them after five minutes, running 55 yards at blistering pace. David Watkins kicked the goal and a penalty because referee Billy Thompson had penalised John Bevan for fouling Fielding after he had touched down. John was always very competitive with rival wingers. That put them 7–0 ahead and they went on to win 10–5.

I played in the replay. It was my first game for a month and I lost the ball a couple of times. I was just getting into my stride in the second half when Murph took me off and sent Brian Brady on instead. The following day I was put on the transfer list for £10,000 – about £100,000 in today's money. The supporters were outraged. Murph said at the time: "Contrary to public opinion, I am not 'anti-Nicholas'. He is a very good forward. If I did not think so he would not be in my first team panel, but we have not been getting consistency from him."

I said: "I do not particularly want to leave Warrington and if a club did come in for me I would not want to leave the area. I have always given my best, but I have also played when not fully fit and I think allowances should be made for that. I am a great admirer of Alex Murphy as a coach. He is ruthless, although that is the way I like it."

I was taken off the transfer list at the start of April, but was put back on it the following week after a misunderstanding. I was substituted after half an hour of the Sunday match against Castleford with a chest infection and pulled out of a Wales session at Bradford on the Tuesday and Warrington's match at Wakefield on the Wednesday. I phoned the club to tell them, but because I had not spoken to Murph directly he put me back on the list.

The return to Australia of Dave Wright had left a massive hole in our second row, but Murph sorted that out when he signed Tommy Martyn from Leigh in January. Warrington paid £7,000 plus my old mate Clive Jones. I loved playing with Tommy. When we played together we could win any game. I used to get in among them and disrupt them while Tommy used to pick up the pieces and be creative. We could control the game. Whenever Tommy and I played we had a chance of beating anybody – even the Aussies. I had great respect for him. He was a really good player. I enjoyed playing with him and used to listen to him. He pulled me out of a few situations when I had lost it. He used to calm me down. He would say in his strong Leigh accent "thy knows Mike..." and I would answer: "There is nothing wrong with my nose Tommy. It's a bit flat, but it's all right."

Tommy had a lovely family. His daughter used to help Ockher clean up the changing rooms after matches and when she had to pick up jock straps she blushed like hell. His son, young Tommy, would be out on the pitch, practising his goalkicking. He later played for Oldham and St Helens and when he won the Lance Todd Trophy with Saints in 1997 I was as proud as Tommy. I saw him in the Hilton hotel after the match and said: "Come on, we have got to celebrate this." We had a party in Gerrards Cross in a pub called the Pack Horse, which was quite apt. We all went back there and had a fantastic evening but, unfortunately, all the public transport had closed by the time we had finished, so Tommy had to get a taxi back to his hotel in Reading. It cost him about 50 quid and he has never forgiven me for it.

Signing Tommy helped us to reach Wembley for the second year in a row. We beat Halifax 32–6 in the first round, with young winger Paul Wharton scoring a hat-trick, and were then drawn to play Wigan at Central Park. Just like the year before, three players were sent off in front of a 20,000 plus crowd – two from Wigan and one from Warrington – but this time it wasn't me in the early bath, it was Bobby Wanbon. He was sent off with Denis Ashcroft for fighting and then Brian Hogan was sent off after an incident with Chissie. John Bevan scored a hat-trick and got another hat-trick in the semi-final against Leeds, so we were heading back to the Twin Towers to play Widnes. Semi-final week was busy for me. I had a minor operation to clear up sinus trouble on the Monday, played for the 'A' team at Oldham on the Tuesday to prove my fitness and then played in the semi-final on the Saturday.

Again, we stopped in the Kensington Palace Hotel for the final. On the Thursday night we all went to see the new film *Towering Inferno* at the cinema. By some strange coincidence, one of the stars of the film, Richard Chamberlain, who was playing the villain, was also staying in our hotel. His character threw somebody down a lift shaft or something and I remember booing him in the hotel. Chissie and Bobby Wanbon went for a pint after the film to help them sleep. They must have developed a thirst because of all the flames.

On the Friday afternoon when we went to Wembley to have a look around, Ken Dodd was waiting for us. He must have been appearing in the West End. His accompanist Stan Clarke lived in Runcorn, was a keen Warrington fan and had brought Doddy to a few games at Wilderspool. That night we went to see Max Bygraves at the Victoria Palace Theatre and were introduced to the audience. Millions of people watched the Challenge Cup final in those days. It was one of the jewels in the crown. Viewers didn't have the options they have now. Everybody watched it and the players became household names.

We were the favourites and we had the same North (No.1) dressing room, but we weren't as prepared as we had been the year before. Barry Philbin had a dodgy back. Tommy Martyn tweaked his hamstring getting out of the bus at Wembley and Bobby Wanbon's knee seized up. I was on the bench, but I wasn't fully fit – and I was still on the transfer list. Parry Gordon was recovering from tonsillitis. He was terribly unlucky. He played in two finals and wasn't fully fit for either one. It was his stage and he could easily have matched Gerry Helme, the Warrington scrum-half from the 1950s, who won the Lance Todd Trophy as man-of-the-match in 1950 and 1954 – but he wasn't right.

We were in a worst state than people realised. We were patched up and did well to keep them to 14–7: one try each. John Bevan scored for us after five minutes and Jim Mills scored for them just before half-time. Ray Dutton's four penalty goals were the difference. Murph, as ever, summed it up perfectly afterwards. "Things can go wrong," he said. "After all, the Titanic sank, didn't it?" At least Frank Reynolds, Tommy Conroy and Wilf Briggs got the chance to play at Wembley and Dave Chisnall got the chance to lead out a Warrington team under the Twin Towers.

Brian Pitchford, the Warrington vice-chairman, said later that we would have beaten Widnes if Murph had played and there definitely was a Murphy factor. We were undercooked and going into the final with injuries. We papered over the cracks. People played who shouldn't have played really – but you will always get that. Even with all his powers I don't think Murph could have made the difference, but it was a close match and so it might have been the type of match he might have swayed with his kicking game. There was always that possibility with Murph. It might have been one of those matches we could have nicked even though they were territorially dominant, especially in the second half.

Wembley 1974

Kevin Ashcroft stretches out to score the first Warrington try,
with Mike and Barry Philbin in close support. (Photo: Eddie Whitham).

Left: Bobby Wanbon gracing the famous Wembley turf. (Photo: Eddie Fuller).
Right: Alex Murphy made his fourth appearance at Wembley. (Photo: Eddie Fuller).

Left: Mike taking the ball forward. (Photo: Eddie Fuller).
Above: Kevin Ashcroft (left) and Alex Murphy celebrate Warrington's win. (Photo: Eddie Whitham).

Brian Brady, Derek Whitehead, Alan Whittle, Bobby Wanbon and Dave Wright do a lap of honour.
Mike was too injured to join them.

The 1974 Challenge Cup winning squad with wives and girlfriends in the banqueting suite at the Wilderspool Leisure Centre. Alex Murphy invited his mentor Jim Sullivan along. Both are seated in the front row. (Courtesy Warrington Wolves).

The Banquet

Before returning to Warrington, the club had a banquet in London. The menu was:

Minestrone Soup

Fried River Trout garnished with Shrimps, Capers and Soft Roes

Roasted Thick Cut of Beef Sirloin with Wine and Mushroom Sauce
Large Round Scooped Roast Potatoes
Browned Cauliflower with Parsley and Egg
Side Salad of Lettuce, Oranges, Grapes, Bananas and Cream

Round Éclair filled with Ice Cream and garnished with Cream

Coffee

There were two toasts:
The Queen – proposed by Mr B.J. Pitchford (Director, Warrington RLFC)
The 'Wires' – Proposed by Mr O. Davies CBE, JP (Chairman, Warrington RLFC)
Responder: Mr A. Murphy Manager/Coach Warrington RLFC

Wembley 1975

The 1975 Challenge Cup Final team in casual attire. From left: Alan Whittle, Parry Gordon, Wilf Briggs, Mike Philbin, Tommy Conroy, Kevin Ashcroft, Mike, Frank Reynolds, Dave Chisnall, Derek Whitehead, Barry Philbin, Tommy Martyn, John Bevan, Bobby Wanbon, Derek Noonan.

The 1975 Challenge Cup final team. Left to right, back: Derek Whitehead, Frank Reynolds, Tommy Conroy, John Bevan, Mike; middle: Kevin Ashcroft, Barry Philbin, Tommy Martyn, Bobby Wanbon, Derek Noonan; front: Mike Philbin, Parry Gordon, Dave Chisnall (capt.), Alan Whittle, Wilf Briggs. (Both photos: Eddie Fuller).

Walking out at Wembley in 1975: Mike following Wilf Briggs, Barry Philbin, Tommy Martyn and Tommy Conroy.

Mike being presented to Princess Alexandra by Warrington chairman Ossie Davies.

Top: John Bevan scored a try after five minutes in the 1975 final to give the Wire a dream start.
Middle right: Powerhouse Welsh winger John Bevan stopped in his tracks by Widnes winger Alan Prescott. (Courtesy Gary Slater)
Bottom: Mike was a substitute with, from left: physio Tommy Lomax, 'A' team coach Tommy Grainey, coach Alex Murphy looking at his watch and assistant coach Derek Clarke.

10. Warrington captain

The 1975–76 season was Joe Price's testimonial year and I helped him organise things. One of the first events was a 16-mile, fancy dress, sponsored walk starting at Wilderspool and going through Winwick, Newton-le-Willows and Earlestown. Dennis Curling was dressed as a fairy godmother, complete with a magic wand. Joe was popular with the fans and the whole year raised £3,000 – about £30,000 in today's money.

Dennis, of course, had played with me at Aberavon and we were great mates. I went to his wedding and everything, but he started having a few problems off the pitch and wasn't playing that well. He was distracted and in one particular game at Wilderspool we had taken about 20 minutes to get up the pitch. The forwards had grafted away and it was hard work getting field position. It was like a First World War battle for territory and then one of their players kicked the ball down field and Dennis just let it go into touch and we lost 70 or 80 yards in just a stroke. It was a schoolboy error. I ran back and remonstrated with him vehemently as a mate would. I said: "Get your act together." But his problems must have been building up inside him and he just lost it. He came running at me, swinging wildly and missing. Everybody saw it and Murph obviously saw it. Shortly after that it was half-time. We left the field and, as we got in the dressing room, Murph coat hangered him, hooked him with a high tackle, told him I was in the right and he was totally in the wrong. Murph was absolutely livid with him and could see my frustration. I had never seen that before, the coach trying to knock the head off one of his own players at half-time. But nothing surprised you with Murph.

Dennis Curling, the former Aberavon and Warrington winger, recalls: *"Mike is a very complex character to say the least. He is fanatical. Everything he did was to get bigger, stronger and faster and he was very aggressive. Obviously, he was a good player and because he was a scrum-half who played in the back row he had all the footballing ability. I played on the wing, could run and was fairly elusive. I was only 11 stones and I was fearless, but if you put a high ball in the air I couldn't bloody catch it and Mike used to hate that. He thought I'd let him down. At Warrington he always had a go at me if I didn't do something right and the ball went into touch. He used to really get on my nerves and one time I smacked him. I was frustrated. I didn't feel it was my fault. He started having a go at me and so I smacked him. To be fair to Mike he never tried to retaliate or hit me back; he just stood there in amazement. Mike didn't speak to me for about a year after that, but then they made him captain, so he had to talk to me and we became friends again."*

Sad to say, the great team of 1972, 1973 and 1974 started to break up. Kevin Ashcroft returned to Leigh as player-coach and took Wilf Briggs with him. Dave Chisnall joined Swinton, with Warrington receiving a transfer fee plus Brian Butler in return. Warrington were going to sign Bill Ashurst, the former Wigan and Great Britain forward, as a guest player from Penrith, but the deal fell through. I would have enjoyed playing with Bill.

Warrington pack 1975-76: Brian Butler, Tony Miller and Bobby Wanbon form the front row; Mike, Tommy Martyn and Peter Connell are the back row.

John Bevan scoring a try against Wakefield at Wilderspool in March 1976 with a young Ian Potter in the background. (Both photos: Eddie Fuller).

Top left: Ready for a tackle. Top right: Setting up a play, with Mike's hero, Parry Gordon, in the background. (Both photos: Eddie Fuller). Bottom: Joe Price and Derek Finnigan are in support as Mike takes on the St Helens forwards in April 1976. (Photo: Eddie Whitham)

Brian Brady and Tommy Conroy retired. Alan Whittle signed for Wigan. Derek Noonan joined his hometown team St Helens, with scrum-half Alan Gwilliam joining Warrington in exchange.

New players arrived, including a goalkicking utility back and former goalkeeper by the name of Steve Hesford who was signed from Fleetwood Rugby Union Club. Steve increased our attendances overnight because it seemed that every young woman in Warrington wanted to look at him on the pitch – and Steve was more than happy to be admired. In his testimonial brochure, John Bevan described Steve as the "Robert Redford of the team" and, again, Steve was more than happy to take the compliment. On top of that, he was a magnificent goalkicker.

Steve and Dai Watkins were the best goalkickers I played with, but Derek Whitehead was no slouch. They just had different styles. Recently, Wigan's Frano Botica was the best I saw. He never seemed to miss. Today I am a big fan of Kevin Sinfield. He is a fantastic kicker with a wonderful technique, like a golfer, holding his head still and standing over the ball.

Steve made his debut at Wakefield in October 1975. I missed the match through injury, but was told all about it. Steve kicked two penalty goals to put Warrington 4–0 ahead before we collapsed and lost 47–4. Murph was furious and lashed out in all directions. John Dickens, the sports editor of the *Warrington Guardian*, used to travel on the team coach in those days and found himself under fire until he could slide down his seat and avoid eye contact. Murph offered to resign at the following Tuesday's board meeting, but the players backed him and the offer was refused.

Murph also signed two teenage forwards from the Blackbrook amateur club in St Helens, Brian Case and Ian Potter. When they arrived for training I could not believe how fresh-faced they looked and wondered if they would be tough enough to make it. Both, of course, went on to play for Great Britain and appear in three Challenge Cup finals for Wigan. Murph got it right again.

All this change was not a recipe for success and we only finished 10th in the league. We were still expected to thrash the amateur side, Leigh Miners Welfare, at Wilderspool in the first round of the Challenge Cup, but it was nearly a big shock. Deep into the second half, we were losing 12–11 before Derek Whitehead crossed for the match-winning try and kicked the goal. It would have been one of the most embarrassing defeats of my career. John Whittaker played for them that day and later Warrington signed him. They also had the terrible twins, Paul and Bob Dowling. Paul was the first-team coach, Bob was the club secretary and they were great amateur players. It was a wake-up call. We took it too easy, obviously. It was almost the ultimate example of taking a team too lightly – simple as that. I also think we might have socialised a bit that week, on the Friday night – but not on the Saturday night. We never did that.

We lost 6–0 to Widnes at Wilderspool in the quarter-finals, three Ray Dutton penalties ended our dream of three successive Wembley finals, but Murph wasn't impressed with the Chemics. Far from it; after the match, he came out with one of his most famous one-liners: "If Widnes win the cup, I'll jump off Runcorn Bridge." Widnes were furious – and they reached the final, but an ageing St Helens team, nicknamed 'Dad's Army', beat them 20–5 to save Murph from the Mersey. Derek Noonan played in his third successive final and picked up a second winners' medal.

We played Dave Chisnall's Swinton, who had already been relegated, in the last game of the season on what turned out to be a memorable afternoon. Bobby Wanbon was thinking about retiring, but then scored a hat-trick of tries and changed his mind, which was great news for us, but less good news for his dodgy knee.

The first game of the 1976–77 season was a Lancashire Cup tie at Barrow and our new stand-off, Glenn Knight, scored four tries, but that is not what the match is remembered for. The groundsman must have put sea water on the pitch because the surface had gone and it was just like a dust bowl. Every time we got tackled we were covered in dust. We looked like the Homepride flour men from the 'graded grains make finer flour' advert. Frank Foster, the Barrow coach, had been unbelievably rough, tough and raw-boned in his playing days and had modelled the team in his image. Phil Hogan came out with a headband on and flared nostrils, wide-eyed, like a bull in a china shop. He had a go at me, had a go at Tommy Martyn and, stupidly, had a go at Joe Price. There was dust everywhere and Joe got up and said: "I have had enough of this."

The next time Hogan came through on a short ball, Joe put him in Never Never Land. It was an execution really. It was like a scene out of *Psycho*. He dropped in the line and scurried along and when Hogan came on the short ball and came on to Joe's shoulder, Joe bounced into him and delivered his guided missile, his elbow, and then bounced out and back into the line. Peter Geraghty was the referee and I thought was running around like a headless chicken. He knew that something heinous had happened, but he never saw it and the touch judges never saw it. Joe was an artist. I know it was bad, but that's what you had to live with. You adapted your game. You got your act together or you got out. I became slightly unhinged myself because you became good at it. You started off trying to combat foul play and it ended up becoming part of your arsenal. Hogan went up in the air, came down and the dust settled all over him. His jaw was absolutely mangled. They came to take him off and it was surreal, like when the horses drag off a bull after a bull fight and the bells are ringing. Two guys dragged him off and his legs were dragging behind.

We went on to win the game 40–7 after that. None of their players wanted to know any more. Their team had been totally deflated. Joe said "give me the ball, give me the ball" and he ran straight into their pack. They all wanted to kill him, but nobody laid a finger on him. The job was done. I was covering across and saw it all. I was the witness for the prosecution. It was amazing to see it in the cold light of day, nothing short of an execution. Phil Hogan was a top player and he went on to be a world record signing when Hull Kingston Rovers paid £35,000 for him in 1978.

A lot of people disagreed with the way Joe went about his work. Ken Kelly wouldn't speak to him when he signed for Warrington in December 1976 because Joe had broken his jaw in a Warrington versus St Helens match in 1970. Joe didn't care who they were.

Left: Taking on Castleford at Wilderspool with Derek Finnigan looking on. John Joyner is the Castleford player, Gerry Kershaw is the referee.
(Photo: courtesy *Warrington Guardian*).

Bottom left: Tommy Martyn and Mike formed a fine second-row partnership and he kept Mike out of trouble. Here he is about to set up a try for Tony Miller (not pictured) despite the attentions of Salford loose-forward Eric Prescott in a Lancashire Cup tie at Wilderspool in August 1976.

Bottom right: Leading the Warrington team in two minutes' silence for the great Jim Challinor before they played Leeds in December 1976. Mike was the man-of-the-match that day.
(Both photos: Eddie Fuller).

Tommy Martyn escapes the clutches of two would-be tacklers to score a try against
Rochdale Hornets at Wilderspool in January 1977. Ken Kelly is backing up.
Wally Jones, the former Warrington forward, is the nearest Rochdale man.

Heading for a gap at Hull Kingston Rovers in the Premiership first round in May 1977. Phil Lowe is the Hull KR player with Warrington's Steve Hesford in support. Warrington lost 18–13 but were reinstated in the competition when Hull KR were kicked out for playing Lowe, who was not eligible. (Both photos: Eddie Fuller).

Steve 'Knocker' Norton came unstuck with him on a couple of occasions, but he was always 'Joking Joe' and was good for team morale. It was a shame that he died so young, in 2006 aged 60, after an 18-month battle against cancer. He was a character to the day he died. Because of his lack of computer skills he booked three holidays instead of one by pressing the wrong button and when he asked the holiday firm if he could be refunded, they said 'no'. So he went and chained himself to the gate at the airport and started shouting: "You can't treat a dying man like this." He was true to himself right to the end as a person who stood up for himself and wasn't frightened of anything.

I used to kick goals for Aberavon. Alan Martin was the main kicker and I was the reserve and used to practise for hours with him after training. So when Steve Hesford was injured in September 1976 I stepped in. I kicked eight goals for Warrington altogether, including three in the Lancashire Cup semi-final against Workington Town at Wilderspool. I was named the man-of-the-match, but I must have been the most miserable ever recipient of the award – a barrel of beer – because the match finished in a 9–9 draw and that meant we had to go up to Workington the following week for the replay. Big Jim was playing for Workington at the time and, in the replay, I made the mistake of waking him up with a high tackle. It cut him across the face. He went berserk after that and flattened half of the Warrington team in the rest of the match. He smashed Barry Philbin, he might even have perforated his ear drum, and knocked Tommy Martyn into the stand. They were all moaning at me because I had woken him up. We lost 26–15.

The following week we had Wales training at Swinton and Jim still had the cut across his face. I was in the dressing room, getting changed with Dai Watkins, Colin Dixon and Tony Fisher. All of a sudden the dressing room went dark and Jim walked in. Everybody turned around, saw the cut and asked "When are they burying him" – meaning the player who had given him the cut. I was cringing and thinking: "This could all kick off here." Everybody was laughing and asking Jim who had done it, but he never said a word.

Ronnie Simpson from Castleford, who was our manager, went round taking measurements for suits and jerseys. He asked Jim for his measurements and Jim said "56 inch chest, 25 inch neck" and that sort of thing. Then Jim asked: "Have you got Mike Nicholas's measurements because you will need them for his coffin!" Jim looked at me and said: "You're dead. Next time we play against each other, you've had it."

We lost at Leigh in the BBC2 Floodlit Trophy, despite two goals from me, but after the match I briefly met one of my heroes, Cliff Morgan, who was the head of BBC Television Sport and outside broadcasts. He was one of my favourite Welshmen and I became friendly with him later through Ken Jones of *The Independent*. Cliff's programmes on Radio 4, such as *Sport on Four* and *My Heroes*, were mandatory listening. I met him at golf events and the boxing writers' dinners at the Savoy and facilitated people for him to interview in his programmes, such as Jonathan Davies. He was a great Welshman and the stories about him are legendary. One of my favourites is about when he made his debut for Wales in 1951 and travelled from his home village of Trebanog to Cardiff on the bus, standing up all the way. Needless to say, he had a blinder. Afterwards he went to collect his expenses from the secretary of the Welsh Rugby Union and asked for five shillings bus fare. The secretary went mad and said: "Morgan, you are a liar and a cheat – the bus fare is only four shillings and 10 pence." At least the people on the bus let him sit down on the way back. I was taking my son Morgan to Wales rugby league training at Taff's Well in August 2013 when I heard that Cliff had died. I just travelled down to Trebanog in the Rhondda and spent a few minutes there in silence, paying homage.

Despite our occasional differences, Murph appointed me as captain in October 1976. I took over from our hooker Tony Miller, who later announced that he was emigrating to Australia. My first game as skipper was at home to Barrow and we lost 16–15. It was our fourth defeat in a row and, once again, Murph offered to resign. I called a private players' meeting the following week, giving my full support to Murph and asking my team-mates to give their views. I would like to say that the meeting was a huge success, but we lost our next two games as well – at Wakefield and Hull KR – but then John Bevan returned from a broken foot and the tide turned. We won three home games in a row, against Featherstone, Salford and Leeds, and never looked back. I remember the Leeds game very clearly because I was the man-of-the-match, despite having a thumb nail ripped off – and you can imagine how painful that was.

I picked it up and put it back on and bound it up as tight as I could and carried on playing. After the match I had a few pints and went home and the thumb started to throb. I couldn't sleep because the pain was so bad. I got up to go to the toilet and took the bandage off and a blood clot must have been released. It went straight to my head and I fell down a flight of stairs. I realised then I had put the thumb nail on the wrong way round. I was in a hell of a mess and rang my mate Mal Thomas to rescue me. Needless to say, it didn't stop me from playing the following week, but it was a bit of a shock having a blood clot travelling around your body.

Dennis Curling joined in the fun that season too with four tries at Oldham as we climbed up the table to finish fifth. We lost away to Hull KR in the first round of the Premiership and so our season was over. Or so we thought. The following week Hull KR were kicked out of the competition for fielding an ineligible player in Phil Lowe and we were handed a two-legged semi-final against Featherstone. As described earlier, I was harshly sent off in the first leg at Post Office Road when we lost 17–13, but that was only a four-point deficit and we overturned that with an 11–1 victory at Wilderspool four days later.

After that sending off in the first leg I was certain that, with my record, I was going to be banned for the final against St Helens at Swinton. I already had a slight tear in my knee, but stupidly I ran a fun run or half marathon or something in the build-up to the final and my knee ballooned. Still, it didn't matter because the final was the last game of the season and I was going to be banned anyway. Amazingly, when the disciplinary committee met in Leeds they found me guilty, but only punished me with a £10 fine, leaving me free to play in the final, except for the fact that my knee was knackered again.

Featherstone's Jimmy Thompson had also been sent off in the first leg and we made personal appearances before the committee. Jimmy had just been called into the Great

105

Britain squad to tour Australia and New Zealand as a replacement for Eddie Cunningham. They didn't want to ban Jimmy and so we escaped with £10 fines. I had to pull out of the team in the dressing room before the final and Mike Peers took my place. I could only watch as Warrington built up a 5–4 lead by half-time with an Alan Gwilliam try and Steve Hesford goal. The turning point of the match was early in the second half when Alan and Harry Pinner were sent off for fighting. The extra space suited St Helens and they won 32–20.

Barry Philbin and I had both received offers to play for Brisbane Souths that summer. I had also been in touch with Brisbane Brothers, Dave Wright's club, about playing for them. But, in the end, neither of us was able to go because of injury.

As captain, I thought I had a voice for the players and so I let Murph know what I felt about a few things and he didn't like it. Nobody told Murph anything. I was driving down Bridge Street in Warrington one day in my beloved MGB where a bloke used to sell newspapers outside the Packet House pub. I was driving past and the billboard said: "Wires skipper on transfer list." I nearly drove into the Mersey. I stopped the car in the middle of the road, went over, grabbed the billboard and took it into the club and said: "What's this?" Murphy said: "You want to grow up." He put me on the list again, this time for £8,000, about £80,000 in today's money, and then reduced it to £6,000. Hull Kingston Rovers wanted me and Clive Sullivan approached me when we were on Welsh duty, but I didn't want to leave Warrington. York even put in a bid for me. Gary Cooper was their coach and Tommy Harris, the former Welsh hooker, was on the board, but I didn't want to go and Warrington eventually took me off the list again. Gordon Cottier of Whitehaven came in for me as well. I respectfully thanked him, but there was no way I could go to Whitehaven. I have only been a two-club man, Aberavon and Warrington.

Barry Philbin was appointed captain for the 1977–78 season and his first game as skipper was the Locker Cup match at Wigan. Sadly, the only thing that game is remembered for is that Dennis Curling suffered a broken neck – an injury that was to end his career at the age of just 27. He had played 132 games for Warrington, scoring 35 tries, and was rightly awarded a testimonial match.

I returned to training in September after my knee injury and played for an hour at Salford. My right knee swelled up like a balloon afterwards and I was taken to hospital, but I gradually worked my way back to fitness.

Former team-mate Mike Peers recalls: *"I remember an 'A' team game at Barrow when Mike was coming back from injury. They had this young lad they had just signed on called Stephen Kirkby and he had been in the papers. He was making his debut in this 'A' team game and the first time Mike took the ball up, Kirkby smacked him. I said to him: 'Look son, if you want a career in rugby don't do that again because he'll kill you.' He wouldn't listen and he hit him again. Third time he tried it we were attacking on their line and Mike passed the ball and Kirkby hit him again, looked at him and ran off. He was running away from play, down the field, with Mike right behind him and me behind Mike, trying to stop him. So the three of us were going totally against the run of play. This lad was running and running and then he slipped and Mike swung his boot to kick him in the face and missed him and I am so*

106

glad he did because he would just be coming out of jail now. It was a godsend that he missed him because he would have done a lot of damage because of the pace he was going. He had been running for 40 yards. The lad got up and said to me: 'You were right mate.' I said he should have listened 10 minutes earlier. Kirkby didn't play much after that. He was going to be a superstar but it didn't work out that way."

Murph was in the news again in September 1977 when he was stopped from spending a penny at Fylde Rugby Union Club. What made the whole thing even more ridiculous was that Murph had played rugby union for the RAF at Twickenham during his national service. Murph and Albert White, Warrington's chief scout, had gone to watch Fylde play Kilmarnock. They had paid to go in, had paid to buy a programme and gone into the clubhouse before the match and again at half-time. At the end of the match Murph tried to go into the clubhouse again to use the toilet and was stopped by a club official. Murph said at the time: "He told me he recognised me and that it was against the club rules to let me in. I just feel sorry there are still people around in rugby union who cannot accept that rugby league people are quite normal. I enjoy watching both codes, and have some friends in rugby union circles. These people who show such a childish and petty attitude to rugby league are not worth worrying about."

Murph again showed his Midas touch in the transfer market when he signed hooker John Dalgreen from Halifax and two veteran centres: Billy Benyon from St Helens and Frank Wilson from Workington Town. We always seemed to do well in the John Player Trophy and set off on another good run, beating Blackpool Borough, Salford and Featherstone Rovers to reach the semi-finals. The draw for the semi-finals could hardly have been worse: Wakefield Trinity at Belle Vue, a ground where Warrington had not won since 1963, 14 years earlier. We won 15–5 thanks, in part, to a referee who just happened to be watching the match from the sidelines.

Former referee Ronnie Campbell recalls: *"I took charge of the curtain raiser, Yorkshire Colts versus Lancashire Colts, prior to the Warrington versus Wakefield match at Wakefield and stayed to watch the match, standing by the dug-outs. Just before half-time Mike got belted off the ball by the Wakefield hooker Ray Handscombe and, to be honest, it was disgraceful. The lad hit him off the ball, with the elbow, and Mike dropped to the earth. I thought to myself: 'There is no way he is getting up.' He shook his head, looked at the player and I could see the fire in his eyes and I thought: 'Oh God.' At half-time I went to the referee's dressing room and said to the touch judge: 'You should have picked that up. That bloke should be getting a shower now.' Mick Naughton was the referee and I said to him: 'Mike Nicholas got belted and he is going to get the player back. Guaranteed.' Ten minutes into the second half, Mike clouted this fella. Mick called him over and just gave him a bit of a talking to. Normally he would have sent him off."*

Perhaps referees did know their fathers after all. Anyway, thanks to Ronnie, I had one of my best games of the season, setting up tries for Bob Eccles, Ken Kelly and Tommy Martyn. Bob was only 20 and regards that match as his breakthrough game. Our opponents in the final would be Widnes and, just to make things interesting, Big Jim had rejoined them after his spell at Workington Town and, of course, he still wanted to kill me for cutting his face in the Lancashire Cup semi-final replay the year before.

Thankfully, Jim was sent off in the build-up to the final for attacking Wigan's Bill Ashurst at Naughton Park. It was the 16th sending off of his career and he was banned for two matches, ruling him out of the final. He covers the sending off in his excellent biography *Big Jim* and it goes something like this. Vince Karalius, the Wigan coach, instructed Ashurst to wind Big Jim up to try to get him sent off. The plan worked perfectly and Big Jim was indeed sent off, but Bill was carried off on a stretcher unconscious and later said to his coach: "Next time can someone else get the job of winding Big Jim up."

We had our problems too. John Bevan pulled a hamstring at Workington three weeks before the final and it was touch-and-go whether he would make it. He played, of course, at a rain-soaked and muddy Knowsley Road, but he wasn't fit, although that did not stop him from scoring the match-winning try.

Two Steve Hesford penalty goals put us 4–0 ahead at half-time and, in the second half, he put in a towering cross-field kick. The ball swerved and Widnes winger Stuart Wright appeared to knock it into the path of Bevan, who was clearly struggling. John tapped the ball ahead, shrugged off an attempted bodycheck from Widnes full-back David Eckersley and touched down. Hesford kicked the goal and we won 9–4.

That was the mud and blood final. They were atrocious conditions and I was up against a novice prop from Wales in Glyn Shaw, who had only signed for Widnes from Neath three months before, and gave him his rites of passage. I gave him his welcome to rugby league, like I used to do with all the Welsh boys, showing them what they would have to put up with. A lot of people didn't quite see it that way. The final became a war of attrition, with dirty tricks thrown in to try to establish dominance. I picked a lump of mud up before a scrum and shoved it in his eyes and up his nose. He was led off because he couldn't see through the mud. There were physical asides going on all the time in those days. Scrums used to be like two octopi mating. It was like being on a waltzer as the scrums went up and down. The number 8 was the key man and Kevin Ashcroft had shown me all the dark arts. Without the four flankers, the rugby league scrum was not as stable as the rugby union one and it became a lottery, but a disciplined lottery. There was still a method of getting the ball. It looked poor to the eye, but we knew what was going on – complete with stray punches and head butts.

As far as Widnes were concerned, the turning point of the match came on the hour mark when Glyn went over, but referee Billy Thompson ruled that he had not grounded the ball properly. John Dalgreen said at the time: "I couldn't reach Shaw to tackle him, so I just slid under him. He put the ball down on my legs."

The Widnes players did not see it that way. Murph said: "We played to the conditions and adapted our game. This should certainly put us in the mood for another trip to Wembley in the Challenge Cup."

Parry Gordon holds aloft the John Player Trophy at Knowsley Road in January 1978. Mike is standing next to him covered in mud and blood. Ken Kelly's nose is just in the picture. Ken recalls: "I am whispering to him 'Don't frighten them' because he looked like something out of a Hammer Horror movie."

Warrington captain Parry Gordon (left), man-of-the-match Steve Hesford (centre) and coach Alex Murphy in the Midland Hotel, Manchester after the 1978 John Player Trophy win over Widnes. (Both photos: Eddie Fuller).

We picked up £300 per man for that – about £2,000 per man in today's money – and Eddie Fuller, the *Warrington Guardian's* chief photographer, took a brilliant picture of Parry Gordon and myself (and Ken Kelly's nose) covered in mud and blood, with Parry holding up the trophy. Derek Whitehead and Bob Eccles were the Warrington substitutes in the final, but Murph never used them. The 13 players who started the match were the 13 who finished it, despite the terrible conditions. You wouldn't get that now.

Ken Kelly recollects: *"We would not have won the John Player final without forwards like Mike Nicholas. It wasn't a backs' type of game. We had a set of forwards that relished the dirt. There was no grass on the Knowsley Road pitch. Nicko had a storming game and loved it. John Bevan scored a typical try, a kick up field and the ball stopped because there was that much slutch about. Twelve months later we played Widnes in the final again and it was dry and they hammered us because they were the footballing team, but in 1978 the ground suited us. It would be no good now with summer rugby, we'd get beat."*

After one of the finals, we were invited to a civic reception at the County Hall in Chester in March, but nobody knew us. Warrington and Widnes had both been put into Cheshire under local government reorganisation in 1974. People in Chester hardly supported soccer, let alone rugby league, and it was a bit embarrassing actually. We couldn't get out of there quick enough. They were doing their best to be cordial and polite and everything, but I doubt if any of them had actually watched the match. Chester and the north of England are not that compatible. We left as early as we could and went back to the Brown Cow pub – now called the Helsby Arms – and had a knees-up. Warrington had always been a Lancashire town and always will be.

We were drawn to play Widnes again at Wilderspool in the Challenge Cup quarter-finals. It turned out to be a really bad-tempered match with four sent off – including me. As I mentioned earlier, my unofficial job was to take their best ball player, Doug Laughton, out of the equation. I did just that. We were both sent off and Warrington won 6–0, thanks to three Steve Hesford penalties. That dismissal cost me a two-match ban which ruled me out of the semi-final against St Helens at Central Park and so I could only watch from the sidelines as we lost a thrilling match 12–8.

We were ahead 8–6 at half-time after tries from John Dalgreen and John Bevan and, in the second half, were convinced that referee Billy Thompson got it wrong when he decided that a try-scoring pass from Barry Philbin to Ken Kelly was forward. George Nicholls, the St Helens second row, was the man-of-the-match and stopped Bevan in his tracks with a try-saving, last-ditch tackle. It wasn't our day and I wonder if I could have made a difference.

Still, we had the makings of another good team, with young forwards like Brian Case, John Dalgreen, Bob Eccles and Ian Potter and quality backs like John Bevan, Ken Kelly and Parry Gordon. Some people were surprised in May when Murph resigned to become Salford coach. I wasn't surprised because he had been to see me in hospital, where I was having a knee operation, and asked me to go with him.

When Murph came to see me, I thought: "What does he want?" We didn't get on that well, we were always at loggerheads, but he was warming to me a bit, especially when I played with broken fingers and stuff like that. He said: "I'm going to Salford. Do you want to come with me?" I was tempted, but I said: "No. I'll stay at Warrington. There's only one club for me." Murph thought he could do at Salford what he had done at Leigh and Warrington. They were ambitious and trying to rebuild the team which had won the league in 1973–74 and 1975–76. He should have been the man for the job.

My knee operation was another legacy of the 1974 Challenge Cup Final. Bits had broken off and were floating around. I used to strap my knee every game in such a way that kept the pieces up in my thigh, up in my quads. It was all right unless I got a tackle that loosened the bandages because the pieces would come into my knee and it would swell up. This started to happen more and more and they would do an aspiration after every match, putting a needle – like a knitting needle – into the knee, drawing off the fluid and then putting a cortisone injection in. That was happening after every game and so in May I had another operation to clean it all up.

I was in hospital at the same time as Wigan's Keiron O'Loughlin and up-and-coming Widnes prop John Wood. John had an operation and was in the bed opposite me. The nurses were kidding him, saying that I had had a massive operation and didn't need painkillers. He said: "If Mike doesn't need them, I don't." We were both in agony and trying to stay the longest without asking for painkillers. I heard him in the middle of the night whimper: "Nurse, nurse, I need painkillers." He took some; then I shouted: "Nurse, nurse."

Away from the game, I was looking for a business to get into. A friend of mine had a taxi firm and I started off by putting a couple of cars on his rank for extra income. Then I branched out on my own. Wire Wheels was born and it became a brand in Warrington. Everybody knew Wire Wheels and it became a tough 10 years of my life, working 24/7. It took its toll; I had a garage in Stockton Heath as well. I gave up alcohol and flung myself into the old work ethic – 14 hours a day, seven days a week. I made a few bob, but went into social isolation to a degree. I became a workaholic. I was driven – as usual. I had a good business going, had a white Rolls Royce for weddings and did mini-buses. I ran Mercedes. We had a workshop; we used to do everything. It was a one-stop business, but was very demanding.

The white Rolls Royce had the number plate WED 72 and I drove it back to Port Talbot once to take my mum to the social club. The locals thought Richard Burton had come back from the dead. You don't see too many Rolls Royces on council house estate drives.

Ken Kelly recollects: *"I'll always remember an away match at Featherstone Rovers, at Post Office Road, which was always a hard match. They were a top-class team. Featherstone was just a village; blink and you were through it. There was only one pub in the place. We were over halfway there and somebody on the bus shouted: 'We are missing somebody.' Someone else asked: 'Who's missing?' Another said: 'Mike Nick.' And Nicko was a big part of the pack. Next thing, there was a grunt from the back seat and a hand went up: 'I'm here. I had a long night on the taxis.' He had been having a sleep. So we got there* with a full complement and Nicko lasted five minutes before he was sent off. He probably thought he was dreaming."

Mike Peers recalls: "*I did a bit of work for him on the taxis. Warrington was being redeveloped and you couldn't move. It was gridlocked all the time. Mike had some big contracts and used to be on the radio to you every minute: 'Where are you now wire seven? Where are you now wire seven?' He gave me a job to go up to Daresbury Laboratories and pick some Chinese people up. They had to be at Bank Quay Station at 4.30pm. All the way there it was: 'Where are you now wire seven?' He was losing his temper and so I turned the radio off. It was almost impossible, but I managed to get through and picked them up; dashed to the station and made sure they got on the train. I drove all the way back, parked in the taxi yard at Winwick Road and turned the radio back on at about half past five. Mike shouted 'Where are you now wire seven?' and I said I had just picked them up and I thought they would miss the train. He went berserk and then I said: 'Look through the window.'*"

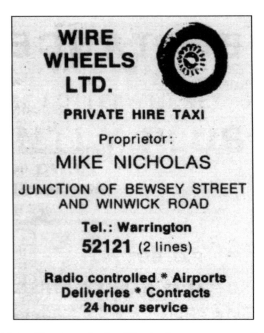

Mike advertised his taxi business in the Warrington programme from 1978 to 1983.
He kept asking them to abbreviate proprietor to prop.

11. Beating Australia

Billy Benyon was named player-coach and was introduced to the supporters at a "Meet Billy Benyon" night at the Wilderspool Leisure Centre in July 1978. I was the MC and we showed highlights of the John Player Trophy final against Widnes. Wilderspool Leisure Centre was a top venue at the time.

On one occasion, Terry Venables, Tony Book of Manchester City and Alan Durban, the former Derby County player who was from Port Talbot like me and was a great all-round sportsman, were all at St Helens College doing a coaching course and Phil Worthington, the Warrington secretary, organised something for them at the Leisure Centre which was absolutely flying. You could have a brilliant night out there. The comedians Bernard Manning, Tom O'Connor, Bob Monkhouse, Colin Crompton and George Roper all performed there as did the Drifters, Showaddywaddy, Gerry and the Pacemakers, Georgie Fame, the Tremeloes and Acker Bilk.

I joined Terry, Tony and Alan for the night and after one of the acts Terry got up on stage and sang *I left my heart in San Francisco* – the Tony Bennett song. He was a really good crooner and brought the house down. We all ended up going to a party in Orford.

Alec Lindsay was quite a good friend of the Warrington players at the time when he was at Liverpool. Kevin Keegan used to come over with him for a drink and we went to the Hamlet nightclub. One time Kevin brought a signed Liverpool ball with him for them to raffle and they still charged him to go in. Kevin didn't mind, but what a small-town mentality. Who wouldn't want Kevin Keegan in their club? I was banned from there sine die for knocking the bouncer out with my crutch, the incident Dougie Laughton described in Chapter 2, but then my mate Wilf Roylance bought it, renamed it Tracy's and I managed it for him.

One night Workington played at Wilderspool in the Lancashire Cup and they all came to the club afterwards. They must have thought I owned it, but I wouldn't let them in and they weren't too happy. They were shouting "Let us in" and "Come on Nicholas." I was behind the door. The owner didn't want them in in case they caused any trouble and I was happy with that. They were a rough bunch those Cumbrians.

I remember throwing people out of the club at two in the morning before playing in a John Player final in St Helens that afternoon. I wasn't drinking, so I went home, got to bed at three and had a sleep until about 11, got up and played in the final. I never punched any customers, but I dragged a few out by their heads. I never fired a shot in anger. I didn't have to really. My reputation saw to that.

One incident could have turned nasty. We had a receptionist called Margaret who was really efficient and handled drunks brilliantly, turning them away, but this particular night she was really abused and broke down in tears. I had never seen her like that before. I said "What's up?" but I could hear the vile abuse she was getting. Then I could hear the lads kicking the cars outside and so I went to the door and they ran off. There were two or three of them and they stopped up the alley and shouted: "Come up here, we will sort you out." I said "All right" and went after them, but they ran off again and I chased them through Market Gate. They turned and stood their ground and I went "Bang, bang, bang" as if I was playing and scattered them. I jogged back to the club and went on the door. An hour later I heard they were in hospital and so I went straight down to the police station with a solicitor and told them about the incident. The police said they had already been to the hospital and investigated and the lads had said they deserved what they got.

Billy Benyon's reign as player-coach got off to an unlucky start when our hooker John Dalgreen broke his leg very badly against Blackpool at Wilderspool in September. The leg was turned the wrong way and I feared his career might be over. Thankfully, it wasn't quite that bad, but he was still out of the first team for a year. John was from a place called Hanging Heaton, between Dewsbury and Batley, where they used to hang highwaymen. I was over there on business, getting an illuminated sign fitted to one of my cabs, and I thought I would call in to see how he was doing. I got to his place on the hillside and it was a lovely cottage. His wife came to the door and said John wasn't in because he had gone to pick up his daughter from school. I had a cup of tea while I waited for him and saw all his awards and trophies on the mantelpiece from his time at Halifax. His wife said: "When John broke his leg, when we got home, his player-of-the-year trophy from Halifax had fallen off the mantelpiece and was in the middle of the floor with a broken leg – the same leg he had broken that afternoon in exactly the same spot." I thought she was having me on at first, but she was deadly serious. That is spooky. How do you explain that?

I had had a knee operation during the summer and then I broke a thumb playing away to Hull Kingston Rovers. I broke it on Geoff Clarkson's head and he had a hard head. It was a bitter blow because Warrington were playing the Kangaroos at Wilderspool on Wednesday, 11 October and I was now almost certain to miss it. I trained with the team the night before the match and Ronnie Clark maintains that I punched him during the training session, which is probably true. If I felt young players weren't pulling their weight I would give them a bit of a slap to wake them up. To add to Warrington's problems, the RFL said that John Bevan and Ken Kelly couldn't play because they were needed by Wales and Lancashire and Parry Gordon had not recovered from an ankle injury.

I went to hospital on the day of the match and had the plaster taken off my broken thumb. I went straight from the hospital to Wilderspool and popped into the dressing room, looking forward to watching the game. I could see Billy Benyon and his assistant Tony Barrow in a huddle at the end and obviously they were struggling. So he looked at me and he must have had a brain wave of some kind.

Anyway he came over and said: "Do you fancy a game?" I said: "Yes, OK, it's only against the best team in the world." Sometimes you can go into a game really relaxed and I just got ready for a normal game, bound my previously broken thumb up like in a boxing glove to protect it and went out to play. I got buried in the first tackle. Three Australians hit me – one, two, three – it was like being hit by three Exocet missiles. I went to town after that. I had nothing to lose really. They were a very physical team and had some great players.

Left: The match programme from Warrington's famous victory (Courtesy Warrington Wolves RLFC).
Above: Warrington captain / coach Billy Benyon handing over a club pennant to Australia skipper Bob Fulton before the kick-off. Joe Jackson is the referee. (Photo: Eddie Whitham).

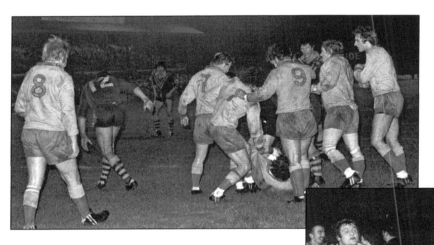

Above: Taking on Australia at Wilderspool in October 1978 are Roy Lester (8), Alan Gwilliam (7), Derek Finnigan (1), Tommy Cunningham (9), Mike and Steve Hesford. (Photo: Eddie Whitham).

Right: Running off the pitch with Australia's Steve Rogers after Warrington's 15–12 win over the Kangaroos. (Photo: Eddie Fuller).

They scored two tries through scrum-half Tommy Raudonikis and second-row forward Geoff Gerard, but Steve Hesford kicked five penalty goals to make the score 12–10 early in the second half. The Kangaroos were rattled, the noise from the crowd was deafening and Alan McMahon, the Australian full-back, was sent off for biting Billy Benyon.

With 10 minutes to go, Ronnie Clark, who was playing stand-off, made a break deep into the Australian half. Ronnie was having his best game for the club. Perhaps I should have punched him before every game. Scrum-half Alan Gwilliam then chipped ahead and made a desperate lunge to score the match-winning try. Hesford kicked the conversion and we had won 15–12. I always thought that when I played with Tommy Martyn we could beat anybody – including the Australians – and we had done just that. It was the first time Warrington had beaten the Kangaroos since 1948 – 30 years before – and it was a bitter blow to the Australians who had been talking about winning every game on the tour.

Bobby Wanbon remembers: "I was in the crowd for Mike's famous match against Australia in 1978. He had a great game. Australia had some really tough characters playing for them and Mike matched them stride for stride all the way. In fact, he knocked them back a little bit. It was a great win and Mike had one of his best games for Warrington. I just wished I was out there with him because I had just retired."

Mike Peers recalls: "He actually took my spot against Australia. We trained on the Tuesday night and Billy announced the team and I was in the second row with Tommy Martyn. My mother had had a heart attack and I had gone to the hospital to see her on the Wednesday afternoon and she said: 'It doesn't matter, I have got the match on tonight on hospital radio. I will be able to listen to that.' We had to be at the ground at 5pm because of the crowd. I got to the ground and Billy Benyon walked in with Tony Barrow and Mike Nicholas with no plaster on. Billy pulled me to one side and said: 'I am putting him in for his size. You're not playing.' So I had gone from being in the team on the Tuesday night to standing with the fans on the terraces under the clock.

Obviously, the rest is history, how the game went and how well Mike played and how well everybody played. Tommy Martyn was outstanding as well. It was a fantastic night, but I was slightly disappointed obviously because it would have been nice to play. I got paid for it, got a medal for it and was invited to the reunion, but it wasn't the same as being a part of that. Mike came in and made the difference, so I couldn't complain really. I would have been too light to play against the Aussies. They were a massive side. The lads stood up to them that night and when the going got tough Nicko was at the forefront. Mike playing probably won the game, because even the Aussies were a bit frightened of him. It was a big plus for the team for him to play, but it wasn't for Mike Peers. But Mike Peers wasn't important that night, it was about beating the Australians. That was on the Wednesday and I played on the Sunday and the two Sundays before and the six or seven Sundays after, but not in that one. It was definitely the right decision. It was a killer at the time, but I got over it. I felt more sorry for my mother because she was in the hospital. I had been to see her and then I wasn't on the radio. I couldn't get a message to her that I wasn't playing."

Alan Gwilliam remembers: *"It was a very physical match and Mike was in his element. Our forwards all played very well. They got stuck into the Aussies and gave them a good hiding – which they didn't like. Steve Hesford kept us in the game with his kicks. It was one of those games that seemed to fly by. You were involved all the time, running, tackling, you were out of breath, you were fighting, you were falling over. I think I did touch the ball for the try. The Aussies think I didn't, but we are not worried about that, are we? We had a little girl the following day. My wife had about 10 double Bacardi and Cokes to celebrate the win – which is frowned upon now – and the baby flew out! Anne-Marie is 35 now with a teenage daughter, Casey, and lives in Warrington."*

As you probably all know by now, I was sent off 15 times in my career, but it could easily have been 17. Billy Thompson sent me off twice, but quickly changed his mind on each occasion and reversed the decision. The first time was against Leigh at Wilderspool in December 1978 and involved the Cumbrian forward Eddie Bowman, who had joined them from Workington. I was always clashing with Eddie. Like a lot of Cumbrians, he always had a lot to say and I charged in to hit him hard, but he covered up and I ran straight on to his elbow. His elbow hit me on the temple and I knew it was pretty serious. The skin opened up straight away and blood started to flow. I had still flattened him and turned to the referee and Billy was saying: "Get off." When I turned some blood sprayed on to Billy and he said: "Get off...and get it seen to." So he reversed his decision and I staggered off. I remember going into the side room where Jackie Hamblett, the groundsman, kept his stuff. You could hardly call it a medical room. I sat there with one eye completely glazed over for about an hour, waiting for the eyesight to come back. You can still see the cut. The second time Billy sent me off and changed his mind was at Bradford and I outlined that earlier.

Just like the previous season, we reached the final of the John Player Trophy and, also just like the previous season, played Widnes at Knowsley Road. This time, however, I stupidly played in the final with a fractured jaw. One of my old sparring partners, Keith Bridges of Bradford, had broken the jaw and a tooth nine days before at Odsal. I had the tooth taken out the next day and was diagnosed with a fractured left mandible, but I kept it quiet. I thought nobody knew I had a busted jaw but, in the very first tackle against Widnes, Mick Adams hit it and I was seeing stars. I hit him; penalty to Widnes; two points. I was fed up then. I shouldn't have been on the field. I was just creating mayhem and having a go at everybody. I put Big Jim Mills down on his bum and Jim went berserk. He missed me a couple of times, as Fred Lindop said earlier, but he hit me a few times too. I was on the deck, on my back and he pinned me down. He went bananas. Fred Lindop sent him off and I stayed on, but it was a dry ground and we got beat 16–4 even with the extra man. Big Jim and Doug Laughton weren't very happy in the club house after the match and we were having a go at each other. I shouldn't have played. The final should have been played in January, like the previous year, and that would have suited us. But the winter of 1978–79 was a bad one and lots of matches were postponed, including our semi-final against Hull Kingston Rovers, and so the final was put back to the end of April.

From top left, clockwise: Ian Potter, Brian Case, Bob Eccles and John Dalgreen. (Photos: Eddie Fuller)

Mike showing his skills as a former scrum-half to send Mike Peers through a gap against Swinton in the Lancashire Cup in August 1978. Mike Peers was the man-of-the-match that afternoon.
(Courtesy Mike Peers)

Widnes scrum-half Reg Bowden attempts a hand-off at Naughton Park in August 1978 under the watchful gaze of Mike Peers. Mike is lining up a shoulder charge, a tackle which is now banned.
(Courtesy Mike Peers)

Tangling with Widnes loose-forward Mick Adams (Courtesy *Warrington Guardian*).

Jogging back into line against Workington in October 1978 (Photo: Eddie Whitham).

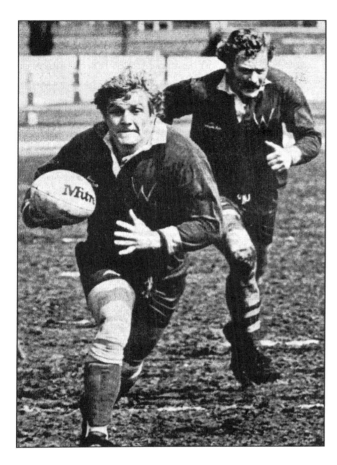

Left: Mike taking the ball up against Castleford at Wilderspool in the first round of the Premiership in May 1979. Fellow prop Steve Hogan is in support.
(Photo: Eddie Fuller).

Bottom left: The match programme from Mike's last first team game with Warrington.

Bottom right: The kicking king – Steve Hesford.

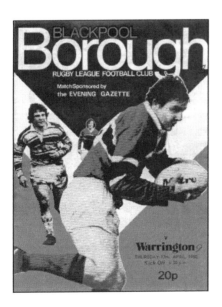

121

If the final had been played in January, Big Jim would have been banned. He was sent off by Billy Thompson two minutes from the end of our league match at Wilderspool for elbowing John Whittaker in the jaw. The Warrington fans were incensed. John was stretchered off and although the jaw was not broken, it was very sore and he couldn't eat properly for days. Big Jim was banned for four matches, but had completed his suspension by the time the John Player Final came around.

I scored my 14th and final try for Warrington at Widnes in December 1979 and it was different to all the rest. Every other time when I scored a try we won. This time we lost 30–13, despite two tries from John Bevan. The following week I played a part in one of the fastest tries ever scored at Wilderspool – after just 35 seconds. We were playing Hunslet in the league and the kick-off was delayed by 15 minutes because they arrived late. When the match finally started, we wasted no time. I collected the ball from the kick-off, Ken Kelly made a break from halfway and Mike Kelly touched down on the right. Warrington had just started video recording every match and if any supporter has still got that tape I would like to watch that try again. It will only take a minute.

I was also helping out the 'A' team and I remember one match at Wilderspool in March 1980, a Lancashire Combination Shield semi-final second leg against Salford 'A'. John Dalgreen played in that one too and we won 11–9, which wasn't quite enough because Salford had won the first leg 26–21. It was a good game but it reached boiling point in the second half when Warrington winger Peter Taylor and Salford forward David Major were sent off for fighting. Trouble was following me around.

Paul Cullen, the former Warrington captain and coach, recalls: "*I saw Nicko play as a supporter and had the privilege of playing with him at 'A' team level as a 17-year-old after signing for the Wire when Nicko was just coming to the back end of his career. So I had the pleasure of watching him as a fan, then playing with him and, probably more importantly, training with him. He was ahead of his time.*

As a supporter, I watched Mike Nicholas rampage through the Australians and almost take them on single-handed – and I know no man ever does in any single game, but he appeared to in that match. He absolutely terrified them. I remember standing on the terraces with my dad as a boy awestruck with how he literally just rampaged through.

Nicko had an aura about him. I knew him as a star of the Warrington side, I was aware of him as a businessman with Wire Wheels – he had a presence about him. When I signed for Warrington as a 17-year-old I peeped into the first-team dressing room and John Bevan, Mike Nicholas and Billy Benyon welcomed me in and then sent me to the other end of the stand where the 'A' team changed. I couldn't believe my luck.

We then ran down Wilderspool Causeway to train at Loushers Lane – the entire first-team squad and the entire reserve team. There must have been 50 men galloping around Loushers Lane field like a herd of wildebeest as a warm-up before we broke into two separate sides – first team and reserves – to play a game of tick and pass which seemed to last for hours. It started off nice and gentle and then got more and more brutal with every minute that passed and Nicko just rampaged through a game of tick-and-pass.

What you saw was what you got. You just left him alone. He was as serious in training as he was when he played. There was no pretence. I remember a few weeks later a very lively, a very quick and a very cheeky scrum-half from Wigan – I will leave his name out so as not to embarrass him – chip-kicked Nicko, left him for dead in the mud at Loushers Lane and ran away and scored in the corner and made fun and laughed all the way to putting the ball down. Nicko wiped him out on the way back. I remember watching it and thinking: 'My God, what have I come into?'

You learned from things like that. Nicko never took a backward step in anything he did. That dressing room, that environment, was brutal and very cynical. You could be bullied – if you allowed yourself to be – and I learned lessons from it: be the hardest trainer. You could see this skulking figure running around the pitch on his own, hood up, wrapped up against the winter, and it was Nicko. No one was speaking to him, him speaking to no one and absolutely flogging himself before the training session, during the training session and after the training session.

Everyone treated him with respect because that is what he demanded – literally. If anyone said anything to him they got a mouthful; if anyone crossed him they got belted. People left him alone and as I grew in my career I came across people like that. When I first saw Nicko I did not really know what message he was sending me but I got it later loud and clear – if you allowed people to take liberties, they would – and no one ever did.

That's why he had that presence in a training session, in a dressing room. No one ever made fun, no one ever took the mickey, no one ever took liberties and if they did it was confrontation time and he revelled in it. I am sure Nicko never got that completely right and I never but the message was very clear: don't back off, don't be put on, don't be bullied and if there's anything in the air get at it and sort it out – and he did.

It was a bizarre relationship. I was a massive fan of Mike Nicholas and all of a sudden I was training with him and playing with him and we were living around the corner from each other in Stockton Heath. I saw him on a daily basis and he was never short of a smile and positive advice and encouragement.

I remember in those first days in 1980 when I first signed, weightlifting was something that was unknown in the game. In the old wooden stand at Wilderspool there was a door that led to a corridor that led to another door with a secret little place inside and in there was a gymnasium, crafted out of iron and old bits of wood. Nicko had built an old wooden bench and there were some old iron bars, borrowed or grabbed from Walter O'Malley. It was like a dungeon more than anything else and Nicko was smashing the place to pieces – doing cleans, dead lifts, split squats. It was unheard of at the time and he dragged in Bob Eccles, who had a reputation for being all glamour and glitz and not that much sweat, but that was never the case. He was just a bit smarter, faster and better than everybody else and he was in those training sessions.

Carl Webb was dragged in – along with Phil Ford, me and John Fieldhouse. I remember we were almost being laughed at by the other players. We were told we would be too slow, weights would ruin us. Nicko had been doing it for years. He was miles ahead of the game.

It wasn't bodybuilding; it was power weight-training to the point where your fingers were bleeding because the bars were that rough. He would have you doing 10 sets of 10 on clean and press. I didn't even know what clean and press was then. But he had a captive audience and we absolutely revelled in it. We were a small club within the club.

The conditioning then was to either run to Loushers Lane and flog yourself around in the mud or run to Victoria Park. It is hard to credit these days that the entire Warrington team would be running either down Knutsford Road to Victoria Park or running down Wilderspool Causeway to Loushers Lane, train for an hour or two, then run back, all jump into a couple of big baths and all go for a drink together. It staggers you when you think how it used to be. That wasn't unusual and it was a great time actually.

Nicko took his game very seriously. He had a 1,000 yard stare. You couldn't break his focus, you couldn't break his concentration. He wouldn't suffer fools. If you were in his company you had earned the right to be in his company and I took great comfort from that. The message that he sent out subliminally was picked up by me very early on: don't be a victim, get on the front foot, retaliate first – all those one-liners were Nicko-esque.

It was about finding out who was their biggest player, who was their best player and we are here to earn money. In those days we were getting two or three times the average working man's wage for winning a game of rugby league and next to nothing if you got beat – and that, in itself, set the tone. You were fighting for mortgages, for two or three weeks' wages against a man doing a full week's graft on a building site. There is something beautiful in that.

Nicko had a massive work ethic. He would work before training, go straight back to work after training and was proud that he had come from a tough environment. He was doing it the hard way and there is some great satisfaction in that."

In case you are wondering, the very lively, very quick and very cheeky scrum-half from Wigan that Paul decided not to name had the initials JF and his name was Jimmy Fairhurst. He showed me a lot more respect after I wiped him out.

The 1979–80 season finished on a sour note for me with a sending off at Blackpool for fighting with John Corcoran. I was banned for six matches for that and that was a punishment that came back to haunt me. It meant that at the start of the following season I wasn't really available to play until October. Warrington had a settled team and winning team by then, playing good rugby under Billy Benyon, and an unprecedented injury-free run. So I couldn't get back into the team. Tommy Martyn took on the mantle as pack leader and they had Brian Case, Ian Potter and Eddie Hunter. I played in the 'A' team and was happy to play in the 'A' team. I realised I was coming to the end of the line. Warrington won the Lancashire Cup in October and the John Player Trophy in January.

It wasn't until February and March that they started picking injuries up. By that time I thought that Billy had alienated the rest of the squad and put all his eggs in one basket, his chosen few. People wouldn't play for him. I realised this and went to see him and volunteered to play, but he still didn't pick me. He obviously felt I was surplus to requirements. Warrington lost at home to Barrow, away to Castleford and away to Leigh because people were out on their feet and playing with injuries. Bradford Northern won the league by two points, I thought because Billy was too stubborn. Billy was named *Coach-of-the-Year* but I think he threw the league away because of the way he treated the rest of the squad. I was particularly unhappy with him because I thought I deserved more respect than that. I was due a testimonial season in 1982, but I didn't get a testimonial, I got a free transfer and walked out. I thought you got a free transfer the year after your benefit season, not the year before. I was treated shabbily. It broke my heart, leaving under those circumstances.

Obviously, John Bevan, who was signed six months after me, had more shelf life and so he got the benefit. Derek Finnigan found himself in the same position as me in 1984. He was due a benefit and got a free transfer to Mansfield instead. I say hello to Billy now, but I wouldn't speak to him for years.

Ken Kelly recalls: *"When Mike finished playing we always got into Tracy's night club for free and then he would get you home in his Wire Wheels taxis. I have only got good things to say about him."*

In August 1981, I signed for Cardiff City Blue Dragons. Dai Watkins, who was the managing director, promised to compensate me for missing out on a benefit, but he had overspent on Steve Fenwick, Paul Ringer and Tommy David and so there was no money left in the pot. We trained at RAF St Athan and a lot of the lads were new to rugby league. We had to get a team together and had a trial game among ourselves. I thought I had better let these guys know how tough the game was. I introduced a bit of realism into training, flattened Paul Ringer and Chris Seldon had to have five or six stitches above his eye as the result of a clash with me. Our first game was against Salford at Ninian Park and we had almost 10,000 there, creating a great atmosphere, but we lost a thrilling match 26–21. Our first win came two weeks later when we beat Hunslet 32–19 at Ninian Park and I was sent off 15 minutes from time; I only played six games for the Blue Dragons.

Billy Benyon was sacked as Warrington coach in March 1982. Kevin Ashcroft got the job and wanted me to re-sign. He said that Brian Pitchford, the new chairman, would reinstate the testimonial. I was 35 and was tempted, but in the end I said: "It doesn't matter Kev. I am out of it now." I think he signed Tony Cooke instead. I could have gone back for another 18 months because I was playing rugby union for Warrington Vikings and London Welsh Vets, but I didn't want all that negativity. My health was beginning to suffer. I was getting old. I realised I couldn't keep up this super machismo. I was starting to get black patches, mini blackouts, after big hits on the head. I was getting concussed, but kept running through a black patch and coming out the other side like a tunnel and the black patches were coming closer together and more frequent. It was like a boxer getting punch drunk.

Kevin Ashcroft and I used to call it 'The Magic Roundabout', the ceiling spinning round when you went to bed. It wasn't through drink. It was through concussion. I had it quite a few times. Kevin and I used to laugh about it and he would say: "Have you been on 'The

Magic Roundabout' lately?" I had it quite a few times. It was a bit like vertigo. When you looked up you nearly lost your balance and, one time, I was 300 feet up at the steelworks.

Frank Reynolds and I kept fit by playing tick-and-pass at Walton and had one last hurrah by winning the B&H Chester Sevens tournament with Aberavon ARLFC in August 1984. I was 38 and Frank was 39. In the group stages we beat Irlam Town, the favourites, Clowne from Sheffield and Fulham. We then hit top form in the semi-finals to thrash Stockport 44–8. Winger Paul Thomas scored four tries, while Frank and myself scored one each as did the Sheehy brothers, Danny and Kerry, Bobby Wanbon's cousins.

The following week's *Port Talbot Guardian* takes up the story: "In the final Aberavon once again met Clowne, who had qualified from the same group in second place. Almost from the kick-off Mike Nicholas scored a try from his own 22 metre line. Shortly after Paul Thomas was put clear by centre Francis Reynolds to score another 75-yard try. Strong running by Aberavon props Darren Godbear and Steve Skwarecki combined with slick handling from Francis Reynolds and Kerry Sheehy led quickly to a third try scored by Mike Nicholas." Further tries were scored by Paul Thomas and Darren Godbear and Danny Sheehy kicked four conversions and we won 28–10.

Frank Reynolds recalls: "*It was a pleasure watching Mike play because he was a human dynamo. His dedication to the game was second to none. Following Saturday games at Aberavon, most of the team would rest on the Sunday morning, but Mike would be at the Afan Lido fields, running laps of the pitch. During the final of the Chester Sevens, one of the Clowne players broke away and was going to score in the corner until Mike came out of nowhere and poleaxed him into touch. The crowd erupted into boos and hisses, nearly causing a riot. That was Mike for you: as competitive as ever at the age of 38.*"

I also went to Germany, Spain, Canada and America on tour with London Welsh Vets. We went to Canada and America for three weeks. A guy named Carter Croft dropped out and so Clive Jones came with me instead and he was known as Carter Croft throughout the tour. I took my golf clubs with me and had all these wonderful courses lined up to play, but Clive gave me a hospital pass in Seattle and I ended up in Seattle Infirmary with damaged ribs. Clive was the worst passer of a ball you have ever seen, every pass from Clive came with a red cross on it, and two former line-backers cleaned me out. Back in the hotel, I stood up in the corridor, trying to make a golf swing but it was just too painful. I had taken my clubs 6,000 miles and was desperate to play, but couldn't. Thanks Clive! I was aged 43 and that was my last game of rugby.

12. Playing for Wales

My father Geoff took me to my first international match, Wales versus France at the National Stadium, in March 1956 when I was nine. It was my first visit to Cardiff, the big city; I remember going up to Quay Street prior to the match and having fish, chips and peas. We stood on the West Terrace in the days when the crowds used to sway forward and people were passed over the top. I remember being at the front and it got pretty scary. It was 0–0 at half-time, but Wales won 5–3 with a try from Charles Derek 'CD' Williams, converted by Garfield Owen, to secure the Five Nations title. Soon after this Garfield switched codes and starred with Halifax and then Keighley.

Four years later, we went to see Wales versus England at Twickenham because two Aberavon players, Cliff Ashton and John Collins, were in the Wales team. I remember it clearly because we all went up to London – my uncle, my father, my cousin Gary and me – and stayed with my father's sister in Kingston. It took us ages on the train, about five hours, and Gary and I had to share a single bed. Richard Sharp made his debut for England, scored a try and they beat us 14–6. It was a fantastic occasion. I remember coming out and leaving the ground at the end and the crowd control was shocking. I remember being carried by the crowd, with my feet not touching the ground.

From then on, like most young boys in the valleys, I wanted to play for Wales and I got very close. John Simonson and I even got pulled into a couple of training sessions with coach Clive Rowlands and the Welsh team at the Afan Lido. But I was so competitive that I even had a go at some of the Wales players during those sessions, and they didn't like it. Still, my one big regret on signing for Warrington was that I would never win a Wales cap. So I was delighted when the Wales rugby league team was relaunched with a match against France at the St Helen's ground in Swansea in February 1975.

It was the first game back in Wales since the 1950s. It wasn't the greatest venue because the crowd were away from the pitch, which was shared with the Glamorgan cricket team, but it was very special for me because I used to go there and watch Glamorgan. In fact, the first Glamorgan match I saw was against the Australian touring team at St Helen's in August 1956. My father took me there for my 10th birthday. I had also played there for Aberavon many times, such as the semi-final of the Welsh Cup against Llanelli in 1972.

William Harries 'Bill' Clement, the secretary of the Welsh Rugby Union, did not want the rugby league match to be played there because it was the home of the Swansea rugby union team, but was powerless to stop it going ahead because the ground was owned by Swansea Council and they gave permission. That was typical of how rugby league was seen in those days. Today, that would be unacceptable and it should have been then.

The crowd was massive, there were more than 20,000 there, and because people arrived en masse near to kick-off time they had to open the gates and let people in for free to stop them getting crushed. It was emotional, but if you look at photographs of the way we walked on to the pitch – we didn't run on like we normally would – you can see from our body language that we weren't really sure what kind of welcome we would receive. We needn't have worried; we received a tremendous welcome. It was a tough game and we took a while to stamp our authority on the match, but we won 21–8 with two tries from John Bevan and one each from Roy Mathias and Big Jim Mills. Kel Coslett kicked four goals and Dai Watkins added a drop-goal.

England also beat France, 11–9 in Perpignan, and so the match between England and Wales at Salford in February would decide who won the Triangular Tournament and receive the Jean Galia Trophy. I started on the substitutes' bench and came on for the second half – just before Big Jim was sent off. John Bevan also suffered a suspected broken leg after a clash with Derek Noonan, but played on until near the end of the match. Thankfully, the suspected broken leg just turned out to be severe bruising. Despite that, it was still a close game, but we lost 12–8 with Derek Noonan and John Atkinson scoring tries for England and Dai Watkins scoring for us. The most important thing, however, was that the Triangular Tournament had been a success and Wales were back on the international scene.

Murph was the England coach and he picked four Warrington players for the World Championship games in Australia and New Zealand: Dave Chisnall, Parry Gordon, Tommy Martyn and Derek Noonan. The England boys looked like they had just come out of the RAF because they all had light blue suits. Murph was in the RAF during his national service and it looked like he had picked the suits. Bobby Wanbon and I were picked for the trip by Wales, with John Bevan taking a rare summer off because his wife Rhiannon was pregnant. How we missed him. The England squad flew out at the end of May and we followed three days later – but we well and truly caught them up in Brisbane on 10 June.

We were sponsored by KLM and were due to fly from Amsterdam Schipol to Frankfurt to Beirut to Bangkok to Singapore to Sydney to Brisbane. But our flight was delayed for about 12 hours in Amsterdam because of fighting in Beirut. The bonus was that we could watch the European Cup final between Leeds United and Bayern Munich in Paris in a bar. Peter Lorimer hit the bar, there was a lot of trouble and we got so caught up in the match that we nearly missed the plane. They had called the flight and we had to run to catch it. When we finally got to Beirut, there was a ceasefire and soldiers shepherded us off the plane and into the transit lounge. There was a civil war going on and there were palls of smoke on the horizon. We couldn't get out of there quick enough. The whole flight took 35 hours. Bobby Wanbon and I were room-mates and when we finally got to our hotel room at 8pm we decided we would have an hour's sleep before we went out. We couldn't wait to have a drink after two days in transit – and woke up 13 hours later, just in time for training. On the way back we went via Bahrain because they had started fighting in Beirut again.

I was in Brisbane on 1 June to see Dave Wright make his debut for Australia against New Zealand. Australia won 36–8, but Dave had to go off with a hamstring injury. He told me he felt a twinge before the match, but wasn't going to miss out on playing for the Kangaroos by admitting it. Dave watched the England versus Wales game on 10 June and I still remember how shocked he was. He thought it was going to be all matey, but it turned out like a State of Origin game in terms of ferocity and became known as the Battle of Brisbane.

Mike taking to the field for Wales against France at Swansea in February 1975, with (from the front) Roy Mathias, Peter Banner, John Bevan, Jim Mills and Bill Francis.

Wales 1977: Left to right, back: Johnny Malpass (physio), Maurice Richards, Peter Rowe, John Mantle, Mick Murphy, Jim Mills, Colin Dixon, Tony Fisher, Mike; front: Paul Woods, Ray Wilkins, Bill Francis, Ron Simpson (manager), David Watkins, Eddie Cunningham, Roy Mathias. (Photo: Eddie Fuller).

In the build-up to the match, Murph said something along the lines that none of the Wales players would get into the England team and that fired us up. It was a savage game. I would have loved to have played in it. Mick Morgan, the England hooker, was knocked out three times, but kept coming back. Bobby Wanbon had a blinder. The Wales pack was tremendous and we won 12–7 with tries from Clive Sullivan and David Treasure and three goals from Dai Watkins. Ultimately, that defeat cost England – and Murph – the World Cup. It was a good Wales team, with really good players, but it was an ageing team, and four days later we had to play Australia in Sydney. It was asking too much and we lost 30–13, although I think with a few more days of rest it would have been much closer. I watched them line up at the Sydney Cricket Ground and I saw the Australian winger Mark Harris. His nose was flat against his face and I thought: "This is going to be tough if the winger looks like that."

I only played in two club games on the tour. I pulled my thigh muscles training on the hard ground on the Gold Coast and never really got going. I played at Wellington on 18 June and Canterbury on 24 June. We won both games and I scored tries in both games. Wales won five of the six club games on tour, but also lost to New Zealand 13–8. For that match I worked with the television commentator who was struggling to identify the players. However, and I may have mentioned this already, we beat England in Brisbane to cost them – and Murph – the World Cup.

Bobby Wanbon remembers: *"Mike and I were room-mates for the Wales World Cup tour in 1975. The press were talking as though we didn't get on with the England boys, but we had a few pints with them. We trained every morning and had a few pints at night. It was totally relaxed as long as you didn't go overboard. I remember we had an 11pm curfew one night. I got back at 11pm after going to the pictures and I was first back, they were all still out."*

Frank Wilson of St Helens was on the tour and he was a great guy, a lovely guy. He never swore, he said "basket" instead of using expletives. You could say he was a basket case and there were two incidents on that tour involving Frank that I will never forget. The first came when we were on the terrace of the Tower Mill hotel in Brisbane, which was our headquarters, for a long and boring team meeting. We couldn't wait to get out and Frank got up and walked straight through the window and cut his nose and everything. The window had obviously been designed to be a door, but they had put a window in instead and left off the skirting board. Frank thought it was an open door.

Frank was also very careful about revealing his age. He was the Archie Moore of centres, nobody really knew his age. I knew he had come to prominence when he played for East Wales against the All Blacks at Cardiff Arms Park in 1967 and scored a try in a 3–3 draw. It was the only match on the tour that the All Blacks failed to win. Coming back from Australia we landed at Schiphol Airport in Amsterdam with KLM and to clear customs quickly we did a group collection of passports. Frank was reluctant to give his passport to the manager, Ron Simpson, because Ron would then know how old he was. Frank disappeared and came back with it and he had altered his date of birth. This was picked up by customs – the ink was still wet – and he got arrested. So we were delayed for a few hours until it was all sorted out. They took Frank away and wanted to know why he had altered his passport, but we eventually got home.

My next appearance for Wales was again against England, at Headingley in January 1977. I was doubtful to play. I wasn't feeling too good and I had been up all night, but Dai Watkins, now the player-coach, talked me into playing. It was a terrible game, but I must have done all right because Murph picked me as his man-of-the-match. We won 6–2, with a try from Eddie Cunningham, a goal from Paul Woods and a drop-goal from Peter Rowe. Ray Wilkins, who had played with me at Aberavon, made his international debut as a substitute.

The following month we played France in Toulouse and I have a very good reason to remember that match: my Toulouse finger. I broke my little finger in the first tackle. I should have gone off really, but I never went off. I played the whole game with it broken. It kept dislocating out of the side and I kept pushing it back in. You should see the state of it now. Big Jim reduced the French to cardboard cut-outs, but we still lost 13–2 after having a couple of tries disallowed. Another former Aberavon player, my mate Dennis Curling, made his international debut as a substitute in this one. We avenged that defeat the following year when we beat France 29–7 at Naughton Park with three Widnes players lifting the crowd. Glyn Shaw did well on his international debut, Big Jim scored a try and Paul Woods kicked seven goals. My next Wales appearance should also have been against France, at Narbonne as hooker in February 1979, but – and I know this is difficult to believe – I was suspended.

I will never forget my final appearance for Wales: as a substitute against England at Widnes in March 1979. Our hooker Tommy Cunningham, who was my Warrington team-mate as well, was kicked in the face and had to go off injured. I replaced him in the front row. Big Jim was furious at Tommy's injury and thought Harry Beverley had done it. He said: "Come on, let's go to town on them." So me, Big Jim and the other Wales prop, Mel James of St Helens, weighed in and went to work on their pack. The first thing I did was to kick Graham Liptrot in the testicles. Harry Beverley copped for a lot of rough stuff and it turns out it wasn't him who had smashed Tommy. To be fair to Harry, he stuck at it despite a nasty cut under his eye. It was a brutal game and we lost 15–7. Tommy Martyn was playing for England and it did feel strange playing against him.

Ken Kelly, former team-mate and England international, recalls: *"We were training with Warrington at Wilderspool the week before the England versus Wales game and Nicko shouted me over and said: 'Ken, we are down here now training, you are my team-mate, no problems, but next week at Widnes, England against Wales, if you come anywhere near me I am going to flatten you.' I said: 'Mike, why the hell would I come anywhere near you? I am playing stand-off and so I will keep as far away from you as I possibly can.' Gary Stephens of Castleford was the England scrum-half, but he got hurt early on and I ended up there. Wales had a tremendous pack of forwards, Nicko was one of them and Tommy Cunningham was hooking. At the next scrum the pack went down; Tommy was flat out and was taken off unconscious and at the scrum after that Harry Beverley copped for one. A fist or boot came up from somewhere and he had an egg on the side of his head as big as Humpty Dumpty. He was off. Nicko didn't need to tell me to keep away from him. I didn't want to go anywhere near him. He was very passionate about playing for his country and so was I, but you don't go chasing forwards like Nicko."*

My good friend Mal Thomas is a nostalgic Welshman. He was snatched from the cradle really. He was a Welsh schoolboy cap, but had only played a couple of games for Bridgend when Warrington signed him. He signed in 1959 and is still homesick. He tells a good story that when he first arrived in Warrington he went the wrong way out of Bank Quay station. He turned left instead of right and walked straight into 5,000 young women who were leaving the Crosfields soap factory. They were saying "What are you doing here lovely?" and "Are you lost love?" He was swept off his feet and that's where he stayed. I would sometimes find him slumped in his car listening to David Alexander songs, with tears rolling down his cheeks. David was a fantastic Welsh singer but, unfortunately for him, he was around at the same time as Tom Jones and so didn't get the recognition he deserved. One of his songs was called *Working Man* – a song about a miner – and it used to reduce Mal to tears because all his family were miners and he spent 12 months underground himself. He said it was like working in hell.

In October 1976, Mal took me to see Max Boyce, a real Welsh troubadour, at the Liverpool Empire and we met him backstage afterwards. The Liverpool footballers Emlyn Hughes and John Toshack were there. We were playing Castleford at Wilderspool on the Sunday and I invited him along. Lo and behold, he turned up. Peter Robinson, the comedian, who was the stadium announcer, recognised him straight away, claimed him and got him in the directors' box. They made a big fuss of him. It was an exciting match; we had a drink together afterwards and I remember him saying: "It's like a football crowd, the noise, the cacophony. It's not like a rugby union game." Max was appearing at the Free Trade Hall in Manchester next and invited me as his guest. Mal and I went again and Max dedicated a song to me called *I'm going home to Swansea town*. He said: "I'd like to dedicate this song to a friend of mine in the audience: Mike Nicholas." I was from Swansea Bay, albeit the industrial end, and I have been friends with him ever since.

I saw Max perform again at Porthcawl Rugby Football Club in November 1988. Jonathan Davies, the Wales and Llanelli fly-half, was there and signed my programme. He was pumping me for information about rugby league and signed for Widnes the following year. He was the Wales captain at the 1995 Centenary Rugby League World Cup – and what an excellent captain he was.

Left: Mike with a koala bear at the Lone Pine Koala Sanctuary in Brisbane during Wales's World Cup tour in 1975.

Below:
The Wales Rugby League legends lunch at the Halliwell Jones Stadium in October 2013. Mike with Billy Boston and Alex Murphy (Photo: Eddie Whitham).

Mike autographing a football, proudly wearing his Wales Rugby League tie.
(Courtesy *Warrington Guardian*).

13. Welsh Manager and President

The Welsh team was resurrected in 1991 after we had an influx of superstars: Jonathan Davies, John Devereux, Paul Moriarty, Gerald Cordle, Adrian Hadley, Dai Young, Richard Webster, Scott Quinnell, Scott Gibbs, Rowland Phillips, Kevin Ellis, David Bishop and Allan Bateman. They were disillusioned with Welsh rugby union which was in disarray during this period. Once Jonathan came the floodgates opened. Jim Mills was the manager and Clive Griffiths was the coach. The first game was against Papua New Guinea at the Vetch Field, Swansea that October and we won 68–0, with Jonathan scoring 24 points. Even after that, Jim was told Wales were not going to be included in the 1995 Centenary World Cup and resigned in protest. I was looking to get back into the game and Clive, who was assistant coach at Warrington, approached me to see if I was interested in taking over from Jim. I jumped at the chance. I missed the game, the bitterness about leaving Warrington under a cloud had disappeared; I revelled in it and relished it. We were reinstated into the World Cup and it was the start of a really successful period with the Welsh team.

My first match as manager was against New Zealand at the Vetch in October 1993 and it coincided with the Frank Bruno versus Lennox Lewis fight at Cardiff Arms Park. The fight was on the Friday night and the match was on the Sunday afternoon. The boys wanted to go to the fight, but Clive issued strict orders, saying the fight was out of bounds. Clive and I switched the fight on on television and the pre-match interviews live from the Arms Park were with Jonathan Davies and Kevin Ellis with the actress Catherine Zeta-Jones. Clive said: "I'm resigning." I said: "Don't be stupid." The problem we had with Wales was we didn't have any depth and so couldn't be disciplinarians. We had to take a pastoral approach and give the players a bit of licence. We lost to New Zealand 24–19, despite two tries from Gerald Cordle.

We played a full-strength Australian side at Ninian Park in October 1994. Jonathan Davies and Allan Bateman were both injured and so Iestyn Harris and Scott Gibbs both came in for their debuts. Iestyn was only 18, but was probably our best player which was unbelievable. John Devereux went off after only eight minutes with a compound fracture of the jaw after colliding with Mal Meninga. It was like watching two diesel trains collide, but John had been out injured for a few months and his timing was off. His chin practically came away from his jaw and he ran off the pitch holding his chin up to his head. Not surprisingly, after that we got battered 46–4. Kevin Ellis had a fight with Paul Sironen and they were both sent to the sin bin. Kevin looked like a panda later because he had two black eyes. I remember going into the dressing room with Jim Mills at half-time. Stand-in captain Dai Young had left the field with a cut above an eye that needed 12 stitches. He went back on in the second half which was a tremendous show of courage on his part.

Before the World Cup we went to America on a development tour. We went to Philadelphia for two weeks in June 1995 and played two games against the United States, winning 92–4 and 66–10. We were based at Valley Forge, Pennsylvania, which was General

135

George Washington's winter camp in the war of independence. We also visited Atlantic City. It was a nice trip. A guy called John Morgan was trying to promote the game in America, but he was based up in Lake Placid. He was also into skiing and was involved in the film *Cool Runnings*, about the Jamaican bobsleigh team. He had fallen in love with rugby league and was trying to get the game off the floor and that was part of the deal and so Maurice Lindsay, who was chief executive of the Rugby Football League, sent us over. I have always said that rugby league is the closest Americans will get to their own game, American Football. What happens to the players who don't get into the franchises? They would be ideal rugby league players because their techniques and hits are very similar. The Australians have learned a lot from American Football and that fed through to us eventually.

The former Great Britain captain Mike Gregory was qualified for Wales, through a grandparent, although he never played for us. After he suffered a cruciate injury in November 1990, I was instrumental in getting him into a rehabilitation centre at Penoyre in the Brecon Beacons. It was a specialist centre, way ahead of its time and Mike went down there for three or four weeks. I went to meet him at the end of it and went to see the director. He said: "We have had all sorts of international sportsmen coming through here but he is the fittest guy that has ever come through these doors." It was a great tribute. By 1995, Mike was emerging as a talented coach and Clive Griffiths got him on board as his assistant for the World Cup and he was excellent for us. It was devastating when Mike died in 2007, aged just 43. He was a great player and a great guy. It is fantastic that Warrington have remembered him by inducting him into the Hall of Fame and by naming the approach road to the Halliwell Jones Stadium 'Mike Gregory Way' in his honour.

During the World Cup, we had a titanic game against Western Samoa at the Vetch. It was a tremendous match, one of the highlights of the tournament. There was a full house of more than 15,000 and it was such a physical and brutal game. Va'aiga Tuigamala, Vila Matautia and Willie Poching all played for Samoa. Matautia looked like a Japanese suicide pilot with his head gear flapping. He was a monster. Everybody thought they would knock us out, but Scott Quinnell and John Devereux put their bodies on the line and we won 22–10. Scott had a massive game. It was great for rugby league in Wales. S4C, the Welsh Channel Four, had their record viewing figures, about a quarter of a million. It was the first time that the Welsh *Coronation Street*, *Pobol y Cwm*, meaning the Valley People, had been knocked off the top of the charts. The golfer Phillip Price came along, it was one of his first games. A lot of Glamorgan cricketers came as well and said they had never seen anything like it in terms of impacts. Everyone was impressed.

The following week Clive Griffiths and myself had some media stuff to do in Manchester for a couple of days and while we were away the boys partied a bit too long in the build-up to the semi-final against England at Old Trafford. A bit of a drinking culture had developed and that affected us. The semi-final was the first time we had travelling support, about 10,000 followed us from Wales out of a crowd of 30,000. They were rebuilding the stadium at the time. Leading the team out was a massively proud moment for me, but Bobbie

Goulding "bombed" us, and set up two tries for Martin Offiah; both were a bit dodgy. If there had been a video referee neither one would have been given, but they were and we lost 25–10. No one was more upset than Jonathan Davies because it was his last game of rugby league before returning to union. He had so wanted to get to the final at Wembley.

After the success of the World Cup I thought there was an opportunity for a South Wales team in Super League, so I went down there and set up shop. I got a little office and a couple of sponsors and set about putting a team together to play in Division Two. I had about two months to get it on the road before the 1996 season started. The first game was against Hull Kingston Rovers. We played at Aberavon and got a crowd of just under 2,000. Hull KR were formidable and beat us 70–8, but our second game was away to Prescot Panthers and we won 24–22. Our second home game was against Bramley at the Morfa Stadium in Swansea – which is now the Liberty Stadium – and again we won, this time 22–18. It was all hands on deck from a lot of people, friends and volunteers, even Phillip Price the golfer was on one of the turnstiles in his cashmere Crombie selling tickets. It was a really promising start. Clive Griffiths was the coach and we had worked together with Wales. We were trying to take advantage of the success of the national team and build from the bottom up. We also played half-a-dozen games at Cardiff Arms Park, which was as good as any Super League ground at the time, courtesy of my connection with Peter Thomas, the chairman of the Cardiff Blues.

We built through the season and found that transport was the biggest problem, travelling up North every other week, and it didn't help when teams started complaining that they had to come down once to play us. The guy from Carlisle wasn't too happy. We finished the season a creditable sixth out of 12, but were struggling financially and had to go to the Rugby Football League. Maurice Lindsay, the chief executive, said that if anybody wanted to back us financially he would match it with Super League money. I was at home one day when I got a phone call out of the blue from someone I didn't know. He introduced himself as Paul Thompson of Sanderson Electronics. At the time Sanderson Electronics were the shirt sponsors for Southampton and Sheffield Wednesday. He said he might be able to invest in our team. He said he was from Barnsley and worked in Rotherham and so I asked him what was wrong with investing in Sheffield Eagles because they were on his doorstep. He said we would be the only Super League team in Wales. He asked: "When can you come up to visit me?" I said: "Tomorrow." So myself and Jeff Taylor, who was carrying out the duties of the chief executive, drove up to see him in Rotherham. The address was palatial. We were there all day, hammering out a draft heads of agreement, giving me 30 per cent of the club. It was surreal. He had his television on all the time and all of a sudden the Wigan versus Bradford game came on. There were 20,000-plus at Odsal and that helped our cause as well.

I set off back home feeling ebullient and feeling that I had cracked it. The tricky part then was bringing Paul Thompson to the table with the RFL. Jeff Taylor and I had to go to a meeting of the Super League clubs at Wigan and lay out our proposal that we had an investor who was going to put in up to £1.2million, but we got shafted. They ripped us apart and Paul Thompson put his money into Sheffield Eagles instead. I was very bitter about it. It was wrong. Soon afterwards I received a letter from Maurice Lindsay offering us £250,000 and a place in Division One – which was all right, but it wasn't what we were after. It wouldn't have worked. We needed the profile of Super League. I felt I had wasted 12 months of my life. I couldn't carry on any more and South Wales folded after one year.

The 1995 semi-final had been our best chance to get to the final and win the World Cup, but we had another chance in the 2000 tournament when we played Australia in the semi-final at Huddersfield. Again, nobody gave us a chance, but we were ahead 20–8 midway through the first half. Anthony Farrell had a really good game for us in the second row. Lee Briers was magnificent. I will never forget one incident in the match. Iestyn Harris went on the blindside and he had Anthony Sullivan outside him. If he had got Sully away there we would have been 18 points clear, but Wendell Sailor went for the interception and deliberately knocked it down. In rugby union that would have been a penalty to us, but in rugby league it was just a knock-on. We would have been under the posts. As it was we didn't get the ball back for 20 minutes and they went on to win 46–22. They got their act together. I went into the Australian dressing room afterwards with my young son and they were battered. They were all iced up and everything. We gave them a really good game.

After the 2000 World Cup I stepped down as Wales manager and Kel Coslett took over, but it clashed with his duties at St Helens where he was the club's game-day manager and so I returned as manager for a short spell.

When I was Wales manager Trevor Foster used to come to all of the games with his son Simon, pay for himself and his accommodation and literally stay up all night with us. He was a wonderful man, another example of a great Welshman who was totally committed to the Welsh cause and the game in the north. He was from Pill in Newport, but had become a legend at Bradford. I will never forget the 2003 Challenge Cup final at the Millennium Stadium when he led the Bradford Bulls team out against Leeds Rhinos. It was amazing to see this great man come in and the emotion he showed.

Chris O'Callaghan, who was coach of the Aberavon Fighting Irish rugby league team, took over from me as manager in 2004 and I became president of the Wales Rugby League. Chris and I helped found the Celtic Crusaders club in Bridgend in 2005, with support from Niel Wood at the Rugby Football League. The Celtic Warriors rugby union franchise had disbanded in 2004 and it was an ideal opportunity to fill that vacuum, so we decided to give it a go with businessman Leighton Samuel. Sadly, there was a downturn in the economy and the club could not be sustained in Bridgend and moved up to Wrexham.

Phil Davies, founder of the South Wales Scorpions, says: "*As a result of meeting Mike years and years ago, he talked me into starting up a rugby league team in South Wales when the Crusaders moved to North Wales. I ran it for four years and we had a bit of success. The Crusaders had done quite a bit of work with academies and kids playing the game; it would have been a shame to lose it all. It is happening down here, but it is going to take an awful long time. We are competing against rugby union and that is always difficult;*

but there are a lot of schools now playing rugby league. The club has now been handed over to Wales Rugby League to run. Mike is the elder statesman of rugby league in Wales and if there are any questions to be asked he is the guy to go to.

I went up to see him play for Warrington. I played rugby union for Pontrhydyfen at the time and we used to go up on tour and ring Mike to organise the games. On several occasions Mike joined in and played rugby union for us while he was still playing rugby league. On one occasion he had arranged a game against Speke in Liverpool and when we got there the pitch was like a cow field with a razor barbed wire fence around it. They were the craziest bunch of people I have ever met in my life. We were there to enjoy ourselves on tour and ended up in a fighting match. We had the biggest fight ever and Mike came on to play for us because we were short of players, but that was the last time we asked him to organise a tour up there."

After the 2000 World Cup, Niel Wood and I realised that we couldn't keep trawling through players' ancestry to build our team. We couldn't cherry pick big stars anymore, we would have to produce our own players or go out of existence. We spent many hours setting up a league in South Wales, the Welsh Conference, in 2003, and had brilliant support from the Bridgend Blue Bulls ARLFC and Kevin Ellis, the former Wales and Warrington player.

After all that hard work Wales didn't qualify for the 2008 Rugby League World Cup which was a disaster. We played Scotland, home and away, for the right to go Australia and were the favourites, but lost on points difference over the two matches. Scotland beat us 21–14 in Bridgend in 2006 after Iestyn Harris failed a fitness test before the match. Danny Brough was brilliant for Scotland. Despite being sin-binned for 10 minutes for dissent, he scored a try and kicked a drop-goal.

The return leg was in Glasgow the following year and we led 14–4 at half-time, which would have been enough to book our place, and the boys were already looking forward to the Australian beaches, but Scotland scored two tries in the second half. We still won 18–16 but the aggregate score was 37–32 to Scotland. We were out of the World Cup and it was a major setback for us, especially after reaching the previous two semi-finals. Danny Brough had another good game in Glasgow and kicked four goals. I could not understand why he was not playing for England in the 2013 World Cup when they were badly lacking at half-back and Brough was the Super League Man of Steel.

In 2008, not long after I became Wales Rugby League president, Jim Mills contacted me and said I would never guess who had just got in touch with him. "Who?" I asked. He replied: "John Greengrass." For those of you who are too young to remember, John Greengrass was a prop forward for New Zealand and Jim stamped on his head during a World Cup match at Swansea in November 1975. John was taken to hospital for 15 stitches in a gaping head wound and never played for his country again. Jim was sent off and banned for six months by the RFL (subsequently reduced on appeal). He was later banned from playing in New Zealand for life. Jim said that John was coming over with his wife on a European tour and wanted to meet up. I said "that's great" and arranged for John and his wife to stay at the Forest Hills Hotel in Cheshire. Jim and I met up at the Daresbury Hotel beforehand. Jim was in his Mercedes and we went to Liverpool Airport to meet John and his wife. Jim was driving; his hands are massive and made the steering wheel look like a Frisbee. He said: "I don't know Mike. It's a long time since that match, almost 33 years. Look at us, we've aged. We might not recognise him." I said: "Jim, it won't be a problem. Just look for someone who looks like he has auditioned for *Phantom of the Opera* or still has six stud marks on his face and that will give it away." Anyway, they met up, had a fantastic weekend, buried the hatchet and their wives got on well too. The *Daily Mail* interviewed them both, took some pictures and they all had a marvellous time. John said the incident had made him famous in New Zealand because if there were ever any examples of foul play in any sport they used to show the footage of the stamping.

We are used to setbacks in Welsh rugby league. It is two steps forward, one step back all the time. The game against England in October 2012 when we lost 80–12 at Wrexham was another example. England had just returned from high-altitude training in Potchefstroom in South Africa's North West province. I joked that we had been training in North Wales. We went up Snowdon on the train, had a game of tick-and-pass and a picnic and returned to sea level. It isn't a level playing field. Their resources are far superior to ours.

The 2013 Rugby League World Cup only had three teams who were likely to win it, but it worked and was seen as very successful. Unlike most countries, we went down the organic route, growing our own players and not importing them. We only had one NRL player in Tyson Frizzell, from St George Illawarra Dragons, and he had played for us before in 2011.

We were overlooked on a lot of occasions and felt badly treated by the Rugby League World Cup in some respects. If you are held in such low esteem by your own game, how are you going to be taken seriously in your own land against rugby union? I wasn't even invited to the World Cup launch in Manchester in 2010 and I am the president of Wales Rugby League. Our chairman, Mark Rowley, was only in the audience. They invited two what I call 'professional Welshmen' instead, the Olympic athlete Iwan Thomas and the *Blue Peter* presenter Gethin Jones. I didn't understand that. Where were the real rugby league stars like Jonathan Davies, Allan Bateman, Kevin Ellis, John Devereux, Scott Quinnell and Scott Gibbs? Even though we were supposed to be co-hosts and the Welsh Assembly had contributed more than £700,000, I felt that we weren't given the respect we were due.

I am still involved now as president of Wales Rugby League and am hands-on with the development of the game in Wales. I love it so much. One of my main aims is to get rugby league to take its proper place in the pantheon of Welsh sport. Welsh players have been well represented in rugby league in the past, but there is still a lack of acknowledgement of what they achieved. An anti-rugby league myth was perpetuated by the Welsh Rugby Union who, for a sporting body, had a ridiculous amount of power in Wales. The WRU did a magnificent job of indoctrinating the public against rugby league. It was driven by fear and insecurity about their product. I think it was wrong the way everyone who went North was treated. Welsh rugby players going North were worse off than today's European migrants who have freedom to work. The issue used to be professionalism, but even now some people can't come to terms with rugby league when both games are professional. There is a massive block in the psyche of the Welsh people and their perception of rugby league, but when we introduce kids to the game, they love it because they are able to express themselves and that's our biggest asset in breaking down the barriers and bias that are still prevalent today.

Brian Juliff, the chairman of Wales Rugby League and former Wakefield, Wigan and Halifax player, reflects on knowing Mike for more than 40 years: *"My first recollection of Mike Nicholas was in 1972 in the changing rooms at Pontypridd rugby club before a match against Aberavon. Tommy David was a very special player to us and went on to play for Wales. He also came to rugby league and played for the Cardiff City Blue Dragons with success. Tommy was a big, powerful back-row forward and said: 'There are a lot of good players in this Aberavon side and a lot of players who are dangerous and one nutter in the back row called Nicholas – just be careful.' I remember thinking 'Who's that?' and I said to Tommy 'Who's Nicholas?' and he told me: 'He's a nutter with blond, curly hair.' As the game went on it became quite clear who Nicholas was. Every line-out and everywhere Tommy went, Nicko was behind him, tapping him on the shoulder and saying: 'I'm here Tom'. He terrorised our back row that day and in training a couple of weeks later we were in the changing rooms again and somebody came in and said 'Good news. Nicko's gone north,' and there was a big cheer.*

I remember watching him on television before I went north and watching his battles with Jim Mills which were legendary. Eddie Waring would commentate on the 'jousts' between them. I can vividly see in my mind one game on the BBC with them running at each other – one with the ball, one without the ball – with their elbows raised and pointing at each other. Now they are best mates. My interest in rugby league came from watching people like Mike, Dai Watkins, Dennis Curling and all the Welsh boys. I used to watch them and really loved the game – the ball was in play more than in rugby union, as it is today. Thanks to people like Mike I came into the game and never looked back. So I owe him a debt in some ways, but maybe not in others, with all the broken bones and everything that came after.

I played with him for Wales against England in 1979. We stayed at a hotel in Runcorn and before the game Mike came into the restaurant, ate three cream cakes and said to me 'Well, Brian, that's for energy,' and he was on the bench that day. It was a tough game and a scrum broke up and I saw one of the worst injuries I ever saw on a rugby pitch. Tommy Cunningham was the hooker and his nose had been splattered all over his face. He was bleeding and the blood was spurting out. It was a shocking injury and everybody thought Harry Beverley had done the dirty deed – either punched him or kicked him.

Off went Tommy and on came Mike Nicholas and I have never seen such a ritual beating up of one individual in all my life. I have never seen so much physicality, so much aggression, from two men in particular – the redoubtable James Mills and led forcibly by Mike Nicholas. They picked Harry out every time he got the ball but Harry Beverley, what a brave man. He never ever stopped coming and they made an absolute mess of him. He never took a backward step, he kept coming, he kept coming, he kept apologising and saying it wasn't him and he went up in my estimation that day. He was a great player.

My family were there and in the bar afterwards we were having our sandwiches. My father and I were sat together and Mike and Jim were sat just to the left of us and in came the England team and Harry Beverley came straight over and said cheerfully 'Hi Mike, hi Jim, how are you doing?' and sat down with them as if nothing had happened. My father couldn't believe it. That was the nature of the guys. They were fierce competitors on the pitch, but as good as gold off the pitch.

I played in the 1979 Challenge Cup Final for Wakefield and the 1984 Challenge Cup Final for Wigan. I missed the 1985 Challenge Cup Final against Hull through injury and I was thinking of retiring. I had broken my arm that year and my leg the year before that. I was 32 and I thought I wasn't going to play at that level anymore. I was living in Stockton Heath in Warrington and Mike and I used to meet every Friday and have a few drinks. I asked him what I should do and he said: 'I don't think you should retire. You are fit and strong, keep on going as long as you can. You have still got a lot to offer, whether you stay at Wigan or go to another club, maybe Warrington. Someone will come in for you.'

I thought about it and a couple of clubs came in, one of which was Halifax. I joined them and had the time of my life, winning the Challenge Cup against St Helens in 1987. Mike was right with his advice to keep on playing. One thing he said was: 'When you get a bit older Brian you have to be careful and be aware that you lose some elasticity in your joints.' I asked: 'What do you mean?' He said: 'Well, when I was that age, every time I punched somebody I dislocated a finger or a knuckle.' I didn't think for one minute I was going to go around punching people.

Another Friday in 1986 we met up as usual and Halifax were playing Australia the following Wednesday. I said to Mike that Chris Anderson, the Halifax coach, had come to me at training the night before and said Roy Dickinson had pulled his hamstring. I laughed at first because I didn't believe Roy could ever pull a hamstring. Chris said that he needed somebody to play at Number 8 and I was that man. I told Chris I had never played at Number 8 in my life, but he said it didn't matter. 'Just keep coming for the ball and keep tackling and you will be all right.'

I asked Mike if he had any tips for me and he said: 'No problem. Easy. When you go into a scrum, keep your eyes on his eyes, grab him by the shirt collar at the back of his head, keep your arm out straight and solid so he struggles to get down and then, when you are ready, let him go down and nut him straight in the face.' I asked: 'Really?' He said 'yes, simple' and then spent 20 minutes in the pub, showing me how to do it until I got the so-called technique right. Then Mike said: 'There's one thing I forgot to tell you: don't bind too tight with the other arm on the hooker because once you've nutted him, he's going to punch you. So you've got to punch him back quickly.'

Sure enough, on the night, I nutted their prop and we both ended up fighting on the floor and were sent to the sin bin. I was in the changing room feeling a bit forlorn when Peter 'Bullfrog' Moore, the Aussie manager and chief executive of Canterbury Bulldogs, came in. He said: 'Brian, that was fantastic, do you want to come and play for Canterbury?' I said: 'Thank you Peter. I was feeling a bit sorry for myself.' He said: 'Don't worry. It's like that in

142

the front row. Just get back out there and enjoy yourself.' So Mike had taught me something useful after all.

I saw the family side to Mike as well because we lived three minutes' walk away from where he lived for 10 years and I saw him as his children were growing up. Mike lived in Whitefield Road, everybody knew him and so he never locked his doors. Occasionally, every couple of months, I would stroll past there late at night and I could see him, through the window, fast asleep on the settee. I would let myself in through the back door and jump on him and frighten him to death. He'd say: 'I'll have you. I'll have you one night when you come in here.'

I got involved with Wales Rugby League because of Mike. When I retired a couple of years back I was contacted about applying for the job as chairman. Mike Nicholas had said I would be the ideal man to do it. Once they mentioned Mike's name I remembered everything he had done for Wales Rugby League and, frankly, without Mike Nicholas there wouldn't be a Wales Rugby League. He has done some remarkable work to establish the game over the last 10 years. He travels all over the place, works with kids and works with underprivileged communities. He is passionate about Wales and about Wales Rugby League and about keeping the game going in Wales, despite all the problems we get with our union neighbours who are not very supportive, get all of the money and we get very little funding. I purely got involved because his name was mentioned and I thought it was something I had to do. It has become a life's passion – as it is with Mike – and there is something about pride and achievement and not letting people down that ties you in. I work on Wales Rugby League three or four hours most days. It is a labour of love."

By 2012, I had been involved in rugby league for 40 years and I was inducted on to the RFL's roll of honour for outstanding service to the game at a lunch in Bradford in January along with Ray Unsworth, Ron England, Jackie Reid MBE and Andrew Cudbertson. Ray had played a pivotal role in the success of the English Schools Rugby League. Ron was instrumental in establishing the Champion Schools competition, the largest rugby league competition in the world. Jackie had been involved in rugby league in Cumbria for more than 50 years as a player, coach, official and volunteer. Andrew had founded the University Rugby League. I was in good company. Later that year I received another honour when I was presented with a Lifetime Achievement Award by the Wales Rugby League during the Wales versus England match at the Racecourse Ground in Wrexham.

Glyndwr University had bought the Racecourse Ground – where Wrexham and the Crusaders were playing – in 2011 and I met the pro vice-chancellor of the university, Dr Alan Howells, who happened to come from Blaina, the same town as Dai Watkins. We were reminiscing and he said that when Dai came home from Salford he used to train in the park on his own, like I used to; we had no access to rugby facilities because we were professionals. I used to train on the running track in Western Avenue, Port Talbot, next to my old school. Dr Howells said that he fancied himself as a bit of a sprinter and challenged Dai to a race. Dai accepted the challenge and ran backwards and still beat him. Dai said that

143

was how you survived in rugby league, you learned to run backwards as quickly as forwards – away from Mike Nicholas and Dave Chisnall. I threw Dai's boot away in a game once. You couldn't stop him any other way, he was such a good player. His boot came off and I threw it right out of the ground. He said to me: "And I always thought you were a nice bloke."

During the course of my work in rugby development, many people have supported me in my pursuit of establishing rugby league in Wales. I would like to give them a mention and thank them for their help.

Neil Kelly, the managing director of the Warrington Wolves Foundation, came down to help me form the South Wales team in 1996. Initially he came as a half-back from Woolston, who were the top amateur team in the country at the time. Along with Paul Cooper he ran the club from Paul's office in Cardiff. We all mucked in on match day operations; Paul even became the match day announcer at the Arms Park. I would like to think that the overall experience gained by Neil at this time stood him in good stead for his position at the Wolves. We all had some tricky situations to deal with and were in the end abandoned by the RFL hierarchy at the time.

Niel Wood, when he was working for the RFL on development, accompanied me many times up and down the motorways to South Wales in order to implement the grass roots structures which enabled us to thrive as a sport. We would have quizzes to pass the time on the motorways. Gerard Keenan eventually came on board in North Wales and is now a very effective board member for that region.

Latterly Mike Nolan (former Wigan chairman) and Dave Critchley were Welsh sponsors during the 2013 World Cup and we are lucky that they are staying on board for the foreseeable future. I was able to repay Dave by supplying a sprinkling of rugby league lads to play for the struggling colts team he managed at Sandbach RFC. This turned a 116–0 loss at the hands of Caldy from the Wirral into a 22–6 away win in the space of six weeks. What a reversal of fortunes and what does that say about their quality?

In Cardiff, Steve Dew, the managing director of Branagan's (First Leisure) theme bars, was a great supporter of rugby league. Branagan's were a shirt sponsor for the Wales rugby league senior team, who enjoyed all the associated liquid refreshment benefits when celebrating international victories. Steve was a Robbie Coltrane look-alike and I introduced him as 'Robbie' to Shaun Edwards and Billy Boston at a Twickenham Challenge Cup Final as a bit of fun and they were taken in. What a 'cracker' of a joke to play on them; they weren't amused when I told them who he really was.

I met Neil McEvoy, the former deputy leader of Cardiff City Council, at a Warrington versus Crusaders game. He had travelled up to the Halliwell Jones Stadium with a bus full of supporters with his dad, who was originally from Warrington. We went to a Catalan Dragons versus Crusaders match in Perpignan and represented the Crusaders in the pre-match formalities. As the 'maitre' of Cardiff he was introduced to the Mayor of Perpignan in a packed sponsors lounge. He blew them away by addressing them fluently in both Welsh and French, which he had taught at school in Wales. Magnifique!

North Wales development

Development in north Wales started later than down south and gained momentum when the Crusaders moved north to Wrexham. Initially, there was only one team, the North Wales Coasters that promoted rugby league in the area with players drawn from all over the north. What started as a promising competitive team in the 1990s playing opposition from the north-west of England had declined into a rag-bag outfit who failed to turn up for away fixtures and became perennial whipping boys for most opposition.

The team was turned around in the last five or six years by hardworking individuals such as Matt Pritchard, a phenomenally energetic development officer who introduced a very successful 'Street Rugby' programme to the area and found time to be an Olympic Torch bearer to boot.

Lee Blackmore, a steward and coach at Rhyl RUFC, a tough, no-nonsense former miner, who hailed from the same Afan Valley as me, from the village of Abergwynfi (known as 'The Cape') helped create a new side, Prestatyn & Rhyl Panthers, with the help of his two sons, Dale and Jason. Will Morecame was the chairman; he was a Wigan supporter. Later on they were coached by Jon Burgess (formerly of Crosfields), who was ably mentored off the field by former England rugby union captain and coach Dick (Richard) Greenwood. Talk about support coming from unexpected places.

Ray Caldwell, from Widnes, set up the Conwy Celts with David Edwards as chairman. The Celts went on to win the first North Wales Grand Final, with Ray winning the North Wales coach of the year – for all sports – at a prestigious awards ceremony in Llandudno.

The Flint Falcons were set up by Matt Pritchard with Mark Parry running the junior section, and are based at the Deeside Leisure centre, the high performance centre and 'home' of Wales Rugby League.

I am very proud of the Dee Valley Dragons, a rugby league outpost in the Bala – Corwen –Llangollen district. The players are primarily Welsh speaking – sheep shearers, farmers and forestry workers. Led by Mike Parry, they now have two pitches dedicated to rugby league. My good friend Gwilym Hughes, a champion angler, entertained Keiron Cunningham, Eamonn Mcmanus, Daniel Anderson and Harry Pinner on the stretch of the River Dee that he controls, near the rugby field. I organised that little fishing trip as a 'thank you' to Eamonn and the St Helens club, who were very supportive of what I was trying to achieve. They supplied kit and coaching expertise. In particular, Keiron seemed to be in his element in this outdoor environment. I felt that if he hadn't been a world class player, he would have made a great backwoodsman.

Eamonn has become a firm friend and he is one of the new breed of entrepreneurial owners, like Simon Moran, who are taking the game forwards. I think that rugby league is safe in their hands under the stewardship of Nigel Wood – the ultimate fan.

Left: An evening with Max Boyce, signed by Jonathan Davies.

Right: Mike with Jonathan Davies during the 1995 World Cup (Photo: Eddie Witham)

Bottom: Wales manager: Mike at Cardiff's Ninian Park with the 1995 World Cup squad. Left to right, back: Kelvin Skerrett, Daio Powell, Adrian Hadley, Rowland Phillips, Neil Cowie, Paul Moriarty, Dai Young, Martin Hall, Mark Perrett, Richie Eyres, Rob Ackerman; front: Paul Acheson, Allan Bateman, Kevin Ellis, Clive Griffiths (coach), Jonathan Davies (captain), Mike, Iestyn Harris, Phil Ford, Anthony Sullivan.

Left: Mike was added to the Rugby Football League's Roll of Honour in January 2012 for outstanding service to the game. Pictured at the induction ceremony in Bradford are, left to right, back: Mike, Andrew Cudbertson and Ray Unsworth; front: Jackie Reid and Ron England. (Courtesy Rugby Football League).

Bottom: Mike addressing the Wales crowd after he had been presented with his Lifetime Achievement award.
(Photo: Eddie Whitham).

John Williams, from Rhosneigr in Anglesey, became a sponsor of the North Wales Service Area when it was first set up and remains a very valuable contributor to our development programme. He lends his considerable business skills to our cause. 'Billy' and I first met at Colin Metson's Glamorgan CCC benefit golf day at Rhosneigr Golf Club. We joked that it has the longest par 5 in the world – that being the RAF Valley runway, where Prince William trained, which is parallel to the first tee.

I have a theory that the Welsh speaking boys (Corwen, "Ysgol Gyfan" Ystalyfera) are really suited to our game. They are a minority in terms of language themselves, like us, and seem to have an untainted mindset not influenced by the anti-league propaganda and myths perpetuated by some of the people in rugby union.

I have also worked with the teams in South Wales. Torfaen Tigers were a team created from a 'cold call' to the Panteg RUFC in Pontypool, which ended with an appointment with their club secretary. This took place after the wedding cake decoration class in the clubhouse had finished. With the help of their rugby union coach, Kevin Weaver, we managed to get a side together (sort of) in two to three weeks to play in the inaugural match against the Cynon Valley Cougars.

The Cougars had a full squad of 19, but Torfaen were five short, so I had to make a last minute dash down from the north in my van on the day of the game with four Woolston Rovers players, Paul Berry, Bev Povey, Chris Mellor and Wes Lawton. They all played their part in the latest historical attempt to create a Welsh League. Like the boys from Bank Quay Bulls – Al Catterall, the late Al (Bundy) Clare, Lee Smith and Stephen Caley, who turned out for the Swansea Valley Miners, all these lads played for the greater good of the game. Some accommodation and international match tickets helped, and I have the utmost admiration and appreciation of the contribution they made.

Torfaen won that opening encounter and with the help of Gary Baker's match reports in the *South Wales Argus*, soon came to prominence. They had more than 50 players signed on, and a Tiger skinned mascot by the end of their first season.

The other teams in the league that year included:

Aberavon Fighting Irish – were run by the combative O'Callaghan brothers – Chris and John. They were involved in the earlier attempts of the Aberavon Steelers to play rugby league locally. Danny and Kerry Sheehy were involved then. Welsh rugby union international Richard Hibberd played for them in his younger days, and won a cap for the Welsh A rugby league team in 2003. He had trials with St Helens.

Bridgend Blue Bulls – had the 'holy trinity' of John Devereux, Allan Bateman and Kevin Ellis, who were magnificent with their commitment and gave more help than any other league players who came back home. They played until they were nearly 40, and were supported off the field by Alan Evans (former Barrow player), Andrew Smallwood and Simon Green as secretary. They played at the Bridgend football ground. The interest they created helped pave the way for the establishment of the Celtic Crusaders franchise under Chris O'Callaghan and funded by Leighton Samuels until it came to grief in the economic downturn of 2008.

Cynon Valley Cougars (later Valley Cougars) – Mark Rowley, who later went on to be the managing director of the Welsh Rugby League, was responsible for setting up the Valley Cougars. They started off playing at Abercynon. The Cougars, together with the 'Scorpions', their semi-professional counterparts now carry the flag for the game down south in tandem with our junior development programme in Maesteg.

Swansea Valley Miners – Based in Ystalyfera, the home village of Ronnie James, a Halifax rugby league legend. It is also where our latest Welsh speaking school, Ysgol Gyfun, is based. For the club, the Davies twins, Connor and Curtis, starred. The team play under the guidance of Ioan Bebb, a former South Wales RLFC player. It is fast becoming a hotbed for the game, and is making great progress in the Champion Schools Competition. Later they became the South Wales Hornets.

Cardiff Demons – This club did not take part in the first season. Ian Golden was the club secretary and they were already playing in the South West England competition and were not sure that the fledgling Wales League would provide strong enough opposition. However, they joined in the second season and soon found out how strong the competition was when they got beaten a few times.

Newport Titans – were set up again with the help of Paul Cooper and the legendary 'Barco'. They played at Pill RFC, the former club of the legendary Trevor Foster, and were a force to be reckoned with.

Richard Greenwood, the former England rugby union captain and coach, recalls: *"I was meeting somebody at the Daresbury Park hotel in Warrington and Nicko appeared, having been to the gym, and I was introduced to him. He must now regard it as one of the worst days of his life because I have dragged him into all of the charitable stuff that I do, such as Wooden Spoon, the children's charity of rugby. Three weeks later he was playing in a charity golf match for me as a personality and we have become very closely associated with a number of Wooden Spoon events. His levels of support, his loyalty and his integrity have been quite exceptional. Anything I have asked for, such as raffle prizes or affordable wine, he has come up with. I have nothing but praise for him. Through Mike I have also become chairman of the Prestatyn and Rhyl Panthers Amateur Rugby League Football Club. Of course, our honorary president is Mr M. Nicholas himself."*

Ken Kelly comments: *"What Mike has done for Welsh Rugby League is fantastic and a lot of it is unsung. You don't know until people tell you that Nicko has been down there and is trying to get a team going there. He doesn't bleat about it or brag about it, he just gets people to places and raises money and tries to get the game into Wales."*

One change after 1995 was that, along with the other former Aberavon players who had gone to rugby league, I was able to return to the club. We drove down in my Rolls Royce, and – making a statement – parked it outside the clubhouse. Our former team-mate, John Richardson, was by then a successful businessman and sponsored the club on condition that the 'Leaguies' were welcomed back into the fold. Even the president, Lord Heycock, asked for a lift home in the Roller, which I happily obliged. Later, the Aberavon Naval Club, run by the Tolland brothers, lent us their minibus for Wales RL to use.

Left: Ready to sink a short putt and wearing Aberavon colours for luck. (Courtesy *Warrington Guardian*)

Bottom: Mike with Peter Greenall (centre) and St Helens player Jonathan Griffiths (second right) at the Greenalls Northern Pro Am. Mike Maloney (second left) went on to become executive director of The Belfry. Peter became Lord Daresbury and chairman of Aintree Racecourse.

(Courtesy Mike Nicholas).

14. Cricket, canals and golf

Cricket has been a big part of my life, as well as rugby. Growing up I was a massive Glamorgan fan and, as I mentioned earlier, I remember my father taking me to my first Glamorgan match – against the Australia touring team at St Helen's in August 1956 – for my 10th birthday.

My family was very involved with the cricket scene in south Wales. There was a comedy on television in the 1990s called *Outside Edge* with Brenda Blethyn and Timothy Spall. We were the Welsh version. My mother made the tea, my father was the umpire and all the boys played. So on Saturday 30 July 1966, which just happened to be my 20th birthday, I had to play cricket at the Mansel ground, Port Talbot.

Saturday 30 July 1966 also happened to be the day of the World Cup final between England and West Germany at Wembley. Despite being Welsh, I was absolutely devastated that I couldn't watch it, because I was a sports fanatic. The worst part about it was that we lost the toss, so I was fielding in the covers while the game was going on. I could hear shouting from the clubhouse, but I couldn't see anything. I had to watch it the next day to see it properly. I have since become good friends with Roger Hunt and, as a result, he rings me every 30 July and says: "It's that day again Mike."

A few years ago, the England team were in Australia on a speaking tour and I got Dave Wright, the former Warrington player, to look after them and fix them up with some golf. I just said some friends of mine were coming over. When they turned up everyone was all over them like a rash. Dave couldn't believe it. The following 30 July Roger rang and said: "I've got someone who wants to talk to you." I said: "Put him on then." This voice said: "Hi Mike, happy birthday, blah, blah, blah." I said: "Excuse me, who am I speaking to?" The voice answered: "Roger played in the final and I made a bit of a contribution as well, I scored three goals." For the benefit of younger readers, that was Sir Geoff Hurst, and England beat West Germany 4–2.

I got picked for the Port Talbot League to play in a six-a-side tournament against the 1966 West Indies, including Charlie Griffiths and Wes Hall. I won the big hitting competition because, in one match during the knockout stage, I hit the ball out of the ground and over the Cardiff to Swansea main road. Luckily, it started to rain before we were due to play the West Indies and so that saved us from pain, suffering and humiliation.

Everybody used to drop in at the Carlton club in Port Talbot, such as the England captain Tony Lewis, when he was playing for Glamorgan. I was also there the night in August 1968 that Garry Sobers came in after becoming the first batsman to hit six sixes in an over. I was talking to a couple of girls; he fancied them and ended up giving one a lift home.

Malcolm Nash, the unfortunate bowler, wasn't there. He was still recovering and looking for the ball on Swansea beach. Cliff Morgan once said that his ideal Welsh woman was shrewd in the market place, pious in the chapel and frantic in the bedroom. I wonder if Sobers agreed.

I was playing a lot of cricket as an all-rounder and was asked to go for trials with Glamorgan, but sport was frowned upon as a career. The attitude was: you are not going to get anywhere playing sport. Yet sport has been my passport to the world.

Bryn Thomas, my mentor from the Afan Lido, was also a keen cricketer, like I was. 'Bryn bat and ball' they used to call him. He knew everybody and he had his own cricket team called the Sphinx (Afan Lido), who were unbeaten for six years in the local league. I played for the Sphinx, with half the Glamorgan team, like Malcolm Nash and Majid Khan. Bryn bowled a bit like 'Deadly' Derek Underwood and his record of 80 wickets in a summer still stands in the South Wales League.

Another mate of mine, Dave O'Brien, who lived at the bottom of the street, also played. He went to university and used to borrow my Ford Cortina if he met a girl because he had no money. But I didn't mind because he always returned it full of petrol. He ended up going to America, to Silicon Valley via Boston, and became a tycoon. He was in the right place at the right time. I love it when locals come good.

We used to play in all sorts of places and I remember once we played Weston-Super-Mare and went on a paddle steamer across the Bristol Channel. There's not too many people have gone to a cricket match by paddle steamer. When we got there, Brian Rose of Somerset and England was playing for them, but we had Keith Jarrett, the Welsh rugby international, and half the Glamorgan team playing for us and were 200 for no wicket.

In Warrington, I played casually for the Ashall family, for the Appleton Casuals. It was perfect because we had about half-a-dozen games a season and it suited me. We ended up playing in charity events. We used to play at Walton Lea and had a very good side – Paul Agar, Mark London, who was known as 'The Bear', and others who were rugby union players and cricketers and I had a lot in common with them. I played in testimonial matches for Farokh Engineer and Barry Wood and a galaxy of stars used to turn out. I remember bowling against Bumble (David Lloyd) and he hit me for six.

I also took five sixes off the England Test attack at Walton Lea – against England Ladies, captained by Rachael Heyhoe Flint. I hit five sixes into the neighbouring Walton Lea Crematorium and the girl who eventually caught me out was from the next street in Port Talbot. Her name was Shirley Morgan, maiden name Shirley Ellis, and she was a bit of a tomboy. She used to play at Vivian Park in Port Talbot with us to make up the numbers and went on to keep wicket for Wales and England, and played hockey for Wales

I opened the batting in a match for Farokh Engineer in 1976. We put on nearly 100 for the first wicket with David Hughes and he was out before me. I think it was the first game Neil Fairbrother had seen me playing cricket. Paul Allott, the England fast bowler, was steaming in. I was heading and elbowing most of the balls away. I loved my cricket and the Appleton Casuals had various fixtures, some up in Eskdale in the Lake District. We also went to Blubberhouses, a small village near Harrogate, to play against the Hawks, the Yorkshire invitation team sponsored by Featherlite Prams. That was a dynasty against dynasty match. We also went over to play Caythorpe, near RAF Cranwell, in Lincolnshire. I enjoyed it. The game was a welcome break from the rigours of rugby; relaxing, not too competitive.

Left: Peter Jenkins, the Llanelli full-back, and Mike on the paddle steamer 'Waverley' heading to a cricket match in Weston-Super-Mare.
Right: Mike using a Ping driver at the Scottsdale Pro-Am in Arizona.

The Good, the Bad and the Ugly: Harry Pinner, Joe Frazier and Mike
at a sportsman's dinner in Manchester. What a front row!
(Photo courtesy Ray Fisher Promotions)

I'll never forget one match when Ronnie Clark, who played with me in the Warrington team who beat Australia in 1978, looked like a test cricketer. He had all the equipment, the helmet, the gloves, the lot, and was out first ball for a duck. I came in wearing a T-shirt and knocked it all over the place.

Frank Collier, who won the Lance Todd Trophy with Widnes in 1964, was the wicketkeeper and he was shouting: "Come on Mike, get your ton." I didn't quite make it – I was out for 89 or 90. Frank was one of those characters you could only find in rugby league. Big Jim Mills tells a story that before the 1964 Challenge Cup final Collier was introduced to Prince Philip, the Duke of Edinburgh, who was the guest of honour, and Frank asked him: "How's the wife and kids?"

It's not true, of course, because Prince Philip wasn't the guest of honour at Wembley in 1964, but it is funny and Frank was a character. He played for his hometown team Wigan from 1951 to 1963 and appeared in two Challenge Cup finals for them – in 1958 and 1963 – before signing for Widnes. And, just in case you are wondering, Prince Philip wasn't the guest of honour at either of those finals.

I became good friends with Neil Fairbrother and used to tease him throughout the Eighties, Nineties and Noughties that Lancashire had not won the County Championship outright since 1934 – they shared it with Surrey in 1950 – while Glamorgan had won it in 1948, 1969 and 1997. Neil was interviewed on local radio last year and was asked to name his two favourite sports stars. He said George Best and Mike Nicholas!

Neil Fairbrother, the former Lancashire and England batsman, reflects: *"When I was growing up – when I was 10, 11 and 12 – I had two sporting heroes: George Best and Mike Nicholas. Not a cricketer in sight. Warrington Rugby League Club's doctor was Dr Rothwell and he was our family GP too. So the first time I came into contact with Mike was in his surgery. I was at the doctor's one day with my mum; and my mum was quite a fearsome lady. We waited for ages and were sat outside the doctor's door because we were the next in. The door opened, a bloke came out and we were about to stand up and go in when Mike wandered past and knocked on the door. He opened the door and was about to go in when my mum got up, grabbed him and said: 'What do you think you're doing?' I was sat there as an 11-year-old saying: 'It's Mike Nicholas, it's Mike Nicholas.' My mum said: 'I don't care who it is. He's not going in there in front of us.' I was petrified, but he burst out laughing. Doctor Rothwell joined in the joke and that was the first time I really got anywhere close to him.*

After that, amazingly, I was playing for England at Old Trafford in about 1989 or 1990, looked down from the players' balcony and sitting in the members' enclosure downstairs was Mike. I got introduced to him and we became good buddies from then on. He came to a lot of cricket while I was playing and we went to watch a lot of rugby league, obviously. He saved me from a couple of fights at rugby league matches and we played a lot of golf together. I am now godfather to his son Morgan and the two families know each other very well. I am proud to call him a friend.

He is nothing like what I envisaged he was going to be like. I only knew the bloke on the rugby pitch and that's how I formed my image of him. Clearly, when you meet him, he is quietly spoken and nothing like the marauding hero that I had in my mind's eye. But there was no disappointment. He is one of life's characters and great company. We have been to Wembley together, watched Warrington's big matches together and seen some big cricket matches together too.

After NatWest one-day finals with Lancashire he came on a couple of nights out with the lads who all got to know him as well. We had some great times. He is Mr Warrington. When I first met him he was playing a lot of golf and was a very handy partner off about 12. If you were playing a pairs match you would want him as your partner. As you can imagine, he never, ever gave up. If you were six down with seven to play, he still thought you were going to win which was similar to my way of thinking. So we struck a chord there as well. It was great to have met him and become such good friends."

Lifelong friend Tony 'Bushman' Jones recalls: *"I have known Mike and his family for more than 40 years. His brother, Clive, was my best man. I know his daughter is called Evie and his niece is married to Jamie Davies, the Aberavon fly-half. So when I was at Newbury races in May 2007 and there was a horse called Red Evie, ridden by Jamie Spencer, my favourite jockey, it jumped out of the page at me. I backed it big time and it came in at 8–1. So thanks for that Mike. After he turned professional in 1972 I went to most of his home games. I watched Manchester United on the Saturday and Warrington on the Sunday. In the summer we both played cricket for Richard Ashall's team. Mike and I would open the batting. They used to call us the Tafia. We used to have fabulous times and were well looked after. One afternoon we played in a place called Blubberhouses, a beautiful village in Yorkshire. I asked where the showers were; they pointed to the river and they weren't joking."*

When I had the taxi business I once had a driving contract, taking the pilots up and down the Manchester Ship Canal, quite a nice job, picking pilots up at Eastham and taking them to Salford with various drop-off points along the canal. My friend Brian Pownall, the son-in-law of Dai Davies, the former Warrington scrum-half, was a pilot and treated me to a trip along the canal from Eastham Locks. I had the privilege of being on the bridge with the captain, taking the ship up to Latchford. It took about four hours. The ship had arrived from Asia and had a crew of 66 Bangladeshis. I was wearing my beloved sheepskin jacket. We got to Chester Road swing-bridge on the outskirts of Warrington and the bridge started to swing.

I was watching the traffic pulling up; a kid came up on his bike and stopped at the barrier, looked at the ship and shouted: "Bloody hell Nicko, you're not the captain of that are you?" It was unbelievable that he recognised me from that distance. I was shell-shocked and waved to him. Years after, I was in the toilet in a pub and this guy said: "I haven't seen you since you were on the bridge of that ship." His name was Ian Waters and we became friends. I did an interview once and was asked "What is the most unusual place you have been recognised?" "On the bridge of a ship on the Manchester Ship Canal," I replied.

Twice I nearly bought a narrow boat. I saw one advertised in the paper and went over to Leeds to try to buy it. Brian came with me. When we got there, the boat was in the basin behind the Dragonara Hotel, which is where the Kangaroos used to sink their cars in an-end-of tour ritual. They would buy old bangers and then drive them into the canal at the end with the lights still on. British Waterways must have dreaded it every four years. The boat wasn't quite what it said in the advert and so I didn't bother. We were due to take a two-week trip back to Warrington along the Leeds Liverpool Canal, but it never happened.

Instead we took a narrow boat along the Cheshire Ring, which is a circular canal route of 97 miles with 92 locks. It takes in the whole of the Macclesfield Canal and parts of the Trent and Mersey, Bridgewater, Rochdale, Ashton and Peak Forest Canals. It was something I had always wanted to do. It poured down all week, but at least I've done it. It was a great experience. We stopped at Bathpool Park in Kidsgrove, the canal runs really close to it, and stumbled across the manhole cover below which the Black Panther, Donald Neilson, had murdered Lesley Whittle. On the manhole cover, in yellow paint, someone had painted: "Black Panther You Bastard."

I was very attracted to that linear world of canals and nearly bought another narrow boat in Thelwall. They wanted £6,000 for it. Today they are worth £150,000. I read the Alexander Cordell trilogy – *Rape of the Fair Country*, *The Hosts of Rebecca* and *Song of the Earth* – which featured the canals in Wales, felt it was a nice, quiet life and it appealed to me. I also read his other book, *The Fire People*, about iron and steel making in the industrial revolution.

I approached Brian Pitchford, the Warrington vice-chairman, to see if he could help me out with the money, but he thought I was mad to try to live in a barge. John Bevan thought it was a bit strange as well, especially with my broad shoulders. There wasn't much room for manoeuvre in a narrow boat.

After I finished playing rugby I got down to single figures in golf. It was a big part of my life and I worked at four Ryder Cups on the hospitality side for De Vere, the hotels and leisure business. Growing up in Wales I couldn't afford to play golf. There was only one municipal course nearby and that was in Cwmbran, 40 miles away. Golf was white collar and expensive. I couldn't afford club membership and I couldn't buy clubs out of catalogues like you can now. I loved the game and started playing seriously in about 1988 when I met Mike Slater, who was the pro at Walton Hall, a fantastic municipal course on my doorstep.

Mike and I used to play golf every Friday for money. One week we ended up at the Star and Garter pub in a beautiful little village called Kirkby Overblow, near Harrogate, for something to eat. There was a bald bloke behind the bar, about my age. I sat down at a table. Mike got the drinks in and said the man behind the bar thought he knew me. He had just asked him who I was. He said: "Is that Mike Nicholas over there? The last time we met he kicked me straight in the teeth." It was Keith Bridges, the former Featherstone Rovers and Bradford Northern hooker. He was the temporary landlord; I went over and we had a chat and a laugh.

On another occasion, I had a run-in with Bryn Terfel, the opera singer, at the Welsh FA golf day at Conwy Golf Club. He is a massive guy, six feet three inches tall, but I didn't recognise him because he had a baseball cap on. Two of the fairways were close together. I teed off and he was coming up the other way and I thought he had hit my ball. I went up to him and said: "Did you just hit my ball?" He said "No. It had BT written all over it" and walked off. I thought he was on about a sponsored golf ball from British Telecom. I went in after and apologised when I found out who he was, my favourite Welsh tenor, and a good friend of Jim Mills.

Mike Slater and I played golf all around the world – South Africa, Morocco, Australia and America – and played at some picturesque venues. I once played on a peninsula in San Francisco and when I was teeing off on one hole, the Golden Gate Bridge was down on my left. I thought to myself: "Is this real?"

In February 1989 we went to Las Vegas for the Mike Tyson versus Frank Bruno world heavyweight title fight. We also visited Fountain Hills, Arizona to watch Bruno train for the fight. Training was rained off and so we all went to a clubhouse and played a card game called Kalooki.

Mickey Duff, Bruno's promoter, was walking through the clubhouse and asked to join in. I dropped out and he took my place. I was just making up the foursome. He cleaned them out and took about £500 off them. He told me he had fought about 80 fights as an amateur, winning 60 odd, before retiring aged 19. He asked me: "Do you think I was born this ugly?"

Mike and I stayed at the Caesars Palace hotel and played golf at a course called Painted Desert, which was basically 18 landing strips. I was paired with a man called Doug Sherman who was the head croupier in the baccarat pit at the Hilton Hotel, the venue for the fight and where Elvis Presley stayed for eight years.

I asked him what was the biggest amount the hotel had lost in the baccarat pit and he told me that a 'big, ugly Australian' called Kerry Packer had once cleaned them out and took them for $20 million. He invited us to see the baccarat pit in action, but warned us that the minimum chip was $1,000.

We went along. He was dealing and there were half-a-dozen people around the pit. They all had mountains of chips worth $10,000 each. I remember thinking: "I hope one of those chips falls into the turn-up of my trousers." We clubbed together for one chip, but the bank won, although, apparently, if you play for long enough baccarat favours the punter.

Doug said that Packer gave him a $100,000 tip, but he had to play with it against the bank. Luckily, he won so he ended up with the tip plus what he won. Apparently, Packer was like that. On one occasion a loud-mouthed Texan was boasting to him about his wealth from the oil business. He was getting on Packer's nerves and so Packer asked him: "How much are you worth?" The Texan replied: "Half a billion dollars." Packer said: "I will toss you for it." The Texan was quiet after that.

My first Ryder Cup was at the Belfry in 1989 with Jonathan Davies and I took celebrity guests down for De Vere. We spent a bit of time with Lord Daresbury and his friends, Nicholas Soames MP, the Duke of Roxburgh, and Lord Stafford, his mates from Eton.

Left: Mike was the chauffeur when Mike Peers and Jan got married in 1983. (Courtesy Mike Peers)

Bottom: Mike with former French rugby union international forward Jean-Pierre Rives (second right) at the Pernod factory in Paris and about to start on the annual Beaujolais run. Businessman John Jones is with them. It was his car! (Courtesy Mike Nicholas)

We were in a stand on the 18th with all these lords-a-leaping and two little boys from housing estates in South Wales, me and Jonathan.

Then I went to Kiawah Island in South Carolina for the 1991 Ryder Cup which became known as the 'War on the Shore'. I went with my mate Mike Slater and joined up with the De Vere party. Stuart Reed, who was the chief executive, was a good friend of mine. He was from Newport and had started off as a third porter at the Royal Hotel in Cardiff. He was a larger than life character and we used to call him the Fat Controller. He was famous for his bacon butties at 4am at the Belfry.

The access we had was unbelievable. We had a house on Seabrook Island, the one next to Kiawah Island. It was so big that Mike and I thought we could have fitted another 20 people in. Mike gave golf lessons to Lord Daresbury (Peter Greenall) and designed a couple of courses for him, including Aintree, which was opened in 1994. He used to travel with De Vere everywhere and ended up giving Prince Andrew golf lessons at Walton as well. The royal Range Rover came in and out. He was a pretty keen golfer. Princess Diana used to stay at Peter Greenall's farm at Daresbury. One of those sports club bores who used to pester him went to his house one day and Princess Diana was in residence. Peter got Diana to greet him and say: "Hello, how are you? We have been expecting you. We have heard all about you. Come in." The man was dumbstruck.

Mike and I also worked at the 1993 Ryder Cup at the Belfry for De Vere. I looked after hospitality and security. They gave me my own Range Rover and had me in PGA livery. They also gave me a charge card and the brief that everybody had to enjoy themselves. What a remit to be given. Neil Fairbrother brought the Lancashire players down. Steve Hampson brought the Wigan players down. Mark Hughes, who was at Manchester United, and Dean Saunders, who was at Aston Villa, came down. Ron Atkinson, the Aston Villa manager, was there. I put them all up in my accommodation and Mike Atherton, the England cricket captain, had to sleep on the floor. They were good times. In fact, it was so good that I never saw a golf shot all week!

Mike Slater was an institution at Walton Hall Golf Club. He was there for more than 20 years as well as playing in tournaments on the European Tour and designing courses like Antrobus, Aintree and High Leigh. In 1997 he had a second bite of the cherry, if you like, when he qualified for the European Senior Tour and I caddied for him a few times. In 1999 he won the Dutch Senior Open and it was the most prize money he had won in his life. Less than a year later he had died of skin cancer at the age of 52. It was a tragedy and I was honoured to speak at his funeral.

The 2001 Ryder Cup at the Belfry was put back until 2002 because of the 9/11 attacks and the security aspect was stepped up. I was due to arrive a week before and Mike Maloney, the executive director of the Belfry, told me my accreditation would be waiting for me at reception and that no one would be able to get in without accreditation because they were expecting Dan Quayle, the American vice president. I decided to put the security to the test and managed to get into the hotel without my accreditation. When Mike saw me he said: "Where have you been? I have been waiting for you with your stuff." I said: "I just walked in." He went bananas. Tiger Woods was playing that week and my young son, Chris, who was eight, wanted to see him. I drove back to Warrington on the Sunday night, picked up him and his friend and took them to the Belfry. I had staff passes made for them and came through the main gate. The security man said: "Are you kidding? What work are they doing?" I said "Chimney sweeps". He let us in and they walked round with Tiger Woods.

Lord Daresbury, the chairman of Aintree Racecourse, says: *"Mike is the most lovely man, very amusing, good company, and we played golf together with Mike Slater. I was brought up in Leicestershire and only moved to the north in 1980. I never saw Mike play rugby because when I got interested he had just finished. I started playing golf and Mike Slater introduced me to Mike and that's how our friendship started. He gave the address at Mike Slater's funeral and it was fantastic. He spoke for 50 minutes and it was very, very funny and very moving. Not only was he a great rugby player, but he is witty, smart and good company and a very good guy. He was a great friend of Stuart Reed, who was the MD of De Vere, and did a lot of work with him which was brilliant. He is very good with people. I think he is a magic man."*

Another favourite golf memory came at a Northern PGA pro-am I played in at Warrington Golf Club. They had two 'longest drive' competitions on the 11th hole – a 450 yards par 4 – one for the pros and one for the amateurs. Jonathan Griffiths, the St Helens player, hit his drive 50 yards longer than the best pro, an amazing shot. He took a drive and a wedge. He was a powerhouse, played cricket and rugby league for Wales, and a terrific games player.

I have had to stop playing golf now because of arthritis, everything jars. The joints are not too bad. One is very painful, my bad knee, where I did my cruciate, but the problem is through the muscles. The muscles are inflamed and it is pretty poor because I have to take painkillers, which is not ideal. I can only work out on the exercise bike now.

My golf connections are many, from my nephew Mike Nicholas junior, who works for Nike, and Malcolm Thorniley in the commercial section. My late, great friend Peter Donoghue, formerly of Warrington RLFC and a Leigh Golf Club member, was nicknamed Growler. He introduced me to the Grappenhall Ex-servicemen's Golf Society; the San Miguel Golf Society (Leigh GC members), led by the irrepressible John ('The Laird') Pigeon and including England 1966 World Cup winner Roger Hunt, Bob Montford, Mike Travers, Nev Dickens and the comedian Stan Boardman among others. Along with the London Bridge Golf Society in Stockton Heath we enjoyed many wonderful trips to Spain, Portugal and Ireland.

My other golfing partners included the De Vere managers Mike Maloney (The Belfry), Paul Clayton (Mottram Hall) and Richard Grey (Lord Daresbury). We all helped to promote the Warrington Classic and many of the company's other venues. I met my great mate Phillip Price, a self-confessed league and Warrington fan, as he left the 16th green at the Belfry in 2002, having just won the pivotal game of the Ryder Cup 3 and 2 against one of the modern golf greats Phil Mickelson. His first words to me were: "Do you think I will get in your Welsh front row after that?"

I spent the rest of the evening celebrating behind (!) the main Belfry bar. The place was crammed, alongside the great Gareth Edwards and Peter Greenall (Lord Daresbury). There was no room anywhere else. I remember listening to Phil being heralded on a table, and proclaiming "Do you know who I just beat?"

Harry Pinner, the former St Helens and Great Britain loose forward, reflects on knowing Mike: *"When I was a young lad coming into the game I had obviously heard of Mike Nicholas of Warrington and how he was a bit mad and ferocious and this and that and so I was a bit wary before I played against him. My third or fourth game for Saints was against Warrington and they had a good side – Tommy Martyn, Barry Philbin and Bobby Wanbon were all playing – and we went to Wilderspool with a young team but I scored in the first minute under the sticks and as I ran back I heard Mike say 'Where's this little blond-haired bastard come from?' and he was ranting and raving. That was my first encounter with Mike and so I kept well away from him I can assure you of that.*

I only got to know him properly after I'd stopped playing. We took to each other straight away and we both played golf. He was a very good golfer and very competitive. Mike is always on the last minute and he rang me one night and said: 'Do you want to play in a pro-am at Gleneagles tomorrow for Steve Redgrave?' I said I did and he arranged to pick me up at 6am, but didn't arrive until 7 and so we were an hour behind already. We were flying up the motorway doing 80mph and he had a cup of coffee in one hand and his phone in the other hand and then he said: 'Will you pass me that pen from over there?' I thought to myself what am I doing in here with him? We got there in one piece and we actually should have won the first prize, which was a holiday. The last hole was a par five and we only needed a seven to win and you could feel the tension. Mike ripped a drive right down the middle but his second shot, which looked fantastic, went through the green and into the rough and he was on his hands and knees looking for his ball. Meanwhile, I five-putted and we never got the points we needed. The lads we were playing with walked off quickly and me and Mike had a two-minute argument about what had gone wrong and then just started laughing.

The following day we were playing in another pro-am at Royal Liverpool at Hoylake where the 2014 Open will be staged and were due to tee off at about 11.30am. We were still in the Gleneagles club at a quarter to six. We finally got in the van and Mike drove and I got in the back to have a sleep. Mike had some memorabilia in the back for the do after the pro-am, a framed and signed picture of Ian Botham. We never stopped once and I slept for three hours. As he swung into the car park at the golf club I rolled over and rolled straight over the memorabilia and broke the glass. I heard Mike say: 'Harry, you've broke the bloody glass.' I pretended that I hadn't heard him and carried on false snoring away. We arrived at the club still wearing our dinner suits from the night before.

Mike knew that I loved boxing and that Joe Frazier was my hero. When Frazier was at a sportsman's evening in Manchester he got tickets for us. We took boxing gloves to get signed and had our picture taken with him. We had a great time. I got the picture framed and put it up on the wall of my pub, the Parr Arms in Grappenhall. Mike said 'That's great' until he noticed that I'd put a caption with it '"The Good, the Bad and the Ugly". You can guess which he was and he certainly wasn't the first one. I breed bulldogs now and Mike got his own back recently when he gave me a framed picture of a bulldog with the caption 'Dirty Harry Pinner'.

Another time, he invited me to a boxing dinner at the Savoy as guests of Ken Jones, Mike's great journalist mate. We had a good meal, a good drink and Colin Jones, the former Welsh welterweight, was on our table. At about 3 in the morning, Colin said he hadn't booked a room and so Nicko said: 'You can sleep in our room with us but you will have to sleep on the floor.' Mike was in one single bed, Colin was on the floor in the middle and I was in the other single bed. At about 5 in the morning I heard some incredibly loud snoring – louder than any of my bulldogs – and opened one eye and looked across at Nicko. Nicko had opened one eye and was looking across at me. Colin, who had fought three times for the world title, was snoring. Nicko said: 'Give him a kick.' I said: 'Do you think I'm stupid? He fought for the world title. You kick him if you want to.' In the end we decided to let him carry on snoring."

15. Sticking together

After I had been at Warrington for a few years I found I couldn't sleep properly. I was as high as a kite all the time from playing and training every day. I was totally adrenalized and couldn't relax. I went to see my GP and he put on medication, but I had a bad reaction to it. I ended up hyperventilating. They took me to Warrington Infirmary and put me on a drip, but that didn't work. They had a different drip that they thought would help at Winwick Hospital, the Victorian mental hospital on the outskirts of town, and so they transferred me there. I ended up spending the night. It was like a scene from the Jack Nicholson film *One flew over the Cuckoo's nest* and I couldn't get out of there fast enough. Ever since then I have been particularly interested in player welfare and, in 2012, I joined the board of trustees of Rugby League Cares, the charity dedicated to supporting the rugby league family and its local communities.

Terry Flanagan, the former Great Britain loose forward and now chairman of Rugby League Cares, reflects: *"I was just starting in the game as Mike was finishing, I entered the pro ranks in 1979–80, but my elder brother, Kevin, played against him for Rochdale. I watched him from afar and appreciated his robust, skilful, hard and uncompromising play with nothing but respect for the guy. As I have got to know him in recent times, through Rugby League Cares, that has confirmed what I thought about him. His love for the game and especially Welsh rugby league is immense. He is on the board driving the past players and is a driving force in re-engaging past players with the game. In some clubs the past players group is great – like Warrington, St Helens and Leeds – but in other clubs it is a bit dormant and so he is using his drive and energy to revitalise the past players movement. We have lunch regularly and knock about socially at games and functions. He is great to be around. Another link with Mike that fascinates me concerns my father, Bill, who played for Belle Vue Rangers in the 1940s when they had six or seven top Welsh internationals in the team, players like Ray Price and Doug Phillips. Mike knows about them all – and their families – and so when we get together we talk about Belle Vue Rangers. These are people I never saw play, but I have pictures of them in my study because my dad played with them. My dad joined them on a tour of Wales once and so Nicko thinks of me and Kevin as honorary Welshmen."*

After I finished playing I didn't watch Warrington for a couple of years. I felt embittered about the way I had been treated. I was a bit disillusioned, but when you love a game and are brought up in that game and it's in your blood and you know nothing else but rugby, you cannot give it up for good. It's like a drug. I soon started watching Warrington again and was at Headingley in November 1986 when they beat Leeds 54–16. They were magnificent that day and I was proud to be a Warrington supporter. It was the best away performance I had ever seen by Warrington. Scrum-half Andy Gregory murdered them. He made eight of the 12 tries and Mark Roberts scored three of them. Peter Fox was the Leeds coach. He had a juggernaut pack and a few good Australians playing for them, including the test centre Andrew Ettingshausen. I went into the Warrington dressing room after the match and put £100 down for them to have a drink because their performance had been so good.

I have already mentioned that I followed the Great Britain tour to Australia in 1988. The footage of the third Test on YouTube shows me on the pitch talking to a delighted Mike Gregory after the final hooter. I was so elated after that 26–12 victory that I just had to get on the field. We hadn't beaten them for 10 years and had so many injury problems. I was in the camp the day before the match, training with them, and it almost looked like a lost cause. They were so patched up. Paul Hulme had to play at hooker, Hugh Waddell came in at the last minute at prop and was outstanding, and Andy Gregory put on another masterclass.

I also went to Milwaukee in June 1989 when Warrington played Wigan at the County Stadium in an American Challenge match designed to promote the game in the United States. Unfortunately, the pitch was that narrow that the players could almost hold hands across it.

Also in the late 1980s I did the Beaujolais Run, the annual race bringing a case or two of that year's vintage back from France to England as quickly as possible on the third Thursday in November. Liverpool's Radio City followed our progress and we did it all for charity. Businessman John Jones, known as JJ, was my partner. However, he had a broken arm and so I had to do all the driving. We took our time going over, went via Paris and met Jean-Pierre Rives, the former French rugby union international flanker, at the Pernod factory. We had our photograph taken with him. We had lunch and then we drove to Beaune in the Beaujolais region ready for the start at 12 noon. We had an E-Type Jaguar which did 140mph. It was 380 miles to Calais and we did it in four hours, going straight through Paris. The only person who passed me was Derek Warwick, the Formula One driver, in a works Jaguar. I was doing 140 and he passed me as if I was standing still. I think the French police must turn a blind eye that day.

I was enjoying the bachelor lifestyle, but then I met Jennifer Hislop, a pretty chartered accountant with Ernst & Young, Ernst & Whinney as it was then, at the Lord Daresbury hotel in Warrington and we started going out together. Events overtook me after that and when we had two children and a third on the way, we decided to take the plunge. We were married at Northwich Register Office on 6 January 1996 with Mike Slater as my best man. We just had a quiet wedding and good old Stuart Reed from De Vere organised the reception at Mottram Hall in Cheshire. It was my 50th year and I was kicking and screaming – only joking.

There were just 12 of us at the wedding. My mother and father were only told the day before but managed to make it. It was typical Nicholas really. My brother Clive has done the same thing to me. He telephoned me in January of this year to say he had got married that morning. He always has been impulsive – he had only known Colleen for 40 years. There were only four people at his wedding. In the Nicholas family we are not particular about ceremony and cant. My brother Geoff, who had a traditional wedding, is still in a state of shock.

Jennifer and I were only married for six years, but we are still good friends. We have a project. We have always been Team Nicko with the three kids and Jennifer has been absolutely brilliant in supporting them. I have supported them fully too, like my mother and father supported me. We have taken them everywhere, but Jennifer has been unbelievable, even becoming team manager at Woolston for a spell.

The Kangaroos came calling at Wilderspool again in October 1990. It was their first visit since we had beaten them 15–12 in 1978 and we got as many players from that Warrington team as possible to attend a Supporters' Club night in the Touchdown Club. Dave Wright was there with the Australian supporters; we had a wonderful time and started thinking that we should meet up more often.

The following December Warrington Museum staged an excellent exhibition called *Now the Wire*, tracing the history of rugby league in the town. I made a speech at the official opening, and said that it was about time we set up a Past Players' Association. Things moved quickly after that and the Warrington Past Players' Association was launched in March 1992. I was chairman and former Man of Steel Ken Kelly was secretary. We wanted Parry Gordon to be the treasurer but, in the end, that post went to supporter Stan Lewandowski and he has done such a superb job that – 22 years later – he is still the treasurer.

We soon recruited more than 100 members and the Past Players' quickly became what it is today: a really strong and vibrant association. I was the chairman until 1995 when I started to have a lot of other commitments as Wales manager and had to step down. Derek 'Nobby' Clarke, the former player, coach and trainer, took over from me until he died in 2006; now it is well led by George Thornton. I am still an active member. They have got a really good committee made up of George, Ken, Stan, Alastair Brindle, Keith Affleck, Paul Ford and Ken Paget who meet on a regular basis. Last year, Keith took over from Ken as secretary and they dropped the word 'Past' from the title so that current players could join. It is one of the strongest associations in the game. I think Murph has agreed to be the life president.

I would have liked to have been more involved with the club, perhaps on the board of directors, but the timing wasn't right. Peter Higham, who became the chairman after Brian Pitchford, tried his best and had a good go, but the crowds didn't really increase as they should have done. It is a thankless task running a rugby league club. There is an old saying in the game: "How do you become a millionaire by owning a rugby league club?" And the answer is: "Start off with £6 million."

When Jonathan Davies moved from Warrington to Widnes in 1993 he lived with me in Stockton Heath for about four months while he moved house. With him being such a superstar the neighbours loved it. Jonathan, his wife Karen and the kids were delightful. He was good company and a fabulous player. He was a success in both codes and while playing for Canterbury in Australia where he scored some great tries.

With Warrington chairman Peter Higham (centre) and former Great Britain coach Maurice Bamford (right) in the late 1980s at a rugby dinner. Back row, left to right: former Warrington players Ken Kelly, Stan McCormick and Bob Jackson. (Photo: courtesy Mike Nicholas).

Bill Shankland is in the centre of the back row at the Wilderspool Centenary. (Photo: Eddie Whitham).

The late Roy 'Ockher' Aspinall, the former Warrington kitman and groundsman, and Mike reminisce about the good old days. (Courtesy *Warrington Guardian*).

Mike sitting with (from the left) Wire past players Alan Whittle, Parry Gordon, Derek Whitehead and Mike Peers before a Challenge Cup tie at Featherstone Rovers in May 2009. Rugby league personalities Tommy Conroy, Dave Chisnall, Clarrie Owen, Roger "the Dodger" Millward, George Thornton, Bob Eccles and John Lowe are also present. (Photo; courtesy Mike Peers).

Welsh wizards John Bevan (centre), Bobby Wanbon (right) and Mike together to celebrate the life of their Wembley team-mate Parry Gordon, who died in November 2009.
(Courtesy *Warrington Guardian*).

Helping Alex Murphy open the extensions to the South Stand at the Halliwell Jones Stadium in March 2012. From the left: past players Mark Forster, John Lowe, Eddie Bowler, George Thornton, Bobby Wanbon and Alastair Brindle. Steven Broomhead, Warrington Wolves chairman, is second right.
(Courtesy *Warrington Guardian*).

At the official opening of the Warrington Wolves Heritage Wall in April 2013 as Paul Cullen, Alastair Brindle, Laurie Gilfedder and Lee Briers cut the primrose and blue ribbons (Photo: Bob Brough).

Mike reading about his record-breaking four sendings off during the 1978–79 season on the Warrington Wolves Heritage Wall. (Courtesy *Warrington Guardian*).

I remember two tries he scored for Warrington at Halifax in the Challenge Cup in January 1994, when it looked like Warrington were about to get knocked out. He had no room to work in and the game was practically lost. Mike Slater and I were sitting in the stand next to a Halifax fan who had dyed his hair blue and painted his face blue and white. He was going on and on about Jonathan being a waste of money when all of a sudden 'boom, boom'; he scored two tries and Warrington had won. The Halifax fan was speechless.

Warrington celebrated the centenary of Wilderspool Stadium with a parade of past players before the Super League match against Huddersfield in September 1998. Bill Shankland, who was 91, was our oldest past player and I arranged for him to come up from Dorset and lead the parade. I believe Bill was the greatest all-round sportsman of all time. Just look at his record. He was a state cricketer and champion boxer in his native Australia. He toured England with the 1929–30 Kangaroos, playing in all four test matches. He won a baseball pitching contest in America. He swam against Johnny Weissmuller, better known as Tarzan. He signed for Warrington and played in two Challenge Cup Finals at Wembley and two Championship Finals, but his greatest successes were still ahead of him – as a golfer. He finished third in the 1939 Open at St Andrews and fourth at Royal Liverpool eight years later. He played his last Open in 1955, aged 48. Then, during the 1960s, he helped to turn one of his assistants at the Potters Bar club, Tony Jacklin, into a major champion. There is a great story that Jacklin arrived at Potters Bar from Scunthorpe during the big freeze of 1963 and found Bill playing cards in the pro's shop. Jacklin asked keenly: "What do you want me to do?" Bill replied: "Come back in three months."

I had a half-hour conversation with Bill before the parade of past players and it was a golden half hour. I asked him lots of questions. He didn't like Jacklin; he thought he was a big head, although he thought his parents were lovely people. Bill was stopping at a hotel in Runcorn, but the following day he slipped and banged his head and never regained consciousness. It was a real tragedy.

I was once on the top table at a golf dinner at the Belfry and the commentator Alex Hay said I used to play for Warrington, like Bill Shankland. Neil Coles, who was the chairman of the PGA European tour, piped up and said: "He had me eight down after nine holes in the Western Division Championship." Peter Alliss said his father, Percy, and Bill were best friends. They were both club pros in Bournemouth, Bill at Parkstone and Percy at Ferndown. Alex Hay had been one of Bill's assistants at Potters Bar. Bill was a genuine superstar.

People

Without the support of the following people, much of what has been written in this book would not have been achieved, and I would like to acknowledge their input.

Richard Ashall, my first sponsor and close friend when I arrived in 1972, is still one of my best mates. He gave me a Triumph TR6 to drive around in. He is now doing stalwart work in addiction rehabilitation and uses me as a guinea pig on occasions. Mike Dolan, Tom Roarke, Dennis Cook and Selwyn London (deceased) – Warrington stalwarts who were always first to be on the phone providing support, advice and encouragement. Nathan Church, who is from Llantwit Major and moved to Appleton Thorn, where Alfie Langer live, has always been on hand in times of need.

Then there was Huw 'Bomber' Thomas, a former Aberavon player and a Cambridge economist, and fondly known to us all as 'Lord Baglan' due to the wonderful comportment he displays. Belated thanks to Huw Eurig (chairman S4C TV) for the coverage of the 1995 World Cup, and his hospitality at 'The Pack' in Cardiff Arms Park. Another good mate is John Mordecai of ABC Tyres of Porthcawl. He lent me a car in 1996 to get back north, even though a tyre blew before Birmingham.

Another important friend was Eddie ('The Hitman') Lamberth, my trusty lieutenant and right-hand-man running Wire Wheels and Stockton Heath Motors. A local hero and talented all-rounder who wrestled professionally in the USA at one time; no one messed with him.

Trevor and David Lloyd – The Chester Boys – A rugby 'rat pack'

I first met Trevor when I was guesting (illegally) for the Warrington Vikings (veterans) team captained by John (Lewey) Lewis, a great character, who I am still in touch with and joins us on 'Nicko's tours'. I arrived late for the game as usual, put on my black balaclava (as a joke) to remain anonymous and took up my position on the pitch against Vauxhalls from Ellesmere Port.

I was harassed throughout by a young Trevor Lloyd playing for the opposition and who wasn't too enamoured with my physical style of play. He set out to let me know this, rugby league hardman or not. These veteran games were usually played a good spirit and were recreation for the senior players. One of the highlights for our club vets was when JPR Williams brought his London Welsh Vets team up to play us. We all then watched the 1986 Great Britain versus Australia match at Old Trafford, and JPR was interviewed on the BBC.

Anyway, Trevor and I ended up after the match having a friendly beer and I discovered he had a Welsh background. His father David, a true gent, was born in Bedlinog, deep in the Welsh valleys, before leaving to play professional soccer for QPR and Wolves.

From that first match, in the spirit of rugby, we became the greatest of friends and over the years he started joining our rugby trips to the Challenge Cup Final at Wembley. We were based in Gerrards Cross, off the newly opened M40, in the De Vere Bull & Bellhouse. Trevor became good mates with Jonathan Davies, Paul Moriarty and John Devereux through sponsorship at Widnes.

His company, Lloyd Motors, were clients of the Mobil 1 Oil brand, a McLaren F1 sponsor. As a result we all enjoyed regular trips to Silverstone for the British Grand Prix with access to all areas (pits, paddock and hospitality) and to the Canon Ashby stately home bash with the drivers. Jiffy and I accompanied the Welsh chairman of Mobil on a short balloon trip, which was surreal. John Monie, Andy Gregory and Bobbie Goulding all came along.

One trip back to Gerrards Cross from Wembley was particularly memorable. We went to the westbound platform at Wembley Stadium station to catch a train back to Gerrards Cross.

The station was very busy. Andy Gregory was with us and was in great demand for his autograph. The train arrived and everyone got on, leaving the station completely empty. The carriages were already full with football fans returning from matches in London. There was lots of banter, and I overheard Trevor Lloyd explaining to one of them that it was an annual visit to the final and we were heading back to our hotel in Gerrards Cross near the motorway and handy for a quick getaway back 'up north' early on Sunday morning.

However, the unimpressed football fan explained to a chastened Trevor that he wouldn't be staying there tonight because the first stop on this particular train was Bicester, in the heart of Oxfordshire, 50 miles past Gerrards Cross. Luckily, due to an unscheduled stop to swap drivers and the illegal use of an emergency door release we got off the train. A hike across the fields followed to a rural taxi rank, and a fleet of taxis delivered us back to Gerrards Cross.

I also had good times with the rest of the Chester boys, Trevor's mates Mike Lee, Peter Spencer (Aintree hospitality on the finishing line), the late Dave Lightfoot, Marko Roberts, John Kelly (a former professional footballer at Oldham with Joe Royle), Des and Craig – the commissars, our in-house entertainment on tour, Steve 'Acko' Acton and Steve (Mavo) Davies.

We all had some great fun at sporting events all over the country. They even owned horses through their syndicate. The Six Nations internationals at Clive Hopkins's marquee, which provided fabulous hospitality at the Cardiff Blues ground was a favourite watering hole, together with his hotels, Blanco's and The Towers. Clive has been a great friend from schooldays, when he played at Cynfig Comp when I was at Sandfields. His wife Valerie is from the bottom of my street. We used to meet up occasionally at Vivian Park to practice goalkicking. He was resplendent in his Kenfig Hill jersey (light blue and dark blue) with me in my beloved red and black B'Ravon. Clive was a really good kicker, with a kick like a 'mule' which was appropriate because the Kenfig Hills nickname was 'The Mules'.

Mal Thorniley is one of my best mates. He was a brilliant ballplayer, number 1 for the Lancashire Squash team, and part of Jonah Barrington's 'train on squads', which were famous for their fitness programmes. I used to join him on 15 mile runs to the Runcorn Bridge and back. He usually left me behind. I got him back by taking him to Wilderspool to train, and paired him up with Dave Chisnall, our 18 stone prop, on the terraces.

Two journalist friends are Ken Jones of the *Independent,* and Simon Jones of the *Daily Mail* – no relation. They helped me get the game of rugby league more coverage; Ken as chief feature writer for the *Independent* and Simon as the Northern sports editor of the *Daily Mail.* Simon enabled me to contribute an online rugby league column to counteract the lack of interest in our game from the rugby union biased London press.

Ken came from a similar background to me in South Wales. He was born in Merthyr and became a professional footballer before he embarked on a media career. I first became aware of him when he worked for the *Sunday Mirror* and eventually met him in Las Vegas for the first Tyson versus Bruno fight. We became great friends immediately, mainly because of our mutual love of all sports. We have spent many happy times together since then.

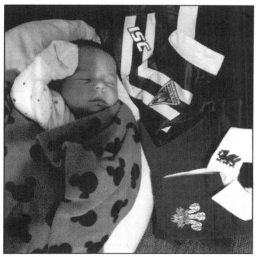

Top: Mike's son Morgan Nicholas playing for a Warrington Wolves junior team against Bradford Bulls at Wilderspool. (Photo: Eddie Whitham)

Left: Mike's grandson, Carter Jai Ross, aged three weeks, with Warrington and Wales shirts.

Top: A family group: Mike, Jennifer, Chris, Evie and Morgan.

Left: Wedding day: Mike and his best man Mike Slater on the big day (Courtesy Sally Slater).

Stockton Heath Motors – Mike's garage in Warrington

Mike and his mum and dad at Margam Castle near where he was born and where he played cricket in the same team as his teacher Cliff David.

We have attended all sorts of major sporting events all around the world. These have included Italia 90, four Ryder Cups, many British Golf Opens, and a multitude of rugby, soccer, cricket and boxing matches. One sad event was the funeral of our much loved national Welsh hero John Charles in Leeds.

Since meeting Ken in 1989, I have had the privilege of attending every Boxing Writers Dinner at the world famous Savoy Hotel, along with Gareth, his son, whose mobile phone company were the sponsors of this great event. I met such luminaries as Sir Henry Cooper, Lennox Lewis, Don King, Ingemar Johansson and many other all-time boxing greats.

One of my funny memories of Simon Jones is when we went together on a stag trip to Valencia. We left the hotel and went into the port area of the city where we came across a lot of banks of tyres in the streets. Our sports editor proclaimed 'what a great go-kart track' we had stumbled upon. It turned out to be one of the composite sections of the F1 European Grand Prix circuits, which was staged there every year. I've never let him forget that gaffe.

Another great friend is Joe Doherty, who played for Warrington, Widnes and Fulham. He ran the tic-and-pass games we used to have every Monday night at the Greenall Whitley recreation centre. It was very popular; sometimes it was 30-a-side. Even Jimmy Nicholl, the former Manchester United footballer used to join in. Frank Reynolds and I used the games to keep fit for veterans rugby union.

When I was at Aberavon I played against Gloucester at the Talbot Athletic Ground and at Kingsholm. They had a hooker called Mike Nicholls, who was about the same age as me, and who went on to become a Gloucester legend. He made 483 first team appearances for the Cherry and Whites in a career that spanned 17 years and later served the club as a coach and a member of the committee. Sadly, and unbeknown to me, Mike died on Christmas Eve 2012 and it was on *Sky Sports News* "rugby legend Mike Nicholls dies" and that led to another surreal episode.

On Christmas Day, I got a message at eight in the morning from John Stanley, a good mate of mine, asking if I was OK. He said there was a rumour going around that I had passed away. It was funny at first, but after three days of phone calls, with people ringing from places like Thailand, Ghana and Australia, the novelty wore off. My daughter, Evie, went bananas over it. Somebody had misread the message on *Sky Sports News* and thought it was me. It just proliferated on the social media, you know what Facebook is like. The next thing I knew there were messages posted like "rest in peace" and "my hero".

Mike Peers recalls: *"It was Christmas Day and I got a phone call from John Lowe and he asked if I had heard anything. I said 'What about?' and he said 'Nicko. They have found him dead.' I rang Bobby Wanbon and he hadn't heard anything. In the end I got a phone call saying that it was a rugby union player called Mike Nicholls who had died. I rang Mike after I knew everything was OK and one of his sons, Morgan, answered. I said: 'Is Mike there please?' He asked: 'Who is it?' I said: 'Mike Peers' and Morgan shouted: 'Dad, there's another one here who thinks you're dead!'"*

I never pushed my kids into sport, but they all played. Chris, my eldest son, who was born in 1991, played for Woolston Rovers as a second-row forward from six or seven years of age up to 16 or 17, when they all meet girls and drink. He was a good player and they had a cracking little team. He is a geologist now, qualified from Leeds University, and is off to Australia and New Zealand, looking for work. My daughter Evie, born in 1994; was a gymnast and got into the national squad. After that she became a shot putter and represented her school in the Cheshire Championships. Before she went into the circle, I used to say "Lose your temper Evie" and she always threw it further. She has got a temper and I don't know where she got that from. Morgan was born in 1997 and started playing rugby union at his school in Altrincham. I went to watch him and he was outstanding. His running was fantastic and he was very strong, like I was. He played rugby league for Latchford Albion, and latterly Rylands, as a second-row and loose-forward, played for Wales Under–16s against England and has been signed by Warrington's Academy, but he has a long way to go. I am probably his harshest critic. He scored two tries for a Warrington Wolves Academy select side against the Australian touring side NRL Group 6 under–18s last October and that's something I never did. I was sat there watching and his name was up in lights at the Halliwell Jones Stadium and I thought: "He has done more than me already." He is training hard and has got a big season coming up. I just keep as low a profile as I can and let him get on with it. I was a late developer and so I think there is more to come from him. I am proud of them all, and of my grandson, Carter, who was born in January to Evie and her partner Jordan. I wonder if he will play rugby.

Appendix 1: Career statistics

Warrington 1972 to 1980

Season	Apps	sub	Tries	Goals	Points
1972–73	16	2	2	0	6
1973–74	26	2	7	0	21
1974–75	13	3	2	0	6
1975–76	21	0	1	0	3
1976–77	28	1	1	8	19
1977–78	13	0	0	0	0
1978–79	16	2	0	0	0
1979–80	9	0	1	0	3
Totals	142	10	14	8	58

6 appearances for the Cardiff City Blue Dragons in 1981–82, without scoring any points.
6 Wales caps between 1975 and 1979, including two as a substitute, again without scoring.
2 non-Test appearances on Wales' 1975 World Championship tour, scoring a try on each occasion.

Sendings off 1972 to 1983

Date	Opponents	Venue	Competition	Referee	Punishment	Result
26-Dec–72	Leigh	Home	League	Sam Shepherd	2 matches	6–6 D
20-Apr–73	Widnes	Away	League	Gerry Kershaw	4 matches	11–17 L
10-Mar–74	Wigan	Away	Challenge Cup	Gerry Kershaw	3 matches	10–6 W
01-Sep–74	Rochdale	Away	Lancs Cup	Fred Lindop	4 matches	12–20 L
16-Nov–75	Huddersfield	Home	League	Bill Allen	4 matches	23–17 W
11-May–77	Featherstone	Away	Premiership	Stan Wall	Fined £10	13–17 L
25-Feb–78	York	Away	Challenge Cup	John McDonald	Sending off sufficient	16–10 W
19-Mar–78	Widnes	Home	Challenge Cup	Fred Lindop	2 matches	6–0 W
03-Dec–78	Featherstone	Away	John Player	Ron Campbell	2 matches	7–0 W
10-Dec–78	Barrow	Home	League	John McDonald	1 match	25–14 W
11-Mar–79	Leigh	Away	League	Joe Jackson	1 match	9–7 W
19-May–79	Bradford	Home	Premiership	Fred Lindop	4 matches	11–14 L
17-Apr–80	Blackpool	Away	League	Harry Hunt	6 matches	9–3 W
13-Sep–81	Hunslet	Cardiff	League	Robin Whitfield		32–19 W
16-Jul–83	Cardiff	Tylorstown	Friendly	Frank Tickle		46–30 W

Mike was also suspended for one match in March 1978 for receiving two recorded cautions, taking his total number of suspensions as a Warrington player to 34 matches.

Appendix 2: Dismissal reports

Competition: Challenge Cup – 3rd Round; Teams: Warrington versus Widnes

Venue: Warrington; Date: 19.3.1978; KO: 3.00pm

I was appointed to referee the above game, during which I had cause to dismiss four players. From the Widnes club, they were Mr D. LAUGHTON, Mr P. WOODS and Mr E. HUGHES. From the Warrington club there was Mr M. NICHOLAS. Laughton, Woods and Hughes were wearing Nos 13, 5 and 3 jerseys respectively. Nicholas was wearing the No. 10 shirt and no addresses were submitted.

The game started on a very heavy pitch and proceeded in the first half in a reasonably fair but hard cup-tie manner with Warrington offending mainly with petty fouls. The first dismissal incident came in the second minute of injury time. Play had proceeded to the Widnes line when I looked back and saw Laughton and Nicholas exchanging blows and head butts. They were separated by Widnes prop Mills and both had to be forcibly restrained. I dismissed them both from the field of play for foul play. As they set off for the tunnel Nicholas went for Laughton and struck him again. They were separated again and I then saw Woods run in from his wing position, some 15 yards and punch a Warrington opponent three times for no reason at all. I dismissed him also from the field of play for foul play, as the hooter sounded for half-time. As I was leaving the field of play and entering the tunnel area I was met by the Warrington coach Mr A. Murphy who appeared to be in a very aggressive state, and he said "Get a f...ing grip of this game Lindop!" I told him I would report him for his remarks and he moved towards me menacingly. Again he repeated the remarks and had to be forcibly restrained by Chief Superintendent Dennis Holland. I passed Murphy at this point and he then seemed to turn on the Widnes captain Bowden.

The second half started in a highly charged manner, but proceeded in a much quieter and cleaner vein until 12 minutes from the end when I cautioned Hughes for striking Warrington player Hesford in the face with the forearm after Hesford had kicked past him. Play deteriorated in the last 10 minutes with petty fouls committed by both teams. During this period Hughes was warned twice for attempted punches on opponents. He was finally dismissed with two minutes to go when he took an almighty swing at a Warrington opponent, which did not connect. As he had been cautioned previously, I dismissed him immediately from the field of play. With Laughton and Nicholas, I do not know who was the aggressor, but both Woods and Hughes were certainly aggressors. I was about 20 yards from Laughton and Nicholas, 10 yards from Woods and four yards from Hughes when they were dismissed and there was no question of mistaken identity.

I would like to place on record, the thanks to Chief Superintendent Dennis Holland for his help during this difficult interval period and also deplore the remarks made by Widnes chairman Mr J. Woodward to the press "that I looked frightened to death" by the Murphy confrontation. I can assure him I was only too aware of Murphy's intentions and it did not affect my performance as a referee. Inflammatory remarks like these only tend to add to the controversy, when calm and reason should prevail.

G.F. Lindop

Game: Blackpool versus Warrington in Div 1; Played: At Blackpool, Thursday, 17 April, 1980

Players Dismissed: J. Corcoran wearing No. 13 jersey for Blackpool; M. Nicholas wearing No. 10 jersey for Warrington

In the 75th minute of the above game I dismissed from the field J. Corcoran and M. Nicholas following incidents which took place around the Blackpool 25 yards line in front of the posts.

After Corcoran was tackled by Nicholas, the latter deliberately struck Corcoran in the face. As I blew my whistle Corcoran stood upright and savagely kicked twice into the prone body of Nicholas. Both players were dismissed from the field. Not content, both players – despite attempts by their colleagues and myself to restrain them – engaged in throwing punches at each other. When separated they moved off the field but as they approached the touchline they again started fighting and had to be stopped. Both players had been warned earlier, Corcoran for a foul tackle on the Warrington No1 and disputing decisions and Nicholas for a foul tackle and also butting in the scrum.

The game was played in a poor spirit with a total lack of discipline shown by several players of both teams. Most of the time I had to referee over each tackle to maintain order. Feeling between both sides was apparent from the start.

H.G. Hunt (REFEREE).

Appendix 3: Aberavon stars in rugby league

Johnny Ring's Wigan career (1922 to 1931)

Season	Apps	Tries	Goals	Pts
1922–23	41	44	1	134
1923–24	40	48	1	146
1924–25	33	52	0	156
1925–26	37	62	0	186
1926–27	38	48	0	144
1927–28	26	18	0	54
1928–29	37	32	0	96
1929–30	26	26	1	80
1930–31	40	33	0	99
1931–32	12	8	0	24
Totals	**330**	**371**	**3**	**1,119**

26 appearances for Rochdale, 12 tries.

Alan Edwards's career (1935 to 1949)
Salford

Season	Apps	Tries	Goals	Pts
1935–36	28	21	0	63
1936–37	33	15	0	45
1937–38	32	21	0	63
1938–39	46	33	0	99
1939–40	26	20	0	60
1940–41	1	2	0	6
1945–46	33	17	29	109
Totals	**199**	**129**	**29**	**445**

Bradford

Season	Apps	Tries	Goals	Pts
1939–40	20	3	0	9
1944–45	16	6	0	18
1946–47	24	13	6	51
1947–48	36	36	2	112
1948–49	32	23	16	101
1949–50	5	2	9	24
Totals	**133**	**83**	**33**	**315**
Overall	**332**	**212**	**62**	**760**

Also played with Dewsbury during the war.

Kel Coslett's St Helens career (1962 to 1976)

Season	Apps	Tries	Goals	Pts
1962–63	44	3	156	321
1963–64	41	5	138	291
1964–65	9	2	26	58
1965–66	26+2	4	57	126
1966–67	15+3	1	3	9
1967–68	38+1	4	84	180
1968–69	46+1	3	154	317
1969–70	42	1	160	323
1970–71	49	3	193	395
1971–72	54	8	214	452
1972–73	46	2	162	330
1973–74	39+2	4	134	280
1974–75	39	2	120	246
1975–76	31+2	3	38	85
Totals	**519+11**	**45**	**1,639**	**3,413**

Wales: 10 matches. Rochdale, 1976 to 1979, 47+2 games, 3 tries, 38 goals, 1 drop-goal, 86 points.

Bobby Wanbon's career (1968 to 1978)
St Helens

Season	Apps	Tries	Pts
1967–68	14+1	2	6
1968–69	5+7	6	18
1969–70	33+3	8	24
1970–71	4+5	1	3
1971–72	6+2	1	3
Totals	**62+18**	**18**	**54**

Warrington

Season	Apps	Tries	Pts
1971–72	34	2	6
1972–73	40	12	36
1973–74	20+7	1	3
1974–75	19	2	6
1975–76	24	4	12
1976–77	3+7	1	3
1977–78	8+1	0	0
Totals	**148+15**	**22**	**66**
Club total	**210+33**	**40**	**120**

Wales: 7 appearances.

Bob Fleay's Swinton career (1970 to 1976)

Season	Apps	Tries	Pts
1970–71	24	10	30
1971–72	33+1	13	39
1972–73	44	20	60
1973–74	37	26	78
1974–75	34	12	36
1975–76	35	6	18
1976–77	3+2	1	3
Totals	**210+3**	**88**	**264**

82 games for the Cardiff City / Bridgend Blue Dragons 1981 to 1985, 26 tries.

Frank Reynolds' Warrington career (1971 to 1975)

Season	Apps	Tries	Pts
1971–72	13+2	3	9
1972–73	37	10	30
1973–74	16+3	1	3
1974–75	7+1	0	0
1975–76	10	2	6
Totals	83+6	16	48

Clive Jones' career (1972 to 1979)

Warrington

Season	Apps	Tries	Pts
1972–73	15+7	5	15
1973–74	9+12	1	3
1974–75	0+2	0	0
Totals	24+21	6	18

Leigh

Season	Apps	Tries	Pts
1974–75	12	2	6
1975–76	23+5	4	12
1976–77	26+11	0	0
1977–78	18+9	5	15
1978–79	4+4	0	0
Totals	83+29	11	33
Club totals	107+50	17	51

Wales: 4 appearances, twice in 1975 and twice in 1978.

Dennis Curling's Warrington career (1972 to 1977)

Season	Apps	Tries	Pts
1972–73	27+4	16	48
1973–74	27+2	1	3
1974–75	3	1	3
1975–76	33	6	18
1976–77	36	11	33
Totals	126+6	35	105

One substitute appearance for Wales against France in 1977.

Statistics compiled by Robert Gate and Gary Slater.

Photo: Alan Edwards (Courtesy Robert Gate)

Bibliography

Books

Murphy's Law, A biography of Alex Murphy, Brian Clarke, Heinemann Kingswood, 1988

Gone North (Volume 1), Robert Gate, self-published, 1986

Gone North (Volume 2), Robert Gate, self-published, 1988

Big Jim, Jim Mills – a rugby giant, Peter Lush & Maurice Bamford, London League Publications Ltd, 2013

John Player Rugby League yearbooks 1973–74 to 1976–77, Jack Winstanley & Malcolm Ryding, Queen Anne Press

Tries in the Valleys – A history of rugby league in Wales, edited by Peter Lush & Dave Farrar, London League Publications Ltd, 1998

Newspapers

Port Talbot Guardian

Western Mail

Warrington Guardian

Daily Express

Various rugby league programmes

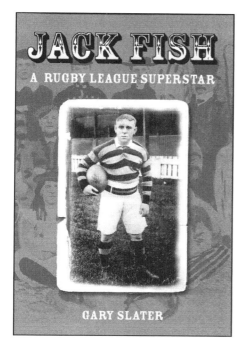

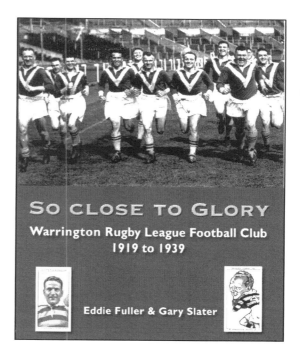

Jack Fish was one of Rugby League's superstars in the sport's early years. He was signed by Warrington in 1898, and soon established himself in the first team. He played in four Challenge Cup Finals, and scored both tries when Warrington beat Hull KR 6–0 in 1905. He captained the team in 1907 when they beat Oldham 17–3 in the Final.

As well as playing 321 games for Warrington, he made 16 appearances for Lancashire and was capped three times by England. He scored a phenomenal 215 tries and kicked 262 goals for the Wire. He is still the only player to score 200 tries and kick 200 goals for Warrington. He coached the Warrington team that reached the 1928 Challenge Cup Final and lived in the town until his death in 1940. This authorised biography is a comprehensive record of Warrington's first superstar. It also provides a vivid portrait of the club's early years in the Northern Union.

Big Jack Arkwright, Jack 'Cod' Miller, Tommy 'Tubby' Thompson, Billy Dingsdale and Bill Shankland are rugby league legends. All five made their names at Wilderspool and are now founder members of the Warrington Wolves Hall of Fame.

So close to Glory is the story of how they and their team-mates in the club's famous primrose and blue colours helped the club to grow in size and popularity during the 1920s and 1930s. In this period the team played in three Challenge Cup Finals and three Championship Finals.

This was a time of poverty, economic hardship and mass unemployment, but Warrington RLFC became a focal point for the town and prospered.

Wilderspool was transformed into a magnificent stadium, the club gained a reputation for signing top-quality Australian players, broke the world record transfer fee and even signed a player from Manchester United. This is the untold story of those two decades and is lavishly illustrated with photographs, cartoons, caricatures and cigarette cards from the period.

Both books are available from London League Publications Ltd: Jack Fish for just £10.95 post free in the UK and So Close to Glory at just £10.00. Visit www.llpshop.co.uk to order or write to London League Publications Ltd, PO Box 65784 London NW2 9NS

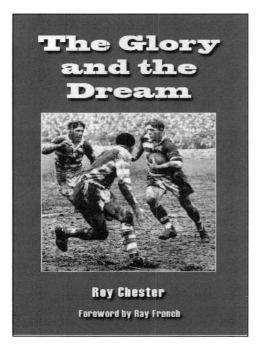

The Glory and the Dream

Roy Chester

Foreword by Ray French

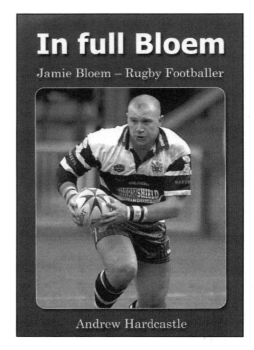

In full Bloem

Jamie Bloem – Rugby Footballer

Andrew Hardcastle

The Glory and the Dream is a great new rugby league novel. It tells the story of a young boy's rite of passage. It is full of rich characters, and is played out against a backdrop of social upheaval in the austere post-war years of rationing and shortages. But it was a time when communities pulled together. Walking days, royal visits, Sunday School outings to the seaside and communal bonfire nights were annual highlights. It was a time when youngsters had to make their own entertainment, including playing rugby league.

It is about Johnny Gregson, the young star of the Garton rugby league team, whose dream is to follow his dad's success in the sport. Johnny lives with his mother in Four Locks, a poor working class area in a grimy northern town. His father died in the Second World War. The story starts in 1945, when Johnny is aged 10. It follows his rise from junior rugby league through playing rugby union as a schoolboy to turning professional with Garton.

However, there is much more to Johnny than rugby league. He faces challenges at every turn, including when he wins a scholarship to a local public school and is labelled as a 'slum kid;' by the class bully. His prowess at rugby helps him deal with this boy. Also, at the tender age of 16, he meets a young woman who becomes very important to him. This is a story about sport, romance and working class life. It includes many humorous incidents, insights and even tragedy in a young man's development.

Published in March 2014 at £9.95. Order for just £9.00 post free in the UK from www.llpshop.co.uk or by post from London League Publications Ltd, PO Box 65784, London NW2 9NS

In full Bloem is an authorised biography of Jamie Bloem. From being a young South African rugby union player, he developed into a star rugby league player. From 1992 to 2005 he played every position on the field in a career that took in Castleford, Oldham, Doncaster, Widnes and Huddersfield, but primarily Halifax. He later became a coach, commentator and Grade 1 referee. He was never far from the headlines, be it for drug taking, an accusation of biting, charges of abusing referees, declining pay cuts, or even sometimes for scoring spectacular tries or kicking touchline goals. This is a frank account of when he was in the wrong and when he was not. Published in 2013 as a hardback @ £14.95, now available direct from London League Publications Ltd at www.llpshop.co.uk for just £9.95 post free in the UK or by post from London League Publications Ltd, PO Box 65784, London NW2 9NS.